THE VOYAGE OF THE
CAP PILAR

The Voyage of the
CAP PILAR

By

ADRIAN SELIGMAN

Seafarer Books

Sheridan House

© Adrian Seligman

First published in 1939 by
Hodder & Stoughton
This edition first published 1993 by
Seafarer Books, 10 Malden Road, London NW5

Distributed in USA by
Sheridan House
145 Palisade Street, Dobbs Ferry, N.Y. 10522

ISBN 085036 438 8

Cover design by Louis Mackay, based on a painting by
the Australian Marine Artist John Allcot

Printed and bound in Great Britain by
Biddles Ltd, Guildford and King's Lynn

CONTENTS

PART I

HOW IT ALL BEGAN

CHAPTER   PAGE
       PROLOGUE   17
   I. IN THE BEGINNING   21
  II. PAPER-CHASE   27
 III. FRENCH LEAVE   32
  IV. BREAD ALONE   40

PART II

DOWN THE ATLANTIC

    V. AWAY   47
   VI. GALES AND GREENHORNS   55
  VII. FIRST BASE   65
 VIII. SALVAGE—OR VERY NEARLY   72
   IX. TENERIFE   78
    X. ROLLING DOWN TO RIO   87
   XI. CALMS AND CATSPAWS   95
  XII. JUNGLE CITY   104
 XIII. MAILS FOR TRISTAN   112
  XIV. THE ISLANDS OF OPPORTUNITY   119
   XV. CRISIS IN CAPETOWN   131

PART III

THE SOUTHERN OCEAN

   XVI. RUNNING THE EASTING DOWN   145
  XVII. ATTEMPT AT HOBART   157
 XVIII. AUSTRALIA FAIR   165
   XIX. AUCKLAND AND JESSICA JANE   173
    XX. DISCONTENT   180
   XXI. THE ROAD TO THE ISLES   186

CONTENTS

PART IV

THE PACIFIC ISLANDS

CHAPTER   PAGE
XXII.   PALM TREES AND CORAL   197
XXIII.   AMONG THE ISLANDS   208
XXIV.   TO NUKUHIVA IN THE MARQUESAS
           ISLANDS   214
XXV.   MARQUESAN MOMENTS   223
XXVI.   HIVA-OA   231
XXVII.   TROPICAL FOOTBALL   241
XXVIII.   THE TUAMOTUS   246
XXIX.   CHRISTMAS ON A CORAL ATOLL   253
XXX.   GOOD-BYE TO THE ISLANDS   261
XXXI.   SNOW ON THE ANDES   267
XXXII.   A GALLEON SAILS FROM CALLAO   277
XXXIII.   PROGRESSO AND WRECK BAY   285
XXXIV.   THE NEVER-NEVER ISLANDS   292
XXXV.   DRIFTING ON   298

PART V

PANAMA AND THE SPANISH MAIN

XXXVI.   THE RED EYE OF CAYMAN   309
XXXVII.   JAMAICA IS SO BRACING   320
XXXVIII.   FOLLOWING THE GULF STREAM   327
XXXIX.   NEW YORK   333
XL.   FOG ON THE BANKS   341
XLI.   HOME FROM HALIFAX   348

ILLUSTRATIONS

Between pages 166 and 167

In a few moments, we were out of earshot and bowling down the river . . .

Outward bound for Rio and Tristan da Cunha . . .

The boys changing sails in the Trade Winds . . .

Once more, the sky began to breathe . . .

Roping a new lower topsail . . .

Colin Potter at the wheel in the Southern Ocean . . .

Lars snapping a sight . . .

Found him feeding Dennis from the saloon teapot . . .

Anchored in Tai-o-Hae . . .

The lagoon of Hao in the Tuamotu Islands . . .

Through the pass into Hao . . .

A pretty South Sea islander . . .

Cap Pilar entering New York . . .

Family Life . . .

Homeward from Halifax . . .

We were home again . . .

MAPS

The Voyage of the *Cap Pilar*   25
Down the Atlantic   51
Cape Town to Simon's Town   135
The Passage of the Southern Ocean   147
The Pacific Islands   196
Gambier Islands   199
Along the Reef   205
Taa Hu Ku Bay   233
Hao Island   247
The Galapagos Islands   287
Panama and Spanish Main   311
Panama to Jamaica   317

PART I

HOW IT ALL BEGAN

PROLOGUE

FROM THE ARGUENON to the Rance in the Gulf of St. Malo, the coast is fringed with rocky islands, and many years ago the Abbey of St. Jacut stood upon one of them. But, for a hundred years or more, the monks carried stones and earth on to the sand spit which used to join this island to the mainland at low tide; so that now St. Jacut lies at the end of a fertile isthmus, enclosed between two dykes.

On either side of this isthmus the grey mud and hard brown sand push deep into the mainland. At the full and change of the moon the sea crawls away out of sight at low water; then, a few hours later, it comes galloping back past the headland—surges in a mighty wave up the river on the western side of the isthmus—past the ruins of an old castle surrounded by huge elms—past steep-sided coves, and yellow beaches—right up to the village of Le Guildo and beyond. On summer evenings the mud flats are alive with whimbrel and curlew, filling the air with their mournful piping, accompanied by the drowsy hum of a distant threshing machine.

My family first visited St. Jacut in 1914, when I was four years old. We stayed at the Abbey for the whole of that summer. After the war we went there every summer, and sometimes at Easter as well. When in 1925 we rented a small stone cottage down by the winter fishing harbour, St. Jacut became our second home.

Each year we spent more and more of our time among the islands, which lay in a great arc protecting the isthmus and the eastern bay, and continued at less frequent intervals right along the coast to St. Malo. The fishing boat we sailed in was the joint property of Marie-Ange Paitrie and of his brother-in-law Jean Bourseul. From these two men we learned how to sail, and the position of every smallest rock and every eddy of tide and current in the bays. Both of them were old " deep-water men ", and they told us stirring tales of the days when they had gone to sea in ships trading to Madagascar and the Indies.

When I was nine years old I went to a preparatory school in Wimbledon. One of my earliest memories is of a certain nature study lesson. Quite early in this lesson a fir cone hit me on the ear, and turning round I just caught sight of George, the headmaster's son, dodging behind a tree. We threw fir cones at each other for the rest of the lesson, and next day we threw stones at each other in the playground. Soon we were firm friends.

At meal times George's younger sister Jane used to sit at one end of the table in a high chair. She was in many ways a remarkable child. She wore huge steel-rimmed spectacles, and had a passion for riddles. Every day during lunch she would recite one riddle out of *Chick's Own*. It was a point of honour among the boys never to guess the answer.

For a few years George and I were inseparable. At the age of fourteen we were sent away to different public schools, but in 1929 we met again at Cambridge, where we spent two happy years. Then, quite suddenly, I went to sea.

In October, 1932, the Finnish four-masted barque *Olivebank* was in the South Atlantic, bound for Australia; I was an ordinary seaman aboard her.

She had been at sea for over sixty days—drifting placidly south before the north-east trades, idling through the Doldrums, then striding out and booming down the full south-easters, from the Equator to the latitude of Monte Video.

For two weeks on end she turned white water from her bows in thundering mountains, and the warm spray went hissing across her decks.

Those were happy days; at night you lay on your back on the main hatch, looking up at the piling canvas, stiff with wind. The sky was black ice set with diamonds; the four mast heads were a group of skaters, making figures upon it in perfect unison. Then came the first of the hard west wind, and, squaring away before it, *Olivebank* laid her shoulder to the sea.

One morning, just after dawn, with the ship making fifteen knots before half a gale of wind, a cloud-bank on the horizon seemed to thicken as we watched it; soon a jet-black pile of rock stood above the mist, rising to a great height. This was Tristan-da-Cunha.

Lars Paersch, also an ordinary seaman, and I stood watching it. It took our imagination; it looked like the loneliest island in the world.

"One day," said Lars solemnly, "we will fit out a ship of our own, and visit Tristan."

For a little more than three years Lars and I sailed in Gustaf Erikson's ships out of Mariehamn—mostly those trading to Australia for wheat, but also in one of his smaller barques bringing timber from the Baltic to London. Then we drifted apart, I to the British tramp *Ramsay*, and he to a Finnish cargo liner, running to South American ports.

The *Ramsay* pounded stolidly along the shortest routes about the world; from North Shields to the Argentine, and on to the West Indies; from Texas to Japan; from Vancouver to Sydney. For a long time I heard no news of Lars; soon even the memory of our first years in sail and four-month passages to and from Australia began to grow dim.

In Vancouver one of the *Ramsay's* officers had to be left

ashore in hospital; and from then on, during the 8–12 watch I paced up and down the bridge alone. At first I enjoyed my new position immensely, but by the time we were homeward bound from South Africa, I had fully made up my mind to give up the sea and become either a doctor or a journalist. Seafaring was leading nowhere; after five years of voyaging about the world in six different ships, I had at last managed to serve enough time to qualify me to sit for my second mate's certificate; but I had been a great deal too old when I first went to sea and now I was many years behind other men of my own age.

On the 8th of December, 1935, the last day of the voyage, the wind was northerly and bitterly cold. The *Ramsay* shouldered her relentless way up the Irish coast from light to light, and from headland to sun-splashed headland. The wind tore at my ears and made my eyes water; it was a day for leather jackets and uproarious song. Tuskar, Cahore and Wicklow Head; then later Slieve Donard and all the mountains of Mourne stood out boldly over Dundrum Bay.

I looked through the glasses at gorse-spattered hillsides, and my spirits rose. I felt that a period of my life was over, and that the very next day would bring a new adventure.

CHAPTER I
IN THE BEGINNING

The BIG MAN received me in a big room. He held in his hand an essay I had written at school, and one of my letters to my mother.

" You want to be a journalist, eh ? "

I nodded apologetically.

" They tell me you've been going to sea."

" Yes."

" Well now, I was at sea until I was twenty-six. I was earning seven pounds a month as an A.B. in a tramp, when I jumped her in Sydney and started free-lance journalism." He paused and glared at me. " Six months ago I gave up a job worth £14,000 a year to come to this one; and I was forty-three last birthday ! "

" You've certainly had all the luck," I suggested timidly.

" Luck be damned ! " he exploded. " I was a sandwich-man on Fleet Street at two shillings a day, for a whole year before I got a newspaper job over here."

As I plodded home that evening, I gazed with interest at the sandwich-men in the Strand, but found them uninspiring. I sat down in the park to consider the future.

My only assets were £3,500 given me by my grandfather, and a certificate of competency as second mate. My only liability—that I wanted to get married to Jane. There seemed to be only one answer—an office.

With £3,500 you can buy and fit out a small ship for a voyage round the world !

The idea came to me at 11 P.M. at the end of a day of weary tramping round the City in search of a job.

Within ten minutes I was at Jane's house. They were all in bed, but I managed to wake Jane by throwing stones through her window. She appeared in a scarlet dressing-gown.

" Hullo, Adrian ! " she said, " have you brought your guitar, or are you going to sing a few simple country songs ? "

" No—listen—I've just had a wonderful idea. . . ."

Next day we went to see George at the school in Essex, where he was teaching. We told him our plans, and suggested that he would become a far better schoolmaster after sailing round the world. He smiled at our enthusiasm, but agreed to join us whatever happened.

We decided that George should spend the following three months in reading up all he could about navigation, so that he would eventually be able to take over that department; Jane was to be responsible for stores; and the next man to get hold of was obviously Lars. I had heard nothing of him for nearly two years, but we hopefully sent a letter to his home in Finland. Then, for ten days, Jane and I met every evening at the " Hoop and Grapes ", where we talked earnestly and interminably about paint, rope, canvas, clothes and crockery; of islands and insect-powder, trade winds, trawls and trousseaux.

At last there came a letter from Lars to say that he was in Helsingfors sitting for an examination, and that he would be ready to come with us in April.

All we needed now was a ship; so a few days later we boarded the channel steamer at Southampton, and the following dawn found us watching the sun rise over the islands in the Gulf of St. Malo.

Later in the morning, as we left our hotel to walk down to the docks, it began to rain; and by the time we reached the water-front a strong nor'-east wind was howling across the harbour in gusts and squalls, snatching the crests from every other wave to fling them, with one hand, into our faces as it passed. We shivered and felt miserable; but in the distance we could make out the spars and rigging of two or three square-rigged sailing ships. Perhaps there would be a small schooner lying amongst them, and anyway Jane and George had never seen a square-rigged vessel; so we trudged on towards them, with heads down and coat-tails flying.

Arrived at the other side of the docks we found, in all, four ships laid up in the same basin. There was a topsail schooner, a great ill-tempered mule of a four-masted barquentine, with a huge beam and a flat square stern, and two three-masted barquentines. Under grey skies and pouring rain, they all presented the most dismal appearance. Their decks were bright green with moss, and foul with all manner of refuse and wreckage. Aloft, frayed ropes and strips of canvas slatted miserably about the rusty shrouds and backstays. Only here and there a patch or two of greyish white paint showed through the crust of prolonged decay. No sign of life was visible aboard any of the ships. They stood patiently with bowed heads, like senile horses drooping wearily between the shafts. Below the water-line the weed grew thick and long. We left them, and wandered desolately about the docks.

Two hours later we were plodding back towards the hotel. It had stopped raining, and as we approached the barquentines, we saw that a string of many-coloured washing fluttered like banners upon the poop of one of them; a streamer of fresh blue wood-smoke hung from the iron chimney beside her cabin hatch. We read the name CAP PILAR printed upon her counter. She, at least, was not dead after all. As we passed by, a hefty red-faced Frenchwoman appeared on deck; so we hailed her, and asked whether we could come aboard. She gave us a look of rather contemptuous amusement, and we felt like inquisitive tourists as we stumbled over the gangway.

At close quarters the *Cap Pilar* looked even more of a wreck than we had expected. Decay had so changed the very shape of things, that much of her gear was barely recognisable. Rust inches thick bulged all over her pre-historic-looking windlass, and over every square inch of ironwork on deck and aloft. Nuts had lost their shape and bolts their character. In every dark corner little clusters of bolt-heads seemed to grow like fantastic mushrooms, flourishing in the damp and desolation.

The Frenchwoman took us down into the forecastle. At first sight we found it impossible to believe that this reeking ill-lit prison had ever supported human life, far less that it had been the cosy home of twenty healthy men. Rotting remnants of clothing, old oilskins, boots, pieces of mildewed bread and bits of newspaper lay everywhere. The smell was appalling, and after a few moments we decided that we could stand it no longer. But the French-woman was merciless; we had asked to see her ship, and she was determined that we should see everything: she snatched off one of the hatches on the main deck, and in-sisted that we should climb down and inspect the hold. We peered into the dank and cavernous depths; everything was covered with a salty slime, and a stench of decaying fish and bilgewater smote us in the face. Heavens! a cod-fishing schooner from the Newfoundland Grand Banks! Hastily we said good-bye and made for the nearest quay-side café.

For a week we searched the harbours, bays and estuaries of the Brittany coast, and throughout that week it rained incessantly. Soon we felt as though the weed of all the ships we had visited was beginning to grow behind our ears, and our hearts grew mouldy within us.

We tried several times to calculate the probable cost of our intended expedition, and on each occasion the figure we arrived at considerably exceeded the capital we pos-

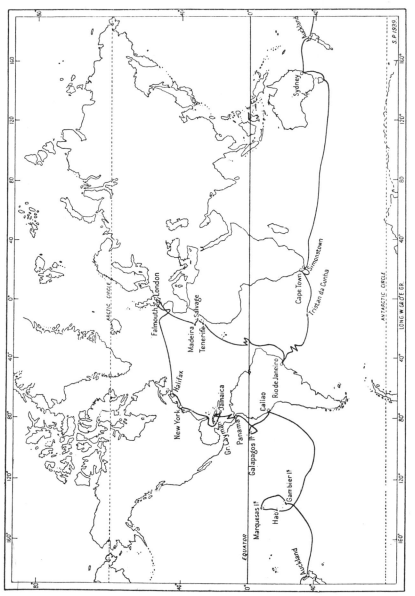

THE VOYAGE OF THE *CAP PILAR*

sessed; we came to the conclusion that we must find a crew of adventurous young men, who would each be willing to subscribe a certain amount to the cost of the voyage. But how on earth could we persuade a crew to join us before we even had a ship? On the other hand, how could we buy a ship and embark upon a re-fit that would undoubtedly run us into two or three thousand pounds, until we were certain that we should be able to find a crew?

On our last day in Brittany we were once more sitting in a dockside café. The floor of this café was of stone, the tables had stone tops with cast-iron legs, and the crudely coloured advertisements only accentuated the bareness of the walls. All was bleak and cold as the quay outside.

As the rain dripped down our necks and made puddles on the floor beneath our feet, we wondered whether it might not still be possible to withdraw gracefully from the whole business. We knew at once that it was not, so we ordered cognac. Soon we began to feel a little warmer; and then we remembered that we had only just started on our search for a vessel: somewhere on the coast of Brittany, or perhaps in the Baltic, there *must* be just the very ship we were looking for. So we ordered more cognac. Then, in a flash, we all thought of it together. "What fools we had been! What paltry, second-rate holiday cruisers! We had not yet taken the absolutely essential, the only decent ' first step to adventure '."

We drank a last hasty cognac all round, and hurried back to our hotel. There we wrote out the following advertisement and sent it off to *The Times*:

> Voyage to South Seas in sail: schooner leaving August for about a year. SIX YOUNG MEN WANTED to crew, each contribute £100 towards expenses.

CHAPTER II
PAPER-CHASE

THE RESULT WAS terrific and unexpected.

Our advertisement appeared on a Friday morning two days later, and at 11 A.M. on the same day a reporter from the *News Chronicle* rang me up. He wanted to know all about us and our intentions, and would Jane and I report at once at the office in Fleet Street. We realised that publicity on the centre page of the *Chronicle* would bring us all the applications we wanted for berths in our ship; so we wasted no time in getting to the City.

We were pardonably startled when we read our "write-up" in the paper next morning. I had been described as a keen-featured, square-rigged young man, and the head-lines ran:

BRIDE AT WHEEL IN ADVENTURE CRUISE
They Left College to See Life
Romance of School Comes True

But the main facts were accurately and reasonably set out, with the result that the first post on Monday brought us over a hundred letters. Many were from young lads in or out of work, who offered their £40 or £50 of hard-won savings and begged to be signed on. Some were from people of fifty or sixty, and among these was a charmingly encouraging letter from an old sailing-ship captain, and one from a maiden lady, who said that she could imagine "nothing more restful than sitting upon the heaving deck of a ship with the white sails blowing out overhead."

In a very different category were the letters which demanded full references and guarantees, and usually ended somewhat on these lines:

I don't propose to offer any contribution towards expenses, but would be willing to accompany you for a comparatively nominal share in the profits.

And also the one which read:

I am twenty-eight years old, weight 11 stone 7 oz., chest 39"—expanded 42½". I am writing to you as man to man with the suggestion that one of my type will be of great value to you on the tough trip you intend to make. For the past ten years I have knocked about all over the place, and am used to roughing it under all conditions. I can use a revolver, and have looked after myself in several tight corners, including water-front fights. I can definitely call myself tough (on one occasion I slept through a gale on the deck of a fishing-boat). I have always managed to prove myself a man who is not to be trifled with ashore or afloat.

Several women applied for berths, but it was impossible even to consider their applications. One poor girl offered to join the ship as stewardess, and finished her appeal with the pathetic remark: "I don't eat much, and I can swim a little."

Before we even began to sort out the applications, Jane and I took a day off in which to get married, and then hurried to Finland to see Lars and to continue our search for a ship. In Helsingfors we hired a small cutter and set out to sail to Stockholm, with the intention of looking for a schooner on the way. For a week we settled down to enjoy the scent of pine forests and the sound of wavelets tinkling beneath the forefoot of our tiny craft. But nowhere could we find a schooner. Incidentally this was Jane's first trip in a boat of any sort.

We returned to England in June, and there followed weeks of furious activity; but, at the end of the month, we were still shipless, and over three hundred people had applied for berths. We had to make a hasty choice of forty or fifty of those who appeared to be the most suitable, and contrive to keep them interested, hopeful, *and at home*, while we carried the hue-and-cry after a ship into every European port north of Brest.

For a fortnight I travelled up and down Brittany and Normandy without an hour to spare in which to look at the scenery. I tried without success at Dieppe, Le Havre, Fécamp, Cherbourg, and Paimpol.

At Nantes I drove twenty miles along a river in a very old Citröen, with the marine superintendent of a steamship company—a small weather-beaten Frenchman. He was exceedingly polite and friendly—remarkably so in fact, since he appeared to imagine that I was the agent for some hastily formed company, who was buying up old ships in order to sell them to the unsuspecting natives of the remoter tropics.

He eyed me quizzically as we clambered about the two little steel ketches he had brought me to see.

"Fine leetle ships, hein?" he said, with a prodigious wink. "Some painture 'ere and dere, a few fadoms rope, and zey would be wort a fortune in Tahiti, hein?"

"-I'm not going to Tahiti," I answered, a little puzzled.

"Ah, no! Of course. I forget. You make ze voyage round ze Cape 'Orn vis your wife and seex childs as ze crew. Ho! ho! ho! Of course, yes, I am so stupide."

And he winked again, horribly.

We put an advertisement in Lloyd's List, but received only one reply—from an unknown but enthusiastic firm of "ship brokers and valuers". Throughout the remainder of the summer this firm bombarded us with specifications of trawlers, fishing smacks, whale-chasers, obsolete destroyers, paddle-steamers, tugs, and even spritsail barges—in fact every kind of vessel but the one we wanted. At any moment of the day the telephone might ring, and I would hear that urgent, hurried voice at the other end.

"That you, mister? Listen, quick. I got you a boat. Best bargain on the market. Can't think why I don't buy her myself. Listen to this: twin-screw motor vessel; five hundred tons; seven hundred and fifty horse-power, excellent. . . ."

"But I'm looking for a schooner!"

"This one's better than a schooner; seven hundred and fifty horse-power. Get you anywhere in the world."

"I want a schooner."

"You want a schooner. Yes, yes, I get you one. I get you the last schooner in Europe. You wait."

We could not afford to wait. Already the first crew we had chosen had lost heart, and we had been forced to send urgent requests to some of those whom we had turned down, asking them to renew their applications. This occurred three times; by the middle of July, we were left with a fast dwindling capital and a crew consisting of *four men*. All the others had written, one after the other, to say that their mothers had begged them to withdraw, or that they had found a good job, or suddenly decided to get married. Actually, of course, the rumour that our whole enterprise was nothing but a cunning swindle was fast gaining ground; even the faithful four who still remained, did so in the face of continual advice "not to touch it" or "get out while there was still time" from their more knowing acquaintances.

At this stage we owed more than we shall ever be able to repay to the *News Chronicle* and their staff, who did not hesitate to risk their reputation as a reliable newspaper, by continuing to give us far more publicity than we deserved. Everywhere else we came up against destructive criticism, incredulity and even open contempt. Gradually the colour of romance and the atmosphere of adventure faded; the whole undertaking became a weary struggle against time and blind prejudice.

At last the game seemed nearly up; and one gloomy evening we gathered for what we all thought would be our final council of war.

" We'll have to send everyone a letter saying that the thing's off, I suppose. It's a good thing we didn't ask for any money in advance."

" Are you sure you haven't seen a single ship anywhere that might possibly do ? " said George.

" Not a smell of one."

" Talking of smells, what about the *Cap Pilar* ? " said Jane.

" Ough ! "

" She wasn't so bad after a cognac or two."

" Good heavens ! It'd cost us a fortune in cognac to live aboard her for a month."

" Well, let's have a couple now, and then see what we think about it."

CHAPTER III
FRENCH LEAVE

ONE BRILLIANT SUMMER'S MORNING we came back to St. Malo. In the early sunshine the medieval town, with its ramparts and cathedral spire, stood out like a fairy-tale castle from the iron-bound coast of Brittany. The grey slate roofs shone brightly, the air was fresh, and from the quay a crowd of blue-smocked porters winked and beckoned to all the passengers on the steamer. It had been a smooth crossing, and everyone was in great good humour.

We spent an hour over breakfast, and when we eventually set off for the docks, it was in a mood of hearty optimism that we clattered along the cobbled streets. How different everything looked from the day on which we had first come to St. Malo to search for a ship, nearly three months before. Each tree was now a bulging cloud of leaves, the streets were dry, the sea bright blue, and the people were gaily dressed.

When we came within sight of the docks we halted, amazed at what we saw. A quarter of a mile away, where once had lain a group of rain-draggled derelicts, was now a stately company of ships! And the *Cap Pilar* stood out among them, with tall raking masts, square yards and a noble sheer. At this distance, even her meagrely painted topsides showed up white in the morning sun; and for the first time we saw her, not as what she was, but as what she might one day become.

We hurried eagerly towards her. When we got aboard we found that the rubbish had been cleared from off her decks, and all her hatches lay open. Jane poked her head below.

32

"There's hardly any smell at all now," she cried excitedly, "and there's no wet either."

"I believe they've scrubbed all the salt off the walls," said George. "Let's go downstairs, and see if the old girl's got the coffee-pot on."

We trooped into the cabin aft, and within ten minutes we were arguing about "alterations".

There followed a week of feverish negotiations. It seemed that I had never talked so much and done so little in all my life. My arms grew numb with endless arguments in French.

In the end the ship went into dry-dock for survey, and as the water ebbed, clean lines and powerful bows appeared; she looked a wonderful sea boat. But she still had to be surveyed, and for this purpose a very quiet and unemotional gentleman from England came to St. Malo. It took two whole days to strip the ship for survey: planks were torn from her hull, spider bands and wedges removed from the masts, and the whole of one morning was spent in unshipping the rudder. For two more days the surveyor went over her from stem to stern; we dared hardly speak to him lest he should tell us something we were afraid to hear.

At the end of those two days he nodded, handed in his report, and left us; three minutes later I was inside the ship-broker's office.

"*Je l'accepte!*"

"You accept her? Ah! but now we are going to see something of formidable."

Accompanied by the ship-broker we all swept out of the office, like children out of school. Down aboard the ship we encountered a host of shipwrights, ship chandlers, master riggers, master caulkers, master sail-makers, master onlookers and master arm wavers, all talking together and elbowing each other aside. It was over a year since the old ship had felt the clatter of so many feet upon her decks. She heaved and trembled beneath them, as though a new hope were waking in her weathered timbers.

"Regard me that," roared the shipwright, his trouser legs jerking half-way to his knees through trying to talk with his hands in his pockets, "the planking is so hard that not a worm has got into her."

"I'll put a zinc sheath round her that will break the nose of a crocodile!" said the master caulker.

"I know every faulty block," cried the master rigger. "Is it not I that have put them there?"

They started work within the hour. In a little over a month, they promised me, the *Cap Pilar* would be ready for sea.

For a day or two we felt quite drunk with excitement and relief. We were going south on a long voyage after all; south and by west, and then south, to forgotten oceans, to the kingdom of the whales and flying fishes.

Lars arrived from Finland, and we rented a small flat in a narrow back street of the town. Jane insisted on doing every bit of the cooking and housework for all of us. Every morning she trotted off to market with a shiny black bag upon her arm, looking the picture of a contented little French housewife as she clattered down the cobbled streets and alleys. A 8 o'clock each day the rest of us rode down to the ship on bicycles, and worked there until close on sunset. Jane used to roast large juicy joints of veal and mutton for our meals, and in the evenings we always brought home red wine at four francs the bottle. In this way we passed two hard, happy months, during which time the ship was almost gutted and rebuilt.

Throughout the re-fit we were lucky to have the advice and encouragement of a famous seaman in Commander J. R. Stenhouse, R.N.R., who had spent most of his life in sailing ships, and had at one time been master of Shackleton's *Discovery*. His unconquerable optimism and great knowledge carried us through many difficulties.

Here are a few of the *Cap Pilar's* measurements:

Length between uprights	118 feet
Extreme breadth	27 ,,
Depth of hold	13 ,,
Height of main truck above deck	103 ,,
Length of foreyard	50 ,,
Gross tonnage	295 tons

Her frames are of oak 9 inches thick, and her planking of oak and elm 3 inches thick. She is double-skinned, both being of equal thickness.

The only remarkable features of her hull construction are her unusually heavy and close-spaced frames, and the arrangement of her deck, which is broken abreast the mizzen mast, and again amidships. The main deck is 2 ft. 4 in. higher than the foredeck, and the poop 1 ft. 4 in. higher still. This arrangement keeps the main deck clear of heavy water, and the poop completely dry in almost any weather.

About two weeks before the *Cap Pilar* was ready to leave St. Malo the first of the crew began to arrive. Their number had once more increased to nine, of whom seven only were contributing to the expenses of the voyage.

The nine were:

FRANCIS NEWELL, aged 31, ex-Paymaster, R.N., who had left a good job with the Shell Co. to join us.

WILLIE MARSH, 26 years' old builder's labourer and gardener, from Sussex; red faced, short, thick-set and uproariously cheerful.

JOHN DONNELLY, aged 25, who had just passed his final examination as a solicitor; also short, very quiet, with large round spectacles and a gift for whimsicalities.

ALAN BURGESS, 22, tall and athletic, with curly yellow hair, blue eyes and a charming manner; formerly a ventilating engineer in Birmingham.

PETER ROACH, 18 years old, and the youngest of the crew; very thin and spindly; fresh from teaching in his father's preparatory school.

ALEXANDER DRUMMOND SANSON, 24, a biologist from Edinburgh University; so Scotch that we thought, at first, that he was putting it on.

DR. EDMUND ATKINSON, 25, just qualified; very efficient, and possessing an overpowering sense of duty and a habit of humorous pessimisms.

KURT ROMM, aged 28, who came as official photographer; very charming and extremely "artistic"; a refugee from the Nazis.

ALAN ROPER, aged 20, a student of botany from Leeds University; freckled face, short, energetic and aggressive.

A more mixed collection of young men could scarcely have been imagined; and it was perhaps on account of this that they managed to settle down together so well from the very start. The strange existence into which they had fallen must have appeared little short of fantastic to most of them. When the first one arrived the ship presented a more dismantled, dishevelled and disreputable appearance than ever before or since, and, within ten minutes of his arrival, each recruit was set to work at chipping rust, scraping paintwork and scrambling about in the rigging.

For several of them the voyage across to St. Malo had been a major adventure in itself. Willie Marsh afterwards wrote the following account of how he joined the *Cap Pilar*:

Long did I toil and sweat to earn the necessary money, working from dawn to midnight besides my daily work, with mowing lawns, digging gardens, wheeling bath-chairs, and finally selling my few treasured possessions. Grim did I carry on what seemed a never-ending gruesome struggle.

Soon my intentions whizzed like wild-fire round the small village of Lancing; then came the pest of newspaper reporters—in vain little did I spill, yet much they seemed to write. Higher and higher into the limelight I soared, and talk swiftly became very annoying.

I continued work until two hours before setting out for St. Malo. Never had I made such a lengthy journey, so one can well imagine how agitated a country yokel was. I slept on the steamer's deck with my £100 secretly stowed in a specially made arrangement next my skin. Now did the world seem to spread before me, like a land of dreams beyond compare.

After the rust was all chipped and the paint scraped, the next job was to carry on board 150 tons of granite, which was to be our ballast. For a day and a half we carried pieces of rock in each hand from the quay to the ship, and down into the hold. It was a weary business.

But the crew were a healthy looking lot. Romm looked the brawniest of them all, so he surprised everyone, on his arrival, by shyly announcing :

" I know nothing about anything material. I only know about literature, music and art."

Francis Newell arrived several days after the others, and when he came on board, Donnelly met him at the gangway.

" I'm Newell."

" Oh, how do you do. I'm Donnelly, that's Burgess and that's Roach, and that's the pile of stones we've got to carry on board by lunch-time to-morrow. I don't know how long this is going to appeal."

One morning Romm suddenly disappeared. He was eventually found behind the heap of ballast rocks on the quay, a dreamy light in his eyes, patiently picking up one stone at a time and arranging them in a long straight line.

" Hullo Romm. Playing patience ? "

Romm straightened, and answered in kind and cultured accents: " Pardon, I arrange the stones for the others, so that they shall reach them more easily."

Roper had been one of the earliest to apply for a berth, but he had expressed himself in such enthusiastic language that we had feared lest he should be disillusioned by a long voyage in a sailing ship. Everyone who joined us was bound to be something of a romantic, with visions of "bellying white sails " and "sun-blue water "; yet we had to do our best to make our future companions understand that the sea would usually look grey, and that the *Cap Pilar's* sails were, in point of fact, a dirty yellowish colour. We might have saved ourselves the trouble, for not one of the crew believed us; except possibly Sanson, who had made voyages in fishing trawlers in the North Sea and to Greenland.

Roper arrived in St. Malo in heavy hob-nailed boots, with a rucksack on his back. He stood for several minutes upon the quay, gazing enraptured at the masts and rigging of the *Cap Pilar*. Suddenly he vaulted nimbly over the rail, and, without a second's pause, he leaped at the boat skids, where he proceeded to do gymnastics. From the very first Roper was as keen and excited as he had sounded in his letters; but we found that he spoke just as extravagantly as he wrote. Long words seemed to fascinate him, and he took great pains to introduce them into his most everyday remarks.

There are still two of our number whom I have not yet described:

Jane's brother, GEORGE BATTERBURY, was the only realist among us. His first act on arriving in France was to give up shaving for good; and we soon found that even

George—born schoolmaster and intellectual though he was—had in him a streak of harum-scarum, which seemed to grow upon him with his bushy black beard, and subsequently left him when he finally shaved the beard off.

LARS PAERSCH was a tall raw-boned Finn, of very aristocratic descent. He was reserved almost to the point of surliness, and tremendously strong. In bearing and appearance he was a combination of Russian prince and brigand chief; and, despite furious protestations to the contrary, he was sensitive and kind-hearted to a fault.

The afternoon of 9th September was clear and cloudless, with a light wind blowing from the south. The tug put her hawser aboard at 3 P.M., and within twenty minutes we were in the locks.

Although we were only going across to London for stores, a large crowd lined the waterfront to watch our departure. With a tremendous amount of shouting and waving of hands we managed to get all the sails loosened, ready for setting; then the lock gates creaked slowly open.

"Let go for'ard! Let go aft!" The towing hawser lifted dripping from the water and slowly tautened, accompanied by a prodigious grinding and creaking, as the turns hardened round the bitts.

The *Cap Pilar* strained, hesitated, then surged nobly out to sea. The tug blew three long blasts on her whistle; down came our ensign to the dip; the crowd gave us a friendly cheer.

"Well, boys," cried Willie Marsh excitedly, "we're off on our first ride in a sailing boat."

CHAPTER IV
BREAD ALONE

I WILL NOT TRY to describe our feelings during those first moments at sea in the *Cap Pilar*; none of us had leisure at that time to consider them. We were only concerned with making sail.

It came as a real shock to Lars and me that there could be people in the world who had never heard of a reef knot, who had never seen an arrangement of pulleys known as a tackle, who had never even *wondered* how a ship was steered. Of course when we considered it seriously, we realised how remarkable it was that any of them should know anything at all about a ship. But at first the task of establishing any semblance of routine in the ship was a terrific one for all of us; and it was chiefly on account of the keenness of fellows like Roach and Roper that some sort of order was achieved almost at once.

But very few of the crew understood the reason for the various jobs they were told to do. There were many who had imagined that a square-rigged ship could only sail with the wind dead behind her, like the galleons on Christmas cards. Others could see no sense in altering the trim of the sails for different winds; and one man had never realised that a sailing ship could not be steered perpetually upon a given course, irrespective of the direction from which the wind might blow.

The passage from St. Malo to London occupied five days. There was little or no wind the whole way, which gave just the breathing space we needed for all of us to settle down to our strange new life.

Jane shared the duties of cook with her father, who had

40

joined us for this passage. They had a great deal to contend with—their first experience of seafaring, a heavily rolling ship for the whole of one forenoon, and, worst of all, a "patent" stove, which knew no half-measures; on the rare occasions when it could be induced to provide enough heat to boil the water, it would soon get completely out of control, and pour streams of blazing paraffin all over the galley.

The five days passed almost without incident. Roper caused considerable amusement by his pedantic speech. He referred to tea, quite seriously, as the "herbal brew," and asked whether "a little seasoning might not enhance the flavour of the meat pie." At dusk one evening we met a steamer, who blew a short blast on her whistle and shecred away from us. The crew took this to be a friendly greeting, and cheered lustily as she passed. They were answered by a hoarse voice from the steamer's bridge shouting: "Your bloody port light's screened by your foresail, blast you!"

We were only a fortnight in London, but it seemed like six months!

Every day fresh wagon-loads of stores came down to the ship, and soon her hold was half-full of crates and sacks. Some of the stores we carried were to last us for a year; we shipped 6,000 pounds of flour, 2,000 pounds of tinned meat, 1,000 pounds of salt meat in casks, and many other essentials in like proportions.

The only livestock we took with us was a small pink pig—of such an engaging appearance and cheerful character, that it was not until three months later (by which time he had grown too gross to command our affection, and too large for his sty) that we could bring ourselves to eat him.

As soon as the Tristan-da-Cunha Society heard that we intended to visit that island, they asked us to take a considerable quantity of mail and stores for the inhabitants. Apart from the usual foodstuffs and general stores, the consignment included two large crates full of Bibles, 100 pairs of wooden shoes and a great many wire rat-traps. We were also asked by some other philanthropist to take a dozen cats with us to Tristan, since it was feared that the island had become infested with rats.

When news of the cats leaked out, it caused quite a sensation in the Press. " CATS FOR TRISTAN: CAP PILAR HELPS FIGHT PLAGUE ON LONELY ISLAND," was one of the headlines. We felt that it would have been ungracious to refuse; but we waited with deep misgivings for the twelve cats (in twelve " large airy cages " ?) to arrive. We felt sure that by the time they reached Tristan they would be ferocious enough not only to eat every rat on the island, but even a few of the inhabitants as well.

Luckily for us the R.S.P.C.A. eventually stepped in on behalf of the cats themselves, and we sailed without them.

In London three more recruits joined us. The first of them, COLIN POTTER, a sheet-metal worker formerly employed by the L.G.O.C., was 25 years old, and a craftsman. He could make or mend anything; before very long " Send for Potter! " became the ship's slogan, whether it was to make bread or repair the gramophone. But, apart from his cleverness with his hands, Potter was a tower of strength morally. To use George's words : " Potter could always be relied upon to see the reasonable side of any argument—if there was a reasonable side."

A few days later CYRIL MONEY, a furniture draughtsman, came down to the ship. He was a second edition of Potter, but a year older. George and I were sitting on the poop when we first saw him, dressed in motor-cycling overalls, strolling up and down the quay and gazing at the ship. He seemed very shy, but after a long time he eventually approached and said :

" I suppose you're all full up a long time ago ? "
I told him that we were not.
" Well, can you give me two days to go home and get myself ready ? "
He rode straight back to Oxford that evening, and two days later he was aboard the *Cap Pilar* and ready for work.

CHARLES PAYNE also joined us at the last moment. He had been second chef at an hotel on the south coast, so he became the cook of the *Cap Pilar*. He was twenty-two, rather plump and cheerful; and his greatest asset was a beautiful tenor voice, which, unfortunately, he used exclusively for crooning.

During, the whole of that fortnight in London we were up to our eyes in work and worry, and the ship was crowded from morning until night with visitors of every description, who added considerably to the confusion. But among them were a few professional seamen, with many years of experience. Lars and I had been prepared for a great deal of ridicule and even open disapproval from the older members of our profession; but we were delighted to find that these men, above all others, were the ones who gave us the greatest encouragement. Some of them even came down in their spare time to help us get ready for sea.

Then there was Gelder. Gelder was a reporter on the *News Chronicle*, who had been told to " cover " the voyage of the *Cap Pilar*. He was the most energetic and enthusiastic mortal imaginable; for a month before we sailed he voluntarily assumed the duties of honorary secretary to the expedition. He worked tremendously hard—ordering stores, finding more crew, and keeping the " story " alive in the Press. We felt especially grateful to Gelder, but could think of no way of adequately expressing our gratitude. In the end we decided to ask him to come with us as far as Madeira.

At last, on Tuesday, 29th September, we were ready to leave, and in the evening of that day our last recruit, DUNCAN McDONALD, turned up on board. He seemed very young and very keen; he had first heard about us only that morning, and came down to the docks after his day's work, as a clerk in a shipping office, ready to join us at a moment's notice.

We were due to sail next day at 11 A.M., so we arranged with McDonald that if he could settle his affairs in time to meet me at the ship-broker's office at 9 A.M. we would take him.

McDonald met me punctually, and together we hurried down to a second-hand clothes shop in East India Dock Road, where Mac bought a monkey jacket, a pair of sea-boots and a bright red handkerchief. Then we went straight aboard the ship.

Lars was already warping her across the dock when we arrived.

PART II

DOWN THE ATLANTIC

O.K. Boys! Let's Go!

We're off to sea again, me lads,
The ship lies flush and ready.
Jolly roving sailor cads,
Steady, boys, steady!

The captain stands upon the poop,
His face is all aglow.
" Man the windlass! " comes a whoop,
Okay, boys, let's go.

So slam the anchor on the deck,
Good-bye to Flo and Nelly.
We've down'd the final horse's neck,
The sails are all a-belly.

Out across the booming bar,
Where scudding spume makes merry,
We've canvas taut on every spar,
Sing hey, jig-jig, down-derry!

Free from care and madding crowds,
On the boundless main a-rollin',
The wind is in the futtock shrouds,
So haul away the bowline.

Harken to the brave wild waves,
We *parlez-vouz* their lingo.
Britons never shall be slaves,
Rather not, by jingo!

Yours sincerely,
JOHN DONNELLY
Boatswain

CHAPTER V
AWAY

ONLY WHEN THE GAP was widening between ourselves and the quay; only when our moorings splashed into the water for the last time, did we realise that we were actually upon our way. After more than six months of feverish preparations we were at last outward-bound for far countries and the ocean solitudes between.

The tug hooted merrily, the crowd at the dock-gates waved and cheered; we all shouted back, and in a few moments we were out of earshot, and bowling down the river. Now we looked with real interest at every factory and warehouse, the ships moored in the river, the barges with their huge red sails working nimbly between the crowd of shipping, the tugs and coasters, liners and lighters. It would be a long time before we saw any of them again.

As we passed one warehouse a man on the roof shouted: "Why don't you take some *real* sailors?" This was the last word spoken to us from English soil.

Commander Stenhouse and my father were aboard, intending to leave with the pilot. But the latter was not the cheerful and enthusiastic Mr. Clare, who had brought us in from Dungeness. He professed himself in no way interested in sailing, and was anxious to get away as soon as we reached the North East Spit buoy.

Both my father and the Commander, who in different ways had nursed us through every moment of the past six months, were bitterly disappointed at the prospect of having to leave us so soon; and we also were only too anxious to delay the coming of that dreaded moment, when we should be cast off to fend entirely for ourselves;

47

so it was decided that they should remain on board, and we would put them ashore at Plymouth on our way down the Channel.

Eventually, at the mouth of the river, we made all sail, and the tug came sidling alongside for the pilot.

It was already night. The moon was nearly full, but a cold northerly wind carried black boulders of cloud, and kicked up a stiff cross sea against the tide. For a moment, upon the tug's bridge, the faces of my mother and sister and Jane's mother shone whitely in the glare from a hurricane lamp—faces at a window pane—only a few yards away, but already in another world.

"Good-bye! Good-bye!" Their voices came thinly through the wind.

Off went the tug in a thunderous commotion.

"Good-bye and good luck. Good-bye! Good-bye!" fading into the scurrying darkness, like a colony of seagulls upon a rock.

We squared away and stood south past the north Goodwin light vessel. The shore lights winked mysteriously as we passed them by. It was as though they were anxious to share with us the guilty knowledge of our own gross lack of experience. Perhaps they approved of our temerity. We felt suddenly more courageous, more encouraged.

For to us this was indeed a voyage of Discovery and Adventure. Not in the accepted journalistic sense. We did not claim to be attempting anything that had not been done many hundreds of times before, that could not equally well be achieved by any number of others, with no better qualifications than ours. To us this voyage was an adventure in quite a different sphere: we carried no wireless set of any sort; the *Cap Pilar* had no engine. We were out to discover whether a score of healthy young people could live happily together for a long time, without any contact with the world to which they had been accustomed; with no other tie than a common determination to make the voyage a success. We were out to re-discover the world; but, above all, to discover ourselves.

In point of fact we had never had any misgivings concerning our ability to sail the ship. We were all very young, and dead keen to learn. We suffered from no delusions as to the exact extent of our knowledge and abilities; but we felt certain that we could make up for any gaps in our seafaring education, by always taking every possible precaution, even when we knew that an older seaman would probably stand more boldly upon his course. Our determination to do this cleared our consciences of any qualms as to our right to take the ship to sea.

Three of us were sufficiently competent to navigate; two of us knew enough meteorology not to make any bad mistakes. Three of us again understood the broad principles of ship-handling; and, most important of all, we had made certain that the *Cap Pilar* would be a thoroughly strong and seaworthy vessel.

So we bid the lights of Kent a cheery farewell.

Excluding my father and the Commander, we were nineteen all told aboard the *Cap Pilar* at this stage of the voyage. Jane, myself, Lars, Francis Newell, George, the Doc and Allon (of whom more later) all lived aft. In the forecastle were Donnelly, Potter, Money, Sanson, McDonald, Marsh, Roach, Romm, Roper and Burgess. Gelder slept in a small cabin abaft the forecastle, and in one near by was Charles Payne, the cook.

Except for Sanson, none of the crowd forward had ever been to sea before. The youngest of them was Peter Roach, aged eighteen, and the eldest Kurt Romm, who was twenty-eight. Before leaving London they had chosen John Donnelly as their bos'n.

Newell, who was to be second mate, had developed a poisoned finger; and at the last moment Allon, our only yachtsman friend, had volunteered to come with us as far as Madeira, by which time it was hoped that Newell would be on watch again.

We have always felt since, that the cruise would have ended at Madeira but for Allon. He did more to keep up our spirits during the first stormy fortnight of the voyage than anyone else in the ship. Apart from the fact that he was an expert seaman, Allon's most remarkable characteristic was his uncanny flair for making everybody happy.

The wind remained fair, and we sailed down Channel as easily as we had come up two weeks before. We passed the tall finger of Dungeness in the early morning on 1st October. The weather was now cold and miserable; occasionally, too, there was fog, and we saw no more of the coast till we reached St. Catherine's Head on the Isle of Wight. The autumn was definitely settling in, and many of us felt glad that we should soon be in a summer climate.

Gelder was in great spirits. We had warned him that at this time of the year it would probably rain and blow most of the way to Madeira; but he was not to be discouraged, and went round asserting that, now he had at last managed to get us safely to sea, he was going to relax and enjoy himself.

During the afternoon of Friday, 2nd October, the wind drew easterly and freshened. The black cliffs of the Start came out of the mist on the starboard bow, and we stood right in to signal to Lloyd's station on Prawl Point.

The ship was making nine knots before a fine commanding breeze, and we had to hoist and haul down our signals at full speed, to get the whole message away before we were out of sight.

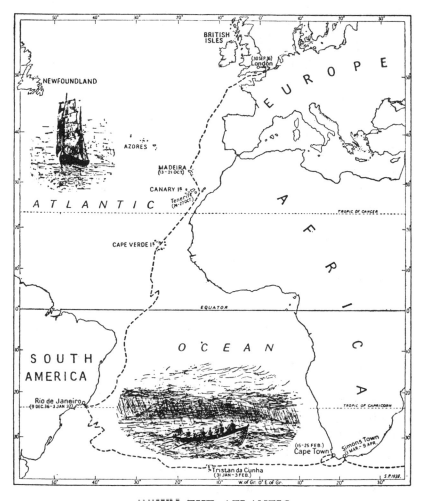

DOWN THE ATLANTIC

This map was drawn by Francis Newell, second mate of the *Cap Pilar*.
The inset pictures give a wonderful impression of: (1) Calm weather in
the tropics. (2) The Tristan Islanders pulling out to us.

Two hours later we were off Plymouth, where the boat for which we had signalled was waiting to take my father and Commander Stenhouse ashore. The wind had freshened a little, and the white caps tumbled on every wave. The boat came up like a cork alongside. My father jumped. Up came the boat again. The Commander jumped. The boat sheered away.

Three hearty cheers from all on board. Three more from the boat; then, "Hard up the helm! Main and spanker sheets!" and once more, after nearly two years within the gates of the Channel, *Cap Pilar* stood away for the open sea.

The light was beginning to fail. The wind shifted into the south-east and freshened more rapidly, the sky to windward darkened.

This was the loneliest, most dismal moment I had ever known. For the past six months there had always been my father or the Commander to share the heaviest responsibilities. More than that, we had been Englishmen in our own country; but I do not believe that any of us had realised before to what an extent we depended upon the quiet, sensible solidity of England. Now we could depend upon it no more; from now on we must face every emergency alone.

By the staggering roll of the ship, we knew already that she was far too stiffly ballasted. For a moment I wondered whether this might be considered a sufficient excuse for putting back into Plymouth—anything to relieve that awful "abandoned" feeling.

Lars and I wandered forward to make sure that all the gear was in its right place, in case we had to shorten sail suddenly during the night.

In the south-east the sky grew darker and more threatening. Soon little stinging needles of rain struck across the deck. The barometer was falling steadily. We could see that we were to be allowed no respite in which to become accustomed to our surroundings; it was going to blow hard before morning.

Right ahead the Eddystone Light rose slowly out of the sea; then shone brilliantly upon us as we passed, making our white spars gleam silver.

Cap Pilar strode on with the wind in her hair. Soon she began to feel the first scend of the big Atlantic swells. She plunged and snorted; the first spray came hissing across her fore-deck. She came to life in the rising sea, as though the smell of blue water had lifted years from her sturdy old shoulders.

I went down into the hold. Here I no longer heard the howling of the wind; only the swish and gurgle of the bilge-water, accompanied by an almighty creaking and groaning, where the new timber chafed against her sides as she worked. Now and then a sea would crash against her; she seemed more than ever alive down here. Every part of her was moving inches as she rolled and plunged. I glanced anxiously round; but the sight of her massive beams and frames made my mind easier. This was my first experience of a wooden ship, so I could only hope that there was some truth in the saying that "while she creaks she swims".

I went on deck again, and for a long time Jane and I stood arm-in-arm upon the poop, saying little but wondering gloomily what the next two years would bring.

We suddenly appreciated for the first time the full magnitude of the responsibility we had so lightly undertaken; and it is certain that if we had once been able, during the previous six months, to view the whole enterprise in the light in which we now saw it the voyage would never have been made.

Into this atmosphere of gloom bounced Gelder: "Off at last!" he said full of boisterous good-fellowship. "I'll bet you're glad to see the last of England for a year or two! All you've got to do now is to sit back and have a real good rest. Let the wind take you where it will. That's what I'm going to do, anyway. Boy, what a life! "

At a moment like this, his high spirits only served to deepen our depression. It was also getting very cold, and soon Jane went below. I stayed to lean on the taffrail, and to stare moodily across the water at the last dark heads of England.

All the worn old descriptions of the English countryside came to my mind: green lanes and sunny meadows, where we had played as children; lazy rivers, shady gardens, woods, moors and mountains—all these seemed suddenly to have assumed their original, their true and important beauty. Why, during the last few years, had I never found time to see and to enjoy all these things? I had become no more than a casual visitor at home. And now England was once more watching me out of sight. England, the thoughtful host watching his departing guests, and Eddystone glowing intermittently like the cigar between his teeth.

CHAPTER VI
GALES AND GREENHORNS

THE MORNING OF THE 3RD OF OCTOBER found us sixty miles west of Ushant, close-hauled under easy canvas to a strong sou'-easterly wind. There was a high sea and every sign of a stormy twenty-four hours ahead.

We realised that we were not giving the old ship a chance; there was 140 tons of rock ballast in the bottom of her hold, and it made her so stiff, that she whipped back at the end of each roll with a jerk that might have taken the masts clean out of a weaker vessel.

Although the topsides had recently been caulked and her pitchpine deck was brand new, she leaked badly; especially at the break of the main deck, where the water poured into the hold in a steady stream. We had to work the bilge pumps for more than half an hour every watch.

There was not a man aboard who did not feel the strain of that first blow. One or two were seasick from the moment we passed the Eddystone; but they came manfully on deck with their watches until, in the end, sheer weakness forbade them the struggle necessary to get out of their bunks.

The cook was terribly ill; but, by means of an heroic self-discipline, he forced himself to continue eating. In this way he found he could maintain just enough bodily strength to stagger into the galley, between periods of hanging over the rail. He always managed to arrive just in time to prevent the stew from burning.

Young Peter Roach stood it longer than most. Eventually he appeared on deck, grinning from ear to ear, with a bucket lashed to his belt. When he went to the wheel he stood his bucket carefully in the most convenient spot for immediate use.

The Doc made a round of the ship regularly each watch; but he could do very little for any of the crew until the time when he came clattering down the forecastle companion, yelled for a bucket, was sick, and staggered out again. At least half of them felt better at once.

The weather, for the Bay of Biscay at that time of year, was not unusually heavy. It blew about force seven according to the log, increasing to nine; but we were close-hauled and punching into a high sea. That night, when the wind became even more contrary, there was no longer any point in over-burdening the ship with canvas, and we set about snugging her right down.

We soon found that there were scarcely enough hands on deck to furl or reef the sails. In fact, even when we had routed out those of the watch off duty, who were still able to crawl up the forecastle ladder, there were only half a dozen in all, including the man at the wheel. After a long struggle with gear to which everyone was unaccustomed, we managed to furl the spanker.

It was almost impossible to make oneself heard, let alone understood, above the uproar of wind and sea. How we wished that we had issued a dictionary of sea terms to each member of the crew when he joined. We tried our best to explain what was required in the simplest possible language. If only a single familiar order could have taken the place of every five minutes of explanation !

To furl the spanker, it is necessary to lie across the boom on your stomach, and pull in the canvas with both hands. This, in a rolling ship, requires a considerable amount of practice, and for anyone who is feeling even slightly seasick it is naturally fatal. Before the job was finished another man was laid out.

I was seriously alarmed. Lars, who has probably never been alarmed by anything in his life, was grinning—grinning at the one or two bodies lying like corpses about the deck—grinning whenever the ship rolled particularly violently, or when a big sea came aboard and washed one of the apparently unconscious forms into the scuppers. Less than two years before I had smiled and laughed with Lars at very similar situations—wondered why the skipper was shortening sail, instead of making the most of a spanking breeze—felt impatient because he didn't stand in towards the land, when the horizon was only *slightly* hazy. Now suddenly I felt about ten years older, and at the same time incredibly young and frightened. True, it was not yet blowing dangerously hard, but at any moment a violent squall might come tearing across the horizon. What crew we had was diminishing at the rate of about one every half hour. I pictured a sudden furious gust—the ship lying flat under a press of sail—a huge sea smashing aboard—the main hatch stove in——!

It was not the time for taking risks. If more than half the crew were sick we must heave to, and wait for them to recover. But, in order to be able to do even this, it was first necessary to shorten sail.

As Lars and I made our way forward to the forecastle a big sea swept the main deck. We had just reached the top of the companion, when another one exploded over the weather rail and the whole foredeck disappeared in a smother of foam. It was a dirty night, but it was essential to get hold of enough men to shorten sail and make the ship safe for the next twelve hours. It would have been silly to expect semi-conscious landsmen to appreciate the exact gravity of the situation, so I shouted:

" All hands on deck ! We want every man who can crawl ! "

It sounded tremendously melodramatic, but in the *Cap Pilar* melodrama was one of the few luxuries we could afford. In any case I was only concerned just then with getting more hands on deck.

Every man who could creep or crawl rolled out of his bunk, and staggered up the companion. It was pitiful to see some of them hurled and bashed about by the wild lurching of the ship. But all of them made the effort, and each one was another eleven-stone on the end of a rope.

We close-reefed the mainsail, furled the foresail and upper topsail, and hauled down the inner jib. It took us two hours; but when it was done we felt that the ship was now safe, and the sick men could go below again. Some of them were too exhausted to move, and they slumped down to spend the rest of the night sprawling about the deck in the rain and cold.

Here is an extract from the diary of the youngest aboard:

October 3rd.
    8 P.M. Blowing hard, but quite pleasant. Some of the watch have disappeared and are lying in grotesque attitudes about the deck or below.
    Midnight. Blowing harder still. Big seas coming over everywhere. Nearly drowned on lookout. Two chaps lying in the scuppers; others in weird positions on the main hatch. Galley a shambles; everything tearing up and down, swilling in a mixture of salt water, paraffin, and split peas.

October 4th.
    4 A.M. When the watches were mustered I was the only one present out of the port watch. I thought of breakfast and a warm dry bunk (not that it had ever occurred to me that a bunk could be wet.) Some scraps of cold bacon and tomatoes (remains of last night's supper) skidding about on the forecastle table. Every now and then a plate or a mug shooting over the fiddle to clatter about the floor. I ate two ship's biscuits with margarine, and drank somebody's cold dregs of tea.
    The smell in the forecastle was terrible, and the

whole place running with water. I went to turn in, and to my horror found my bunk covered with greasy bacon and tomatoes, and a constant drip of water coming through where my head would be.

4.30 A.M. Skipper came down and asked us to give a hand on deck. What we did I don't quite know, but I can remember lying on the spanker boom with one moment the sky and next the swirling black water above my head.

5 A.M. Below again and determined to turn in. Had just got comfortable when the Skipper came down and said all hands were wanted. This meant I had to get up again. We pulled various ropes for an hour or so, after which the ship was apparently no longer in danger.

7 A.M. Had enough of the forecastle. Everything rolling, rolling, rolling—plates, buckets, boots—all together—crashing madly from one side to the other amongst the bacon and tomatoes on the floor.

I went and sat on the storeroom hatch until daylight.

Another diary reads:

October 3rd–4th.
Some time during the night. Unconscious in bunk. Someone shouting, "All hands on deck!"
Later. Hanging on to the hoops of the mainsail, which had jammed half-way down the mast.
Later still. Unconscious on deck.
Much later. Unconscious in bunk.

On Sunday, 5th of October, we were off the middle of the Bay, and about 150 miles to the westward. The wind had died away, but a heavy swell still ran, and *Cap Pilar* rolled more violently than before, without even the wind to steady her.

The Doc, after hanging on grimly for several hours, turned casually to Lars and asked:

" How far *can* a ship roll ? "

Before leaving London, Newell's finger had appeared to be on the mend; but now it suddenly grew worse, and at midday on Sunday the Doc told me that he would have to operate at once—roll or no roll. It was a great effort; and it probably saved Newell his arm, if not his life.

All Sunday morning we lay helpless in the trough of the sea until, softly at first, but growing soon to a fine steady breeze, the easterly weather came back to us. The sea went down, and one by one the "dead" men, having gained strength from food and sleep, came up on deck to enjoy the sunshine.

There was an atmosphere of reprieve over the ship. We sat about on the main deck and the poop. One by one faces that we had almost forgotten appeared blinking at the sun and the bright blue sky, which many of them may have despaired of ever seeing again. Some one began to sing, but he was unsupported; most of us preferred to enjoy in silence the relief from rain and wind and physical strain.

Suddenly somebody asked: "Where's Gelder?" We looked at each other in amazement. None of us had seen or heard of Gelder for nearly two days. Anxiously we went down to his cabin, and looked in. We were appalled at what we saw. Could this be the neat little apartment which had been specially built into the ship in London?

Water had poured in everywhere, making long brown streaks down the paintwork, covering the new varnish with mouldy white stains and patches, soaking through blankets and mattress, which lay, a shapeless steaming mass. Amongst them was Gelder, apparently dead, with water still pouring upon every part of him.

Poor Gelder! After all his energy and enthusiasm; after his anticipations of a glorious yachting holiday to Madeira!

The cabin floor was covered with a congealed layer of oil and water. The heavy sickly smell of bad ventilation was almost suffocating. Somehow we must get him out into the sunshine. This we managed to do, and when he began to look slightly more cheerful, we suggested a little light food. His face brightened at once.

" I think I'll have a nice tender piece of steamed sole, with egg sauce," he said; " or, I know !" he cried eagerly, "what about that case of ox-tongues I ordered for you from the Army and Navy Stores ? "

"You countermanded the order in favour of two extra barrels of salt pork," said Jane gloomily.

He groaned and turned his face away; whereat Jane, feeling she had been a little unsympathetic, bustled off to do something mysterious to an egg, and soon Gelder was himself again.

For two days more the ship strolled pleasantly along her course in brilliant sunshine. Soon half the crew had recovered, and Willie Marsh was heard to swear that he could "eat a horse with the rind on". Almost all the leaks had taken up, and it was no longer necessary to pump out more than once a day. This was just the breathing space we needed to get everything straight for what might follow.

The next blow came suddenly. One moment the ship was almost becalmed, and the next she was lying right over, tearing through the sea at ten knots or more *due north*.

A heavy squall, working up from leeward, had brought the wind round from south-east to north-west in one swoop and a flurry of blinding rain. Before we could get everything ready to put her about, she had made an agonising mile *in the wrong direction*. But when she was on her course once more we found we had a ramping fair wind that freshened to a gale within a few hours.

This time it really blew hard. The wind must have reached force ten during the freshest squalls; at any rate Lars, still grinning, told me that during one hour of his watch she logged eleven miles, carrying less than half her full spread of sails. We heard afterwards that steamers nearer the Portuguese coast had been held up for a full day and night; but to *Cap Pilar* it was a grand fair wind, and she drove headlong, exulting.

Once more she rolled until the sea poured over her lee rail in a great green avalanche. Another of the crew wrote:

> . . . We scramble out of the fo'c'sle and, half-dressed for the task, we shorten sail in a heavy sea, with great gusts of spray soaking all those not completely clad in oilskins. The ship rolls, the work is hard, but it is glorious!
>
> There is no time to consider the quality of your seamanship and capabilities aloft. You just *run* up the rigging quicker than ever before.
>
> On deck you have a certain feeling of helplessness, and can only follow the others from rope to unfamiliar rope. But aloft it is easy. No time to look around and wonder how to get up past the next bit—you are up; and then there is the thrill of fighting to beat the elements.

Away went the *Cap Pilar*, thundering and singing before the wind. The sun shone upon a tumultuous ocean. The sea was a vivid blue. It was a joy to be alive.

Huge combers charged down upon the ship, towering above our heads, but always just in time she lifted and let them pass harmless beneath her. On they went, foaming down her powerful sides, snarling like thwarted monsters. She gathered way and hurled herself after them, burying her head in their glossy backs, hounding them before her.

At noon we had logged 203 miles in twenty-four hours. Allon was so elated that he decorated the saloon lamp with a toy trumpet and pieces of red paper out of a chocolate box. In the afternoon we clung to the weather rail shouting fierce wild choruses of our own composition.

I can remember no more of that passage, but here is Jane's diary:

October 8th.

Woke up very early to find the ship once more like

the "noises-off" department of a pantomime—timber creaking, bilge-water crashing from side to side, and half our library shooting across the saloon.

It was some time before I could get up, and then only with the greatest difficulty and several bruises. The scene on deck took my breath away—brilliantly sunny and clear, the sort of waves one sees in oil paintings, and the ship making ten knots with only about a third of her sails set.

The wake was a wonderful turquoise blue, and at times the waves were flecked with rainbow colours.

Romm struggled into action, and in spite of repeated bouts of seasickness in the fore-top, spent almost the whole morning taking photographs from aloft.

10 A.M. Utterly incapable of moving about. Worn out by the effort of clinging hard to the rail. Went below.

11 A.M. Disturbed by a torrent of water pouring into the cabin, and heard sundry groans and crashes. Arrived on deck just as they were taking in the spanker.

The sight of six of the crew battling with the huge sail filled me with awe and admiration, till Lars, his face one large diabolical grin, pointed at all we could see of Potter—two immensely long pink feet sticking out from his oilskin trousers and kicking wildly at the sky.

October 9th.

We have now crossed the Bay of Biscay at last. To-day everyone seems more cheerful than during the last rough spell, and the seasick ones don't appear to be appreciably worse. The brilliant sunshine makes all the difference.

Allon lashed a deck-chair to the skylight, and I spent the morning there peeling potatoes and carrots. It was like being in the cockpit of a stunting aeroplane, except that I don't suppose they ever peel carrots in an aeroplane.

I was chivvied out again after lunch to make a pudding for supper. George was told off to look after the bread; the result was some peculiar crinkly things, very irregular in shape. Apparently the dough had been flung against the sides of the oven, where it stuck, and was later removed and re-baked.

October 10th.

Cook was given the day off, so I helped Potter cook the breakfast. We managed successfully, even in the scrambling of fifty eggs.

After breakfast I started preparations for an apple pudding. Interrupted by Dennis, the pig, sniffing around, and by most of the ingredients rolling over the deck. The cooking of it was even more difficult, as nothing would induce the stove to remain alight for more than five or ten minutes on end. It alternately blew itself out or caught fire. We struggled with it till nearly I o'clock when, to our joy, everything was cooked.

After lunch Adrian attacked the galley, and I had a grand bath in the laundry tub.

CHAPTER VII
FIRST BASE

AT NOON ON SUNDAY, 11th of October, we were seventy miles from Porto Santo, the northernmost island of the Madeira group. About 5 o'clock in the evening McDonald thought he had seen land, and the hands dashed aloft up the fore rigging to have a look. The cook, who once again wore his white hat at a jaunty angle, was among the first.

It was a false alarm; but at 2 A.M. we raised the light, and at dawn the island of Porto Santo lay dimly like a wisp of grey smoke ahead. As we drew near the land, the dull grey of the island brightened into veins and patches of brown and red and orange-coloured rock. The bulk of Madeira, beneath its bundle of white cloud, was like a huge black bowl of soap-suds in the distance. Next morning at 6 o'clock we drifted into the Bay of Funchal.

As the morning sun crept out from behind a low cloud-bank, details began to grow upon the rugged mountain-side. The red cliff faces and the steep green slopes separated. Misty gorges on the mountain tops fell back from the hillsides, which caught the light first, and soon the whole island was covered with little white-washed red-roofed houses. These little houses thickened towards Funchal like a cluster of stars in the sky.

There came that moment when just the tops of the mountains were capped with orange; clouds hung as if entangled amongst the peaks, and came writhing down the precipitous gorges. Suddenly a rainbow struck through them, and the whole scene was overburdened with colour.

When we anchored we were at once surrounded by a

65

horde of boats. Some of these were piled high with wicker
chairs; others contained small boys gazing patiently up,
and repeating over and over again the monotonous,
mournful ditty, " Sixpence I dive—sixpence I dive, lady—
sixpence I dive." Meanwhile the sellers of tablecloths,
cheap jewellery and curios fell upon us in their hundreds.
Hard-working unanswerable fellows they were, with large
boxes wrapped in cloth, or strapped about with leather
belts.

The Madeira bum-boatman puts every ounce of artistry
and persuasive power into his work. The old disreputable
ones whisper in your ear. Clutching your arm and rolling
their eyes, they pull out a sheaf of filthy, dog-eared papers
with the appearance of being about to disclose to you the
secret of the Pyramids. If you are a ship's officer there
will often be a comparatively clean note addressed to you
personally, and purporting to come from the captain of
another ship:

> DEAR OLD MAN,
> Welcome once more agreeably. I must tell you in
> due course of my lovable colleague Juan Gomez, who
> will devotedly conclude with you unspeakable pre-
> ferences in the matter of: soap, matches, silk pyjamas
> (for any gentleman's Mrs.), jewellery, oranges, cig-
> arettes, brilliantine (most desirous) also all manner of
> especials. Great news if you are always in virile way
> of living since we made merry commonly in the pasture.
> Your humbly adoring accomplice,
> SIR JEROME LASCELLES.
> (High Gentleman.)

Gelder, Allon, the Doc, Newell and some of the crew
went ashore soon after breakfast; but Jane and I were
not free until later on, when we pulled to the jetty in one
of our own dories; leaving Lars and one watch aboard
the ship.

From the sea Funchal is a large patch of red roofs climbing high up a steep green mountainside, like poppies in a field of dark grass. Ashore it is alternately picturesque and crude.

The streets are made of very small cobbles, some of them containing mosaics worked in stones of several colours. One's first impression of Madeira is of beauty and bad hygiene, so closely mingled that it is often difficult to isolate either of them.

We wandered up through the cobbled streets till we came to a square where a line of open cars were parked. We were immediately surrounded by a shouting, grinning mob of drivers. We felt gay and irresponsible and full of friendliness towards the mob. We made a sign to the youngest, most reckless looking brigand, and a few minutes later bright yellow walls were streaking past us, red roofs and brilliant patches of flowers leaped out at us and flashed by, and there was a rush of cool scented air in our faces. Our driver's name was Candido, and his car was a scarlet six-cylinder Dodge. She leaped up the hill, her tyres singing over the cobbles.

Candido was in high spirits too, and kept turning round to grin at us and say complimentary things in very broken English—usually just as we were approaching a nasty corner. We flashed in at a handsome gateway marked Hotel Bella Vista, through a shady garden to a long, low house, which looked old, friendly and peaceful. On a perch beside the front door sat a blue and yellow macaw, watching us obscenely with one eye closed.

In the bar of the Bella Vista we found George, Newell, Gelder and Allon already firmly established, and later we were Allon's guests at what seemed the most wonderful meal we had ever tasted. Beside Jane's place was a bunch of exotic flowers, in keeping with the atmosphere of luxury and extravagance which prevailed throughout the meal. Before we left the table we began to feel like characters out of an Oppenheim novel, and tried to summon the waiters " with a scarcely perceptible lift of the eyebrows ". The waiters winked broadly in reply and remained where they were.

After lunch Candido took Jane to an English hairdresser, where she enjoyed herself in her womanly way for the rest of the afternoon, whilst I rushed from office to office about the business of the ship. My first act was to engage a temporary cabin-boy called José. He had an aristocratic surname and a dazzling smile. He spoke not a word of English, but he was willing to work hard, so we put him aboard and left him almost entirely to his own devices. I engaged him through an interpreter to whom I explained that we only required José while we were in port, and that he must leave the ship before she sailed.

That afternoon I also had my first encounter with the officialdom that has made carefree sea-wandering a thing of the past. I found that it is no longer possible to drift at will about the oceans of the world, calling where and when you please. In these days you must enter a port armed with clearances, bills of health, authorised crew-lists and stamped manifests; in some ports of the world you are even compelled to clear for a specific destination, and you will be heavily fined if you fail to go there.

After three days everything was settled and Jane and I were able to take a few days' holiday. We spent about half the time in great splendour in a large, cool room in the Bella Vista hotel, where we found such relief from our worries, that we even enjoyed the barbarous custom of eating our breakfast in bed. We took hot baths at all hours, and sat during the rest of the time in the back seat of Candido's car. One day he took us high up the mountainside. The next he drove us along the coast road to the westward.

Candido was one of the most charming Madeirans we met, and he was always in the best of spirits. He knew only a few words of English, but he took such pains to interpret our every wish by a process of elimination, that Jane could go out with him for a morning's shopping, and come back with most of what she wanted, having seen almost every shop and street in Funchal into the bargain.

One day we drove along the south coast of the island to Cabo Girao, where the cliff drops sheer from 1,500 feet into the sea. This is the second highest headland in the world. From the top of it we could see the ocean bed in twenty fathoms of water as plainly as you see the bottom of a swimming bath.

We lay for a long time on the cliff-top, watching the falcons wheeling out over the sea. Five-hundred feet below us a narrow ledge seemed greener than the rest; it was somebody's potato patch. No house was visible for miles in any direction, so it must have belonged to people in the village inland. We marvelled at the expenditure of so much effort for the sake of a few vegetables; but Candido also showed us a place where men climbed down a thousand feet of precipice every day to fish.

That is the keynote of Madeiran peasant life, prodigious efforts for small returns. The Madeirans, born in a land where the hills are so steep that it is just as tiring to go down as to go up, appear not to mind how much work they do.

For instance, every day a number of rowing boats are pulled laboriously round the harbour towing dredge nets. We thought at first that they must be dredging for oysters; the amount of work they did suggested that there was a chance of an occasional pearl. We were surprised to find, after a while, that they were collecting nothing more valuable than a few lumps of coal, dropped into the sea from time to time during the bunkering of steamers. Often the unfortunate gleaners dragged up, with infinite labour, a hundredweight or more of broken crockery, old shoes and pebbles, with only one or two lumps of coal amongst them.

But, saddest of all, they invariably threw all the rubbish back again, to be picked up by some other boat, or by themselves next day.

The roads on the island are very steep and tortuous, but Candido was obsessed by two conflicting determinations; that his Dodge should travel faster than any other car on Madeira, and that his patrons should miss nothing which he considered they ought to see. The result was that he never had two hands on the wheel and rarely gave the road ahead more than an occasional glance. His favourite objects of interest were pumpkins, of which every other house had one or two drying upon the roof; so Candido's arms kept shooting out on one side or the other, accompanied by a running fire of :

"One pumpkins ! . . . Two pumpkins ! . . . One pumpkins ! . . . One, two, three, four—*ach!* very plenty pumpkins ! "

Between each ejaculation he would turn round grinning for our approval, which action always caused his right foot to press down on the accelerator. I suppose that the frozen smiles we managed to return confirmed his Latin opinion about the coldness of the English.

"How many years have you old? " asked Candido suddenly.

" Twenty-six," I replied.

" I have twenty-nine."

" You very old."

" You very new," replied Candido simply.

He was delighted at having remembered the English for the opposite to " old "; so, when shortly afterwards we passed a cow with her calf, he pointed and said, " One cow—one new cow."

Allon and Gelder left in the first ship bound for England, and once more a feeling of loneliness oppressed us for a time.

We remained at Funchal in all eight days. During this time half the crew went ashore " seeing the world ", while the other half were working on the ship's ballast, in an attempt to make her easier in a seaway. I believe that they found very little to interest them in Madeira; especially as none of them could speak Portuguese; but they enjoyed eating bananas at a shilling a stem and drinking the wine of the country. This was the first port of their seafaring career, and they must have been the constant butt of every species of water-front shark.

Willie Marsh gave this account of his first night ashore:

" We was sitting in a café, when up comes a posh piece and sits on my knee, and starts stroking my hair. She ought've knowed I didn't want nothing to do with her. And, anyway, it was getting on for tea-time."

CHAPTER VIII
SALVAGE—OR VERY NEARLY

"THERE YOU ARE, CAP! Right on that cross is where you'll anchor in ten fathoms of water, over a clean sandy bottom. There's no better holding ground anywhere round the island."

It was a weathered old chunk of a Portuguese sea captain speaking, and before him was spread a chart of Great Salvage Island, one of those lonely little rocks that crop up here and there, from prodigious depths, in many parts of the Atlantic. We had learned to trust and admire old Fernandez during our stay at Funchal, so it never occurred to us to question his advice on this occasion.

Great Salvage does not attract much tourist traffic. It lies about 150 miles south of Madeira, is not more than a mile square, and uninhabited except by sea-birds and rabbits; moreover it bears a sinister name. But the opportunity for our naturalists to find something unusual as well as our own eagerness to visit strange places proved too great an attraction to be resisted.

Towards evening on Wednesday, 21st of October, the wind died in the Bay of Funchal. The sun was just setting, and the cliffs above us went orange, brown, and yellow by turns. Fifteen miles to the southward the Dezerta Islands, like jagged lumps of iron, cooled through purple to steely black.

Night fell, and the lights of the town blazed out; the air was so still that we could hear the people talking in the streets. To while away the hours of waiting an accordion was brought on deck, and the strains of "Shenandoah"

72

and "The Maid of Amsterdam" fell upon the breathless air, and beat echoes from the cliffs.

In these latitudes we were within the limits of the north-east trade wind, and every day was clear and sunny; we knew also that out at sea the wind would be perpetually fair many hundreds of miles to the southward. I thought the whole ship's company showed a remarkable resilience of temperament. The hardships of the first stage of the voyage appeared to have been forgotten, and everyone was looking forward to the warmth and comfort of tropical seas. But when I looked back at the passage from England to Madeira I was amazed. Lars and I were used to that sort of thing; we had known what to expect. There were half a dozen others, constitutionally free from sea-sickness and ready to take life as it came, to whom the miserable discomfort was all part of the show; but to the rest—hopelessly ill, wet, cold and battered—the first few days of the voyage must have been a horror they will never forget.

I thought of all this as the night wore on, and the murmur of the town grew fainter, then died away. I realised that it was not enough to have warned this company of gay adventurers about the trials they would have to face. Even though they had professed to understand the conditions under which they would have to live, they had *not* understood them fully; and the tropics, I knew, would bring further disillusionment. Not until a year or so of seafaring had dimmed the memory of life as they had been used to living it ashore—not until their impressions and experiences of many parts of the world had cleared their minds of what they had expected to see, would they begin properly to appreciate the cruise. Until then, there would be a great many disappointments and some discontent, nor could any previous warnings on my part clear me of all responsibility for this.

One by one the shore lights went out. The quiet of midnight gave place to dead silence. Without a sound now we also sat waiting.

A dog began to bark incessantly, insistently. All at once the smoke from our cigarettes curved and drifted seaward above our heads. The dog's barking became suddenly louder. "Here's the breeze," said Lars, and stumped off for'ard to man the windlass.

At breakfast-time I was amazed to find the table already laid at half-past seven, and, a moment later, to see José's familiar grin advancing behind a bowl of porridge !

The position was a difficult one : José had stowed away. Why he had done it we were unable to imagine; perhaps he liked the food, but that seemed unlikely : perhaps he wished to learn English—he had never shown any desire to do this; possibly he just wanted to see the world, like everyone else. It was always difficult to understand José's motives. The immediate problem was to make him aware of the enormity of his offence.

We could think of nothing to say except " No good ", which was repeated loudly several times in different tones. José listened attentively for a little, then his face lit up with one of his most brilliant smiles, and in a firm, clear voice he said " All right ", so we gave it up and signed him on the articles.

We made fair sailing all that day. The trade wind blew a steady force four, and a great peace fell upon the ship.

Early the following morning, while it was still dark, a black lump rose upon our starboard bow; and daybreak found us within two or three miles of Salvage Island. The growing light showed it to be a flat forbidding mass of rock, entirely devoid of trees or shrubs, and burned brown by the sub-tropical sun. With the wind abeam we stood straight in for our anchorage.

This was to be a real adventure, we thought. We had

heard among other things that Great Salvage was an island formerly frequented by pirates. It seemed very probable; and we wondered how long a time had elapsed since a sturdy little sailing vessel like ours had stood in upon this rocky shore at dawn. The story went that Salvage had been a favourite rendezvous of buccaneers preying upon the trade route to the East, and that they used to meet here to share the spoils. There was, of course, a fabulous treasure still hidden upon the island, and frankly we welcomed the opportunity of searching for it.

All hands were now on deck, and we were nearing the spot marked by Fernandez with a cross upon our chart. On the poop George was busily engaged in extricating his feet from the coils of the leadline. When finally he made his cast, we were right over our intended anchorage, and he should have found bottom in ten fathoms.

" No bottom at twenty," he sang out. This was the first of many shocks.

We stood on. The cliffs rose higher before us, and the peak of the island disappeared behind them. We were soon no more than a quarter of a mile from the shore; we could see the shoal water stretching out towards us from the rocks. " Still no bottom," called George, and then a little later: " By the deep sixteen ! " About half a mile to leeward an off-shore reef was breaking heavily. We *must* anchor now, and the *anchor must hold*.

" By the deep twelve ! "

" Let go for'ard ! "

Down came Lars's maul, and with a roar of flailing cable our ten hundredweight bower anchor went to the bottom, bringing the ship up less than two hundred yards from the cliffs.

There was a universal sigh of relief; but it came too soon. As the *Cap Pilar* swung, an ominous clank told us that all was far from well. We were now in less than ten fathoms of crystal-clear water, and peering over the bows, we could see our anchor, not lying in a bed of sand, as we had expected, but sliding across a table of smooth rock! Another grating clank from the depths, and we realised there was not a moment to be lost. It was just a question of whether we could get the anchor up and the ship under command before she dragged straight on to the reef astern.

Twelve men hurled themselves upon the windlass, and hove as if possessed, till the decks trembled with their exertions.

"Heyah—ho!" they shouted, and down came the windlass arms, thump! thump! against the deck. Two men scrambled aloft and cleared the lower topsail, two others hauled the sheets.

The huge barrel of the windlass revolved slowly to the chattering of palls; the cable came grinding through the hawse-pipe, the gangs on the two rocker arms were heaving and shouting with all their might. The fore-topsail went creaking aloft, and next the mainsail, thrashing between its lifts. Never before had there been such a storm of furious activity aboard the *Cap Pilar*. "Anchor a-trip," sang Lars. The boys gave a cheer and redoubled their efforts.

Slowly at first, then faster as the jibs filled aback, the ship's head cast to port. Now the nearest land was right ahead, but the *Cap Pilar* had good sternway, and so, for the moment, all was well. There was still that reef to clear, however; but, to our horror, before her head swung clear of this second danger, she began to gather headway and pay off slower and slower. The anchor at her starboard was acting as a rudder and *holding her back towards the wind*! In another minute she was making two or three knots straight for the shoal. We could see the black teeth of rock sticking out of the pother; we could hear the growl of the breakers, like the throaty roar of a great sea-monster hungry for ships.

We dashed to the main halliards, and let them go by the

run. Down came the mainsail with an almighty thunder of slatting canvas, and at the same time, up came the anchor clear of the water. With only fore-topsails and headsails set, and the helm hard up, there was nothing left to do but watch, fascinated, what looked like the certain doom of all our hopes and ambitions. Newell said afterwards that during that handful of seconds, which felt like hours, he was thinking what a fine tent the mainsail would make, and was already planning how best to get the stores ashore in the lifeboat. Lars felt only a bitter disappointment at not having been able to get his ship decently painted before she was lost.

Then the miracle occurred: quite suddenly, her head began to move. The reef shifted from the lee bow to right ahead. For an agonising ten seconds it was hidden by the forepart of the ship; then it flashed into view on the other bow, so near that I was afraid she might turn too fast and scrape her quarter against the rocks.

"Steady the helm. Meet her!" But we were so close that she hardly felt her rudder before the welter of boiling water slid beneath her counter, and we were clear.

We missed the rocks by just half a ship's length, and immediately we were out on the broad Atlantic. Making all sail we bore up upon the wind with the idea of beating back to where another anchorage was marked on the chart. But there was a strong current against us, and we soon saw that it would take us the rest of the day to get back. In any case we felt a very strong desire for deep blue water after our narrow escape; so, without wasting any more time, we squared away and laid a course for Tenerife.

CHAPTER IX
TENERIFE

IN THE PATHETIC little hours before the dawn the wind died to no more than a whisper of far countries and the road to strange adventures. Presently the horizon seemed to lift and harden in the east. Daybreak was at hand.

From right ahead now, the island of Tenerife, towering fantastically to over 12,000 feet out of a sea of even greater depth, strode to meet us across the ocean. We were bound for Santa Cruz, which lies on the eastern side of the island, and at 9 o'clock we anchored in the roadstead about one mile from the town.

Our first visitor from the shore was a tall, fair-haired Scandinavian with striking blue eyes. He wore no hat, and his sandy hair blew about at will, giving him an oddly boyish appearance. He hailed us cheerily in English, but he was so obviously a Norseman that Lars could not resist the temptation of answering him in Swedish. He was surprised but delighted, and swung himself aboard to continue the conversation. He turned out to be a Norwegian doctor, who on account of his health had come to live on Tenerife, where he earned a temporary livelihood as a ship chandler.

After breakfast we went ashore with Dr. Holmboe, who soon disposed of the formalities of the port, and then took us to an open-air restaurant, where we drank beer, and had leisure to watch the life of the town.

It was at Santa Cruz that the first blow of the Spanish revolution had been struck. When we were there, at least 50 per cent of the inhabitants wore uniform—any uniform, and on Sundays there was hardly a civilian to be seen; almost every male and female appeared in khaki or blue.

78

Children of three or four years of age were dressed as soldiers, with toy bayonets in their scabbards; old men shuffled about the streets, wearing caps and tunics—as badges, which they hoped would protect them from molestation. Any, who were old or young enough to lift them, carried carbines as well; some had them slung across their backs, some had them over their shoulders, often holding them by the muzzle, while some trailed their guns like toys behind them.

On Sunday, the day after we arrived, we set off for a drive across the island to visit the central volcano. Dr. Holmboe had found us an immense eight-cylinder Nash and at 9 A.M. seven of us piled into her, and away we went through the narrow streets. We were all in Bank holiday mood, and we cheered lustily for the driver, whose name was Leon, as with shouting klaxon, he scooped the military from before him. Bleak houses echoed the uproar of our passing, harsh curses, screams of laughter, patriotic cries, all tumbled pell-mell after us with the dust from beneath our wheels. We caught the excitement that was in the air, we shouted to the grey, gaunt houses, the people and the sky. Leon responded by driving furiously.

We roared out of the shopping streets into a long shady *avenida*, where a strip of grass with beds of scarlet geraniums ran down the middle of the way. On either side pretty modern villas, one with a bright blue roof, stood buried up to their eyes in trees and flowers.

We turned south towards the outskirts of the town, and Leon slowed down a little to point out the more important buildings. Here was the bull-ring; we wondered whether there were any bull-fights at this season. " No," said Leon, with a glittering eye, " we execute Communists now instead ! " 'A few minutes later we passed a large warehouse, which had been commandeered by the Fascists for a political prison. Old men and women, girls and boys and little children stood in queues outside. They had waited patiently since early morning, for the chance of a hasty word with a husband, father, or a brother whom they might well be seeing for the last time.

"Will all the prisoners be shot?" we asked.

"If God is merciful," answered Leon.

A gloomy silence fell upon us, and we were glad soon to be out upon a fine white highway that took us into the hills, where the prickly pear grew like blackberry bushes at home.

All the way up to the mountain village at Laguna the roads were still alive with Fascists, civil guards, militia, boy scouts, girl guides, and all sorts of nondescript military types. The narrow streets of the township were blocked with people in uniform: all were laughing and singing, and obviously very happy in the new, popular craze of playing at soldiers. But some of them frowned as we passed, and we wished that Leon would keep his hand off the klaxon: we feared that at any moment we might be stopped and asked whether our intentions were honourable.

A mile beyond Laguna we reached the top of the hill, and the sea burst into view again before us. At the same moment we caught our first glimpse of the great volcano, Pico de Teide; the snow streaked his sloping shoulders where he sat, like a senile Buddha, cross-legged upon a platter of cloud. Far below, between us and the farther coast, lay acre upon flat acre of plantains, right round into the valley of Orotava; over a hundred square miles of bananas in an unbroken carpet.

We began, now, the descent of the western slopes, stopping half-way down to stretch our legs and admire the view. As we stood, grouped beside a cactus, for Donnelly to take our photograph, two lorries came coasting down the hill at high speed; in the back of one were standing about twenty men in Fascist uniforms, and in the other as many women similarly clad. The men seemed a little uncertain as to how they ought to answer our shouts and waves; half of them waved back, and half immediately assumed stern, almost injured expressions. The girls appeared to have no doubts.

A few miles farther on we branched off the main coast road and began to climb. Soon we stopped again; this time at a little roadside tavern. Leon disappeared within, returning a moment later with a tray, on which were seven glasses of sweet country wine. We found it very good, and ordered another round; but when we wanted to pay, Leon waved away our money, saying that he had already settled the bill himself. This was a new and welcome experience for us; we wondered whether it would be possible to get London taxi-drivers to follow Leon's example : " Once round Hyde Park and a pint of bitter " would be a very pleasant way of spending a leisure hour. A little farther up the hill we passed another tavern, and this time we insisted on buying Leon a drink. The wine we were given was a different one, but also sweet, and it tasted very innocuous.

This inn was the last of the houses, and now we began to mount steadily towards the clouds, which lay no more than 2,000 feet above us. All at once Jane giggled; in a moment we were all howling with uncontrollable laughter. Donnelly's bright red, glowing countenance beamed upon the company, Newell and George roared, gripping their sides; even the sober Lars began to chuckle. We passed a troop of infant Fascists, boys between the ages of six and ten; they stared at us open mouthed. Then suddenly the boy in them overcame the soldier, and with one accord they broke ranks and came racing down the road after us, yelling and whistling, and no doubt telling Leon that his back wheels were going round. We all stood up in the car and gravely saluted this triumph of Nature.

The air grew cooler. The sun was blotted out, and we plunged into the first bank of mist. Gradually as we climbed still higher, the vegetation changed. We had left a hot gaudy country of palms and brilliant flowers—now we were passing through fields of bracken with clumps of heather. It was as though we had been transported, in the space of half an hour, from the tropics, to the Yorkshire moors or the Highlands of Scotland.

Then down came the rain; softly at first, but soon gaining force, until great gusts and torrents of driving hail and sleet made our fingers numb, and our noses blue with cold. The trees grew thinner, more stunted, then disappeared altogether. Every form of vegetation began to dwindle; soon only the fields of twisted lava and huge boulders of pumice-stone stretched into the mist on either hand. After a little the rain grew lighter, finally dissolving into a windswept drizzle, which enveloped us all the way to the top.

In a pass, at 6,000 feet, we found a nondescript stone building with a kitchen attached. A sullen-mouthed native, wearing about his shoulders a goats-hair cloak, stood upon a rise near by, watching. He came reluctantly down to meet us, and led us into the kitchen, where a blazing fire soon thawed the stiffness out of us. When we offered him a share of our food he merely shook his head, and went out to continue his grim vigil. What he expected to see through the mist and rain we were unable to guess. He seemed to hold himself sombrely aloof from the world, and we felt that he disapproved of our invasion of his mountain solitudes.

After lunch we set off to look about us. Everywhere was a mighty desolation; strange mounds of pumice; immense boulders that looked as if they weighed many tons, yet could be set rolling by the joint efforts of any two of us; and nowhere, in all that wilderness, a single tree or shrub. We trudged across a valley as rugged and lifeless as the canyons of Colorado, and began to climb the outer crater; it was like climbing a pile of coke. Here and there smaller cones of cinders, absolutely regular in shape, had formed round subsidiary vents; we tried to scale one of these, but the surface was so loose that we found it impossible.

When we reached the top of the ridge the clouds had broken up, and, through the gaps between them, we looked down upon the grey sea 9,000 feet below. Sixty miles to the eastward the peaks of Gran Canaria sailed through the clouds like destroyers through a sea of snow, while, above us, huge billows of cumulus drove down and burst upon El Pico de Teide.

We sat here awhile enjoying the sunshine and the fresh, cold air. We felt very remote from hysterical revolutionaries, from ships and from the sea. Sanson collected a few grasshoppers and beetles for subsequent scientific examination; Donnelly took photographs of the peak with a large camera, whose shutter worked with a loud crash and a rattle of powerful machinery; Lars and Newell got busy with an immense boulder, which they eventually succeeded in pushing over a precipice; and George strode away to explore the ridge.

In the evening we drove down again through the clouds, the mist and the drizzle, to the little old-fashioned town of Orotava. Here we found mansions of oak and cedarwood, built in the time of the Inquisition. Some of their immense façades were decorated all over with intricate carved patterns, while a wooden balcony ran from end to end beneath the eaves. Through every magnificent doorway we looked in upon a courtyard filled with palms and tropical flowers. Fountains sang in these " patios ", with monstrous carp swimming lazily beneath them.

At Orotava we saw the most beautiful girls in all Tenerife. They strolled arm in arm upon a shady boulevard before the castle. In the late afternoon the whole town seemed to have collected in this neighbourhood. In groups of two or three they sauntered up and down, up and down. The soldiers guarding the castle brought out chairs, and settled themselves comfortably, their rifles between their legs, to watch the promenade. For the time being every serious thought seemed to have been shelved in favour of the far more important consideration of making the most of the evening air.

We drove home in darkness across the mountains. Every mile or so a pair of soldiers with fixed bayonets stepped into the glare of our headlights, forcing Leon to pull up with a screaming of brakes. They desired to know who we were and whither we were bound.

The headlights of two cars, travelling very fast, appeared over the crest of a hill two miles behind us. In a few minutes they were less than half a mile away. Leon saw them, and increased his speed. Immediately the drive assumed the atmosphere of a flight from justice; we pictured ourselves as a party of gangsters on the way to a killing. George turned to stare grimly into the growing aurora of light from the other cars' headlights: "High-jackers!" he muttered. "Get your rods, boys!"

The cars came roaring up astern, Leon jammed his foot down on the throttle, we leapt forward; but the others were still gaining on us, and next moment the peremptory blare of a klaxon warned us to make way. Leon, like Candido of Madeira, owned the fastest car on his island, and would give way for no one. The summons from behind became more insistent, the cars crowded upon us; George opened an imaginary violin case, and Donnelly made a show of putting on a bullet-proof waistcoat. Next moment the driver of the nearest car, with wonderful skill and daring, took advantage of a curve in the road, and swept abreast on the near side. The road straightened and

Leon opened the Nash full out. For ten seconds we raced side by side, filling the whole roadway, at seventy miles an hour.

In the back seat of the other car, a strange fat figure, with bulging eyes, and dressed in the uniform of the Civil Guard, was bouncing up and down in a frenzy. Now he leaned far out, shouting and gesticulating at us. Suddenly, Leon drew in to the side of the road, and slowed down. Both cars swept by, the second one containing half a dozen soldiers with the muzzles of their rifles sticking out of the windows. It was a general and his bodyguard! Perhaps they were tearing through the night to intercept a landing of government troops, or perhaps to start a counter revolution. Leon looked shaken, and drove us soberly home.

The day after our arrival at Santa Cruz H.M.S. *Leander* anchored in the roadstead. We pulled across to pay our respects, and check our chronometers. For all of us, except Newell, this was our first acquaintance with the Navy, and we were surprised and delighted at the friendliness with which we were received. We brought back to the *Cap Pilar* a fine loaf of good English bread. In the afternoon the *Leander* returned our visit, and at tea-time our guests courageously refused to eat any of their own bread.

One night we had dinner at a restaurant in the main square of the town, and drank our coffee at little tables set upon the side-walk. A military band was playing, and the square, as usual, was packed with people in uniform.

A fanfare of trumpets heralded the national anthem and we rose respectfully to our feet. For an anthem it was exceedingly long, almost a symphony; but all round the square young and old stood rigidly to attention; their arms outstretched in the Fascist salute. Just as our attention was beginning to wander, the music ended amidst a gale of applause. With a sigh of relief we sat down; but almost immediately the band struck up, and we were forced to stand while they played the whole thing through all over again.

We asked them in Tenerife for news of the revolution in Spain. We were told that Madrid would have fallen before the end of the week; that was on 26th of October, 1936.

Next day we left with the sea-breeze, bound for Rio.

CHAPTER X
ROLLING DOWN TO RIO

DAY AFTER BURNING DAY and still the north-east trade held full and steady. On the sixth day after the snow-capped peak of Tenerife had fallen astern, we expected to see the outer islands of the Cape Verde group.

We knew that the atmosphere in the neighbourhood of the islands is often so thick with dust, carried across 500 miles of sea from the Sahara, that you may not see the land before you are almost upon it; so we kept a very sharp look-out.

About three o'clock, the long-awaited cry of "Land ho!" was raised—as a matter of fact it was Roper who first saw land, and he said "Land ahoy!" in a very deep bass voice, which made us all laugh. Yes, there was the land; and our anxiety was almost justified, for the highest peaks of San Antonio seemed to be almost overhead, while the lower part of the island was still invisible.

From the Cape Verde islands our course lay nearly due south, and day after day *Cap Pilar* ambled steadily through brilliant seas. She went as a saw through a sheet of steel, with clouds of flying-fish scattering like sparks from beneath her forefoot.

England was gone; she was no longer behind us, but ahead of us, at the end of the long sea-road we must travel. For the moment all doubts as to the success or failure of the cruise were at rest, and we set about the business of putting the ship in order and trying to improve her very rugged appearance.

All were quickly becoming used to seafaring life; every

day each man found that there was more and more that
he was able to do.

The "patent" galley-stove was a complete failure, so
we had to abandon our attempts to make bread and rely
solely on biscuits. Here is Jane's account of "housekeep-
ing" in a sailing ship:

It is nearly three months now since I signed on as
steward of the *Cap Pilar*, but with lubberly persistence
I still think of myself as "housekeeper". Somehow or
other a steward seems such a very masculine individual,
while the name "stewardess" merely recalls visions of
one's less happy moments on a Channel steamer. But
it's all the same, really, and the big problem is food.

Strictly speaking, a sailor should be so hungry after
his watch on deck that he will eat with avidity any
bucketful of food that may be put before him. But
sometimes our sailors have just been hauled out of
their bunks, and sometimes the sun is very hot; sometimes even, the passing thought of roast-beef or
brussels-sprouts makes pea-soup and salt pork a little
unpalatable. So, to keep everyone happy, quite a deal
of head scratching is necessary over the meal problem.

We have an amazing variety of provisions aboard;
but I remember well the awful sinking feeling when
I ordered the first barrel of salt meat to be opened.
We found enormous chunks of salt-encrusted brown
substance, from which arose a curious odour, that transported the bystander rather abruptly to the slaughter-
house. Cook and I refused to be daunted by this. By
dint of much soaking, and careful boiling, a stew was
eventually produced; and after that we found innumerable uses for "salt-horse". If it is minced, and mixed
with onions and a little herbs, then covered with pastry,
it makes a goodish pie; or in much the same way it
makes a meat pudding or savoury pie, and of course
in stews and curries it is completely at home.

Bully beef is much less frightening, and altogether
easier to deal with. Corned beef is a nautical treat.
The problem of salt meat was our first and biggest,
but there was one other, the breakfast problem.

Often we have neither bacon, eggs, sardines, nor salt fish; and tinned ham and sausages are very, very precious, only to be used once a month. Sometimes, too, it has been too hot for porridge. Payne has become an expert in making salt pork look and taste exactly like bacon, and this we eat with macaroni, potato, or beans and sauce. When any bread can be spared, fried bread and minced bacon is extremely good. Once a week we have tinned herrings; and one day, not one of my most comfortable mornings, we have fish balls.

The whole ship's company, Lars solely excepted, has a grudge against fish balls. I made a bad mistake at the beginning: never having met the species before, I read the tin label carefully, and saw that they were in *bouillon*. I accordingly ordered the cook just to heat them well and serve them. They turned out to be very small and round with a pallor that was almost indecent. Taste they had little or none, and even the cat spurned them. Next time I ordered them to be fried, but everyone recalled their former paleness, and refused to be taken in. A further disguise was tried in the form of kedgeree, but that was little better. However, I felt I must make these men eat fish balls somehow. It was too ignominious to be beaten by a silly little white blob, when one has battled successfully with vast hunks of beef. I found one odd tin of sardines that wasn't enough by itself, and cook carefully mixed this with the fish balls and fried the mixture; and at last they were eaten without suspicion.

A few days later came the great discovery of sausage meat. Three-parts of ship's biscuits to one part of corned beef, very finely minced, judiciously seasoned and then frozen, makes a most excellent substitute for sausage. It went down so well that cook and I hardly dared let on how it materialised, but when they found it out no one seemed to mind its humble origin.

We cannot run to roast-beef and yorkshire pudding on Sundays, but we have excellent tinned boiled mutton and green peas, followed by apple pie. In hot weather it is all served cold, which gives us a change, and the cook a rest.

And here is a description of "A day on board the *Cap Pilar* ", written by one of the crew:

—"Sou'-west a half south," says the man at the wheel. "Sou'-west a half south, " answers the relief, as he takes over for his hour. It is five o'clock in the morning, and the dawn has just broken, with the ship going along at barely three knots under a light south-easterly breeze.

Not long afterwards one of the watch emerges from the galley with two mugs of coffee, which he takes up to the poop; one for the man at the wheel and one for the mate standing beside him. Then he fetches two more mugs, and takes them up to the fo'c'sle head; one for the lookout, and one for a sleeping figure stretched out beside the capstan. He gives the sleeper a shake, and hands him his mug. "What's she doing?" he asks, yawning. "Not much more than two (knots) when I was at the wheel," answers the lookout. "Oh gawd, we'll be another week getting to Rio at this rate."

Soon four-bells are struck. It is six o'clock, broad daylight long ago, and time for the work of the day to begin. The sun is already hot and burning, a promise of melting deck-seams later in the day. The cook is called, and then the watch set about washing down the decks. When the hose is rigged, two men pump the water up, the mate holds the nozzle of the hose, and the third man scrubs vigorously with a deck-broom. The water comes gushing down off the poop on to the maindeck, and then on to the foredeck. The pumpers sing lustily but untunefully as they work; the man with the broom tries to look as though he were working much harder than he really is, and the mate, who is not deceived, swears at him comprehensively but without malice.

When all is finished they turn their attention to cleaning out the pig-sty. The door is flung open, the pumpers redouble their energy, and a jet of water streams into the sty. An infuriated grunting at once ensues, and Dennis, the pig, emerges blinking into the sunlight. The hose is promptly turned on him, and

curiously enough the anger gives place to grunts of
appreciation and delight, for Dennis really loves his
morning shower-bath. So too do the port watch.
When they have finished with Dennis they strip naked,
and turn the hose on each other. Then they go aft to
polish brass till eight o'clock, when they will be
relieved.

About this time the Skipper suddenly appears on
deck in his pyjamas, and takes a look round, scratching himself reflectively as he does so. He has a word
with the mate, leans on the poop rail looking over at
the sea for a while, and as suddenly disappears below
again. Meanwhile the cook has been busy in the
galley; by 7.30 breakfast is ready for the watch below
and the " day men ". Porridge and fried slices of salt
pork are perhaps not very appetising when you are
pulled straight out of your bunk to eat them, but the
coffee is good in spite of condensed milk.

Eight bells! Both watches muster at the break of
the poop. "Relieve the wheel, port watch below,"
calls out the mate. The free watch quickly disappear
below for food and much needed sleep. The mate
remains for a few minutes talking to the second mate
about the work to be done on deck, then makes his
exit down the after-companion ladder.

The morning's work has now begun in earnest. Two
men are dragging out on to the poop long lengths of
stiff new canvas, and soon they are seated on wooden
benches, busily sewing away at a new lower-topsail.
Another man is making a wire splice for an inner-jib
halyard, while the two day-men are painting the boat-
skids. On the poop the navigator is busy with his
sextant taking the sun for a morning sight, in order
to find out the ship's longitude. "Stand by . . . stop,"
he shouts, and the second mate in the chart-room
notes the exact Greenwich time by the chronometer,
then the navigator goes into the chart-room to work
out his sights.

Below in the saloon, the skipper's wife, who acts
as steward and storekeeper, is thinking out the day's
menu. The cook comes aft with a big basket under
his arm to get his orders and fetch the necessary stores.

He is followed shortly by the fo'c'sle orderly, who is given the crews' rations of sugar, jam and milk.

At noon the navigator is again in evidence, as he takes the sun's meridian altitude to find the latitude. Not long after he calls the skipper to show him the noon position plotted on the chart.

Twelve-thirty is dinner-time for the watch below, and the fo'c'sle orderly fetches the fried corned beef and onions (the potatoes ran out two days ago) from the galley, and then goes back for dried apricots and custard. Two bells! (one o'clock); and the watches are changed again; this time it is the starboard watch that dive joyfully below to enjoy a good long afternoon's sleep.

The port watch takes over the various jobs left to them by the others, and the afternoon wears peacefully on. Gradually the wind dies, and the decks become so hot that to walk upon them bare-footed is impossible.

Tea at 3.30 is a welcome break, but, the cook's last batch of bread having been a failure, there are only biscuits to eat. These are good, but rather too full of animal life to please the more squeamish. Out on deck once more, the mate is watching a low bank of cloud coming up very slowly from the east. It hardly seems to be moving, and yet, an hour later, it has blotted out half the sky, and the wind is coming in fitful gusts.

The mate blows two whistles, and the watch come hurrying aft. " In gaff-topsail and flying-jib," he shouts, but before they have finished taking in these sails the squall suddenly strikes the ship with unexpected fury. The rain comes lashing down, and the ship heels far over, streaking through the hissing water. " Call the watch below to take in the t'gallant! " The starboard watch are all blissfully asleep in their bunks, but in a minute they are on deck, some in hastily snatched up clothes, one in underpants, and another in pyjamas. Away aloft they go, and out on to the t'gallant yard, fighting with the canvas, their soaked clothing streaming out behind them in the wind.

For half an hour the ship rushes along at nine knots, then the squall ends as suddenly as it began. The sails taken in are set again, and the port watch cluster round the galley door to chatter with the cook.

"Curry and rice again," moans Willie. "Strike me purple, anyone would think we was blinking Indians."

"Well, if you don't like it you know what to do with it."

"And don't burn the jam tarts like you did the last lot," puts in another man. "Might as well have been filled with Stockholm tar."

"You're not bound to eat 'em," retorts the imperturbable cook.

Five bells! (6.30); time for the watch below to have their supper. "Now then, clear out of my galley," shouts the cook, seizing a large iron spoon, and preparing to do business with it, as the two orderlies crowd round for their food.

Six bells! (7.0 o'clock) and the sun just set as the watches are changed again. Soon the stars come out; the ship glides on leaving a phosphorescent wake. Through the lighted fo'c'sle skylight comes the sound of voices and laughter, and the thin notes of a ukelele.

Soon the lights go out and all is quiet. The second mate and the navigator talk together in low tones on the poop, while, on the fo'c'sle head, the watch are discussing the date of arrival at Rio, and what they will do when they get there. "Roll on the time when we can get a jazz," says Willie, and then turns over for a short doze before his trick at the wheel.

The *Cap Pilar* sailed placidly on. At last one morning another welcome hail was raised:

"Fish under the bowsprit!"

This was the signal for all hands to down tools. Paint brushes, saws, hammers, splicing-spikes—all were forgotten and left to roll where they would about the decks, while the entire ship's company gathered on the forecastle head to watch the fun.

We could easily see the great purple-backed *bonitos* darting here and there just ahead of the bow-wave; and all sorts of fantastic hooks and spinners were tried without effect. Then Lars produced a line on the end of which was a hook garnished with a tuft of white linen, and the moment this lure hit the water two or three of them were after it like a flash.

From the jib-boom end Lars kept the white rag just kissing the surface. The ship was making six or seven knots, and the fish kept pace with the bait, gradually closing in upon it as it danced so temptingly before their noses. We watched, fascinated.

Suddenly one monster darted ahead of the others. There was a brilliant flash, a flurry of white water, and the next minute ten pounds of furious *bonito* was being hauled up hand over hand.

"Sack! Sack! Bring me the sack!" roared Lars. He needed all his strength to keep the great fish from bursting out of his arms.

Before evening seven more were caught, and that night we had a good old fried fish supper, which made us think a little wistfully of King's Road, Chelsea, on a foggy night.

CHAPTER XI
CALMS AND CATSPAWS

TWO DAYS LATER the wind failed. After weeks of the steady drive of the north-easterlies—suddenly flat calm. She lay quite still upon the sea, her canvas slatting as she rolled to the long ocean swells.

Then came the rain, with sudden puffs of wind from every quarter, and clouds like boulders, rolling upon us from all round the horizon; first on one tack, then on the other.

Once again our whole outlook changed. Soon the north-east trades were forgotten and the south-easterlies hardly thought about. The crossing of this muggy strip of dead air between two trades—the notorious calms called the Doldrums—became our only ambition; and day and night we had to use every laborious artifice of sailing in a continual struggle to gain even so much as a mile.

Night and day, with scarcely a pause, the rain fell out of a sky with neither shape nor colour in it. Sometimes it rained so hard that it was difficult for a man to breathe. Rain—rain—rain! and hardly a murmur of wind to get us out of it. In your bunk you lay sweating in the muggy heat. On deck there was nothing to do but stand and look at the sails hanging in ugly sodden bunches, like dirty dishcloths or a scarecrow's overcoat.

The watch ran naked about their work, a piece of soap tied with twine round their necks; and at every pause in the mad rush from the braces to the sheets and back again to the braces, they lathered themselves furiously.

After a day or two the clouds lifted, and the sun beat upon us from a cloudless sky, till the pitch boiled and bubbled from the seams in our decks.

All day long the heat poured down upon a helpless ship. She lay so lifeless that the fish no longer came near her. All through the long day her idle sails hung miserably till the dusk grew out of the sea to hide their shame.

Once a pair of falcons, hailing from some remote crag in the Atlas mountains, stayed to rest awhile on our t'gallant yard; and once a lone hawk thought he had found a castle built in the middle of the ocean.

At night the sea was on fire with phosphorescence; so Sanson, the biologist, streamed a net astern, bringing up hundreds of little beasts and jellies of strange and often horrifying appearance. We used to gather round him at this work, and help him with the trawl. I must say that he always endured our assistance with enormous patience.

A large gathering of dolphins tumbled ponderously round and round the ship; it was as though we had been at the centre of a merry-go-round, and they the painted wooden horses.

A school of whales passed by. They wallowed southward, blowing wispy feathers of steam that turned to rainbows as they fell.

Then, after nearly fourteen days of calm, once more the sky began to breathe. Softly from the south the wind came in. Sweetly the high sails filled and fell asleep. Gently the ship leaned over to the tiny wavelets, talking altogether, whispering of the south and the brave trade winds.

At first it blew but fitfully, and the *Cap Pilar* was kept beating this way and that, like a dog running up and down a fence. One day we gained a mile or two, the next we went back ten. Gradually the world receded, and the ship settled down to a steady untroubled routine. The land, gaudy Spanish towns, a snowy peak, valleys where the dusk was daylight softened by the misty breath of a million flowers; all these were memories too distant to concern us now, too near to be brightened by those colours, with which imagination makes our memories live again. Rio and the jungles of Brazil were ahead, but so far away that they were hardly worth a thought, just names upon a list with Capetown, Melbourne, and the Fiji islands.

It was no longer necessary to give any orders. At sunrise every day the hands turned to; each one found something to be done, and worked contentedly until the evening dew put an end to painting. Now also we began to see each other and ourselves in a very different light.

Peter Roach, who had been at first a somewhat timid, callow boy, began to gain confidence, and showed himself apter than most to learn a sailor's work. But he was also turning fast into a bit of an " old sweat ", loudly self-assertive, although prepared at all times to do his share and half someone else's of any work for the good of the ship.

Willie Marsh soon showed that he was no ordinary yokel. He too developed very strong views, and backed them up with a wealth of picturesque country humour.

But for sheer keenness Duncan McDonald was exceptional. Unfortunately this sometimes tempted him to volunteer advice and instruction to his shipmates, which was more than several of them could enjoy, and they began to refer to him as the " fo'c'sle wizard " and " our miracle man ". There was no rancour in these occasional bickerings. The ship's company was like a hearty young animal, and these were its growing pains.

One Sunday afternoon Roper demonstrated his mountaineering ability by climbing to the very tip of the mainmast, known as the truck.

Our applause of the feat was both loud and sincere; but Willie was not satisfied.

"Garn!" he shouted. "Nar shut yer eyes an' walk abaht a bit."

A month after leaving Tenerife we reached the Equator and crossed it in longitude 26°W. on 22nd of November.

Of course it was unthinkable that a square-rigged ship with a crew of three-months-old sailors should cross the Line without a visit from Neptune; but we were very much handicapped by the fact that Lars and I were the only ones who had done it before, which made the odds 16–2. In the end we decided to turn the proceedings into a sort of carnival.

George, who had the largest beard, was Neptune. He put on an old dressing-gown, seaboots, and a crown made out of cardboard. Newell put on one of Jane's evening-dresses, a female hat and a shawl, to play the part of Neptune's wife. A more hideous old couple it would have been impossible to imagine.

The proceedings started a little tamely, but reached a climax when Neptune ordered the cook to ride Dennis (the pig) twice round the main deck with the hose on him. Unfortunately Dennis had other ideas, and charged at his aquatic majesty followed by a powerful jet of salt water. The mêlée at once became general, and after a few minutes Dennis emerged wearing a long yellow beard and a cardboard crown, both of which he ate as soon as he had regained the safety of his sty.

The equatorial current was now setting us steadily to the westward, and it was very difficult to decide upon which tack it would be best for us to sail. On the port tack we could go south, but must also go west towards the north-eastern shoulder of Brazil, and once we got to leeward of that it would be impossible to get back. On the starboard tack we could lay about east; but this would allow of no southing whatever and we might, on that tack, hang about in the Doldrums for months.

In the end we decided to take a chance on the port tack, and hope to reach the skirt of the true south-east trades before the current drove us into the Caribbean.

The next few days were very exciting. The wind remained southerly, and every day the current set us farther and farther to the westward, till at last on 25th of November we arrived within fifty miles of the island of Fernando Noronha.

All through that day we held on, keeping the ship as close to the wind as she would go without drifting. The sun went down, and for a hour or more a wisp of moon drew patterns on the sea with baby fingers. Somewhere right ahead huge pillars of rock stood in our way, and still our course was the same. Then the moon set, and the night fell creeping black.

Hour after hour we hung about on deck—watching the sails, watching the sky and arguing over and over again about our chances of weathering the land. By midnight we had all but given up hope, the conversation faltered and died, and we stood in heavy silence gazing blankly to windward, our ears straining for the first dull boom of surf upon the outer reefs of the island.

Suddenly the wind flew round! One moment it was a gentle whisper from due south, and the next it was at east-south-east and freshening. The ship burst into life. There were shouts of laughter everywhere. The white wake fluttered out astern like a banner, and the taut wires sang in the rigging. By dawn we were clear of every danger and bowling merrily into the South Atlantic.

It was not until we were well south of the Equator that we saw and caught our first shark. For several hours he swam suspiciously round the ship, and when the rest of us went below for dinner, the cook remained on deck with a shark hook on the end of a stout line.

Suddenly there was a terrific outcry, and all hands came bounding out again to find the cook half-way over the side, still hanging grimly on to the extreme end of his line. There was a rush of willing helpers, and in the first excitement we nearly lost three men as well as the shark. Eventually, however, we hauled him, thrashing and snarling, on to the main deck.

By this time the crew were beside themselves with excitement, and Romm was so overcome that he made eight lightning exposures before he realised that there was no film in his camera. The cook was dancing round with a twelve-inch carving knife, and the shark, still flailing about the deck, missed him by inches with his tail and by centimetres with his snapping jaws.

" How d'you kill it? How d'you kill it? " yelled the cook.

" Ram your foot down his throat and choke 'im," suggested someone.

" Stick yer fingers in 'is ears," howled Willie.

In the end it was Lars who performed the job, and then there was a rush for souvenirs.

That night the breeze freshened and we felt sure that killing a shark had brought us luck.

One day in the south-east trades we came in with a large herd of dolphins; and once more we crowded on to the forecastle-head with cameras and fishing gear.

For a long time we watched the huge fish swimming just ahead of the bow wave. Five of them formed into an exact line abreast, nose to nose, tail to tail, fin to fin, like old gentlemen arm in arm. When they all came up together for air, there was a single great puff as they all blew as one.

It was now nearly a month since we had tasted any fresh

meat, so we rigged the harpoon in the hopes of being able to have dolphin's liver for supper. Our first two casts were unlucky, but the third was a bull. Unfortunately the harpoon came adrift and the stricken dolphin sank before our eyes. We were so appalled at this useless slaughter, that we unrigged the harpoon and, as a matter of fact, we never used it again.

About 200 miles from the coast of Brazil there is a patch of coral called the Victoria Bank, and since we were uncertain about the error on our chronometer, we decided to pass over this bank in order to check our position. On the 2nd of December, in the middle of the afternoon, we reckoned that we had arrived over the edge of the bank, and started sounding. Our first two casts of the lead showed no bottom at a depth of over 100 fathoms.

This did not surprise Willie Marsh, who is essentially a practical man, and puts little faith in modern methods of navigation. "No wonder we gets becalmed," he used to growl at George, the navigator, "with you dancin' round the deck, squintin' at the sky through yer old sexteroon and shoutin' 'Stop!' every time you sees a bit of sunlight. She'll stop quick enough without that!"

On this occasion when our first two soundings gave no results, Willie was heard to mutter : "Lookin' for a bank, are yer, Mr. Navigator? Reckon the banks round 'ere close at three same as they do at 'ome."

At the third cast the wire went suddenly slack, and, upon the brake being applied, began to hum loudly.

"Thirty-five fathoms!" shouted George, in justifiable triumph.

But Willie was not to be beaten without a struggle. He put his ear to the humming wire, then straightened, with a sigh.

"Gawd strike me!" he groaned. "Now 'e 'as done

it—proper. Been and dropped his blasted 'and-grenade right on top of a deep-sea wasps' nest, 'e 'as. I'm off.''

But we had found the bank all right, and when the lead was hove aboard, little crumbs of broken coral were sticking to the tallow with which it was smeared.

Sanson streamed a dredge-net in which he caught strange sea-weeds, bits of coral and tiny animals.

" Any winkles? " asked Willie, returning hopefully. " Gawd love a blind owl—no winkles ! "

As we drew nearer to the Brazilian coast we began to feel the influence of the strong north-easterlies that blow during the summer time in those parts, and on the 8th of December, the day we expected to sight Cape Frio, the wind freshened to a moderate gale from right aft. We stood a good chance of reaching the entrance to Rio harbour before nightfall, but in order to do this we must arrive there before the land breeze failed. We crowded on every stitch of canvas we could set, and under the weight of it the *Cap Pilar* hurled herself through the water.

Before long the sea began to rise, and huge rollers coming up astern made steering difficult. Our patent log registered up to eleven knots, but after that it jumped out of the water on the crest of every wave and was of little further use as a speed indicator.

Soon after midday the outlines of rocky peaks appeared on our starboard bow, and at the same time a small steamer came in sight. By an amazing coincidence this steamer turned out to be the Finnish S.S. *Atlanta*, Lars's last ship. We had heard a great deal about this " fine big steamer ", and were very surprised to see what appeared to be hardly more than a coasting packet, making very heavy weather of it, with every other sea breaking clean over the fore-deck.

The Doc watched her for some time with considerable interest.

" Did you steer her with a rudder, or just a paddle ? " he asked at last.

Two hours later, after forty-one days at sea, we rounded Cape Frio, and in the smooth water in the lee of the land the *Cap Pilar* took the bit between her teeth. She now carried the wind just abaft the starboard beam and, with every sail full, she reached her maximum speed of twelve knots and held it for nearly an hour.

But soon black clouds and lightning warned us that the land breeze had set in squally over Rio harbour, so we shortened sail to two topsails, mainsail, two jibs and the main staysail; even so she was still doing eight.

Later the wind died, and we lay drifting gently down the coast. The scent of heather and wild flowers stole out to us from the mountains, waking vague longings that we had not known for months.

CHAPTER XII
JUNGLE CITY

ALL NIGHT WE LAY MOTIONLESS in the shadow of black mountains, with the glare of Rio spreading like a huge aurora over the western sky; and when daylight came we could just make out the famous Sugar Loaf mountain at the entrance to the harbour.

We still wonder why the Sugar Loaf should be so famous. It stands like a burnt tree-stump, squat and unadorned by any vegetation, while all around it the tortured peaks of Gavea and Corcovada rear themselves to twice the height, like strange monsters writhing in a last agony to escape the jungle that clings to their lower slopes.

It was the middle of the afternoon when we anchored in Botafogo Bay, and the sea breeze had set in quite fresh and cold. At first our arrival appeared to have attracted no attention, but after about half an hour came a launch on whose flag was written *Policia*, and we prepared for trouble. She roared up to the ship's side, and from her bowels was dragged a scared-looking photographer, who began, under a volley of curses and instructions, to take photographs of our crew.

Next the launch came aft to where a rope-ladder hung over the side, and a wildly gesticulating gentleman in a grey homburg, whom we took to be the Chief of Police himself, clambered half aboard and bellowed hoarsely for the captain. With some misgivings I went forward. Immediately he gripped me by the hand, and I expected that at any moment he would produce a pair of handcuffs from his pocket.

It would have been useless to struggle, he held on grimly, his face contorted, and his voice rose to a scream as he beat the air furiously with his free hand in the direction of the photographer. The boat's crew remained ominously calm. One of them began to roll a cigarette, but I felt instinctively that I was covered. Suddenly with a final yell the Chief of Police threw both arms round my neck, the camera clicked, the Chief of Police dropped exhausted into the boat, and her phlegmatic coxswain rang "full astern" on his engines.

In next morning's paper there appeared an account of how an English lord had arrived in his 300-ton luxury yacht. The article was accompanied by a picture of him embracing one of the newspaper's reporters.

After such a hilarious welcome to Brazil we looked forward to a few weeks spent in an atmosphere of grand carnival. We were not disappointed. The ship chandler's clerk, who took our order for fresh provisions, was a youngish man dressed in a howling check suit, a red tie and black-and-white shoes.

"Oh, cri!" he shouted, flinging up his arms. "Oh, cri! Rio in summer, she is marvellous. Se womans—oh, cri!—se dancing, oh, cri!—I will show you how we live in Rio!"

But Jane and I preferred to go ashore alone none the less. We dined sumptuously in a seaside pavilion, and danced on a tiled floor, which was so slippery that I fell flat on my back; the band leader and all the waiters smiled and bowed and winked hugely.

On the topmost pinnacle of Corcovada mountain stands a gigantic figure of Christ with outstretched arms. Land and sea for over twenty miles in every direction, by day and by night, is dominated by it. It is visible from almost every street in Rio, and from every corner of the huge harbour. From twenty miles out upon the Atlantic the statue of Jesus is the first certain landmark for sailors.

We reached the top of Corcovada one evening just before sunset. Below us lay the city fantastically woven between precipitous rocks and hills. In the middle of the business section a huge mass of rock, overgrown by jungle, stood untouched, unconquered by the advance of a jubilant civilisation. The vast natural harbour spread out below us, backed on one side by dense green forest, beyond which more mountains rose in jagged confusion. Bright islands stood humped here and there like beetles on a window pane.

As the sun went down, lights and festoons of lights pricked out the shapes of boulevards, parks and palaces. From where we stood, two thousand feet above the sea, Rio looked like fairyland. On our way down the jungle on either side of the road glittered with a thousand fire-flies, and from the mountain peak overhead the flood-lit figure of Christ followed us home, flying out after us above the trees.

Civilisation in Rio is more than jubilant—almost hysterical. The Carriocas know the art of living above all arts. A good meal can be eaten in many restaurants for as little as 10*d*., while the finest dinner in Brazil costs only 5*s*. Many of the streets are paved with mosaics in black-and-white stone, and there is no need for parks or gardens, because the whole of a large portion of the town consists of a park, where shops and houses stand surrounded by trees, grass and beds of brilliant flowers, with fountains playing amongst them. All night long the water-carts drive at high speed through the streets, until, by morning, every square mile of the city and a good many of its less wary inhabitants have been thoroughly washed down.

Fares in Rio are so ridiculously low that collecting them is, in many cases, a mere formality. On the tramways, for instance, no tickets are issued, because the paper would certainly cost more than half the fare it represented. But the most remarkable instance of the prosperous atmosphere of the capital of Brazil, is the fact that there are no tips. If you give a taxi-driver a bank-note he will give you your change to the nearest 100 reis ($\frac{1}{4}d$.) and drive away without so much as a pleading look.

For a few days we lay at anchor off the city, then one morning we set sail again to cross the harbour. The crews of near-by vessels crowded on deck to watch us pick up our anchor and cast the ship; but we managed to get her headed out into the harbour without much incident. Once out in the bay, however, the ebb tide caught us, and we were driven down dangerously close to the German man-of-war *Schlesien* lying at anchor. She manned her boats as we approached, obviously expecting us to be carried down upon her and sweep away boats, booms and all. We went clear all right, and dipped our ensign as we passed. The salute was ignored.

Arrived on the other side of the harbour we sailed through a narrow passage into the quiet little land-locked bay of Jurujuba, where the jungle came down to the water's edge all round, and steep hills protected us from wind and sea.

In Jurujuba Bay is the headquarters of the Rio Sailing Club which is the pleasantest yacht club in the world. It seems to be a sort of holiday party to which members bring their families every day to have tea, bathe, sail, or just to sit in the shade and talk. There is an atmosphere of peace and good-fellowship about this club which is exceptional.

We soon got into the way of life in the English colony

in Rio. One great institution is the mid-morning gin-and-tonic, which you drink at tables in the back of any sort of shop from an ironmonger's to a tobacconist's. Brazilian hospitality is of a very high order, and when you call for a drink they hand you the bottle for you to help yourself.

One Sunday Jane and I went to lunch with some friends. After lunch they asked us what we would like to do: "we usually go to sleep," they added. We replied that nothing would suit us better, so off went our hosts to their beds, while we disposed ourselves on couches, and slept till it was time for tea. This was our introduction to one of the most sensible items of tropical routine.

The Brazilians are very keen on all forms of sport, whether impromptu or otherwise. One day the ferry in which I was crossing the harbour overtook a cargo ferry upon the upper deck of which a terrific battle was in progress. Apparently it was free-for-all, and men were thrashing, kicking and butting each other all over the deck, while some were dodging here and there in an attempt to keep out of the way. The skipper of our ferry immediately took his vessel alongside the other; not, as I at first imagined, to offer assistance, but merely so that everyone should have a better view of the fight. All the passengers crowded to the side to wave their arms and cheer, and the two ferries finished the journey across the harbour side by side. As soon as we reached the landing-stage the fight miraculously stopped of its own accord. I stayed to watch the men disembark from the other boat, but in spite of the apparent blind fury of their recent conflict, there was not a scratch on any of them.

The Rio boatmen sleep in their boats, and if you wish to be pulled back to the ship late at night you must first wake one of these and bargain with him.

Perhaps you have a Brazilian friend with you, and you

stand at the water's edge, the boats with canopies over them moored in a line below you.

" Who takes us to the *Cap Pilar* to-night?" shouts your friend. Dead silence for a little, then a voice from beneath one of the canopies (you can't tell which): " How much will the señors pay ? "

" Two milreis."

Dead silence again, or perhaps even a few snores, then:
" The señors know that seven milreis is the price."

" Three is all we will give."

At this point one of the canopies is lifted, and a boat is unmoored and brought alongside. You step in without any further reference to the fare, and the boat pushes silently out across the harbour. At the ship's side your friend gives the boatman five milreis, which is the unalterable tariff fee, and honour on both sides is satisfied.

But the boatmen work hard for their living. When we lay in Jurujuba Bay, on the other side of the harbour, one of them used to pull across to us, a distance of four or five miles, with the few pounds of meat and groceries we required for the day, arriving alongside punctually at 8 o'clock every morning.

For a whole week I spent many hours of the day in sweltering heat trying to transact some of the ship's business. In spite of the unremitting efforts of kind English friends I was confronted with obstacle after obstacle, and it seemed that nothing would ever be settled. Then I met a very pleasant young Brazilian, who was the head of a large engineering corporation. I told him my troubles, and he asked me to call at his office on the following afternoon.

I found it difficult to believe that this care-free, kind-spoken, rather plump young man was one of the biggest forces in Brazilian business and politics. Yet so it was; and I was shown further evidence of it when I called at his office.

" What will you do while you wait ? " he asked. " Ah, I know ! Just take my car and drive round for an hour; you will find it very interesting."

I was overwhelmed by such princely hospitality, but accepted it none the less eagerly.

" My car " was a brand new six-cylinder Buick, which leaped away with me before I was even properly seated. At the end of the block was a cross-road. I gave a shy " toot ", whereupon a policeman stepped into the road and stopped all the traffic to let me through. Next I ran down a long street at the end of which the lights were red. I drew up obediently, but immediately the policeman in charge waved me on, and everything else was held up until I had passed. It was the same wherever I went, till I realised that the car must be carrying some government badge, which gave it right of way; so I pressed my foot firmly down upon the accelerator, and tore through the *avenidas* as though on some urgent diplomatic mission.

When I returned I was greeted by the still smiling Mr. ——, who informed me that all my affairs were now arranged. He moreover insisted on taking me aboard in his own speed-boat. In the launch I started to express my gratitude, but before I got more than the first few words out of my mouth, the engine burst into ear-splitting life, and a rush of wind nearly knocked me over backwards. And all the way to the ship we sat nodding and smiling sadly to each other, with now and then a deprecatory wave of the hand or shrug of the shoulders by way of variety.

On one side of the Bay of Jurujuba was a beach, over a mile long, of smooth white sand. Here we bathed and basked and grew fat, and sometimes on cool, misty days it was possible in spite of palms and banyans, to imagine oneself in some sheltered Scottish loch or on the west coast of Ireland.

Occasionally some of us went for long rambles, inland. We chased brilliant blue butterflies as large as dinner plates—thought we saw a snake—thought we saw some monkeys—thought we heard a puma—and knew that we didn't really care.

Every day half the crew were busy painting the ship—she was to be green now instead of white. Those not engaged on ship's work amused themselves ashore according to their various tastes. The Doc used to go ashore every morning and spend almost the entire forenoon at a soda fountain. McDonald went dinghy sailing, while Willie preferred to prowl about in the forest.

Christmas came and went, and we began to think about continuing the voyage. We were already growing tired of the tropical heat, and besides we still had aboard eleven tons of mail and stores for Tristan da Cunha. So one morning we hove up our anchor, and sailed quietly out of the harbour bound for the southern ocean.

Looking back on Rio we saw it again as a city besieged—attacked on all sides by rampant nature—lying within the jaws of the jungle, against which a perpetual war must be waged. The jungle comes down to the very flower-beds and borders in the gardens, it fringes the lawns, snatches with greedy, creeping fingers at fruit trees and shrubs. You must go full speed ahead all the time in Brazil, or the jungle will get you; every enterprise must succeed from the word " go ", for the moment it falters the jungle will swallow it up.

CHAPTER XIII
MAILS FOR TRISTAN

In Rio Romm had left us. Payne, the cook, had also gone, having been called home the day before we were due to sail by news of the death of his mother. So now we were only sixteen all told aboard the *Cap Pilar*.

Romm's departure made very little difference to us, but being without a cook was a serious matter. However, Roper stepped into the breach and volunteered to do the cooking.

The first week out of Rio was uneventful and almost monotonous. The wind was at east-south-east and very light, and since the course we wished to steer was south-east, we made very little progress. Actually we made only 200 miles in that first week, and our course made good was about south.

Slowly the glowing trade-wind skies hardened to the dull metallic grey of higher latitudes. A fresh nip crept into the morning air, and always the long swells came clambering over the south-eastern horizon and muttered in passing the song of the wind that sent them.

During the second week the wind drew round to south-east, and the *Cap Pilar*, on the port tack, went plunging away south-south-west, getting every day farther and farther from Tristan, but we knew that if only we could get down through these " horse latitudes ", we would eventually find steady winds from the westward; so day after day we went on climbing laboriously over the lumbering grey swells that fled cravenly before a wind that never came. At the end of the second week we had sailed another 200 miles.

At last came the shift. First by half points a watch, then faster the ship's head crept round, till, after three more days, she was upon her course for the first time since leaving Rio.

Suddenly one night, like a curved blade flung by the gods, an albatross fell silently across the moon behind us. By morning the wind was freshening from nor'-west, and three albatross and a cloud of little blue ice-birds were following in our wake. At last we knew that we had reached the kingdom of the full west winds. Soon the sleek skuas joined the albatross and all the shearwaters and petrels. Once a whale cruised so close that we feared he would rub himself against the ship's side.

Newell caught a brilliant blue dolphin, so large that it took two men to carry it down the deck, but he spoiled the triumph of the moment somewhat by pacing out the length of the one that got away.

A few days later, during a calm, a large turtle was sighted paddling unconcernedly on the surface within a hundred yards of the ship. We launched a dory, and crept silently upon him, but he saw us and dived. So the voyage went smoothly on, with nothing but an occasional incident to mark the days as they passed.

José, the cabin boy, was the greatest mystery to all of us. He had been in the ship for over two months, but was still unable to speak a word of English. None the less he was always cheerful and usually very willing at his work.

His ideas of cleanliness were strange. He always kept himself and his clothes scrupulously clean, but had very contradictory ideas about general hygiene. He would never voluntarily wash glasses or mugs, because they had never contained anything dirty; when driven to wash them, he would probably dry them off with a floor cloth or a brass-polishing rag.

The Doc, himself a stickler for cleanliness, was the most affected by José's methods; but we usually smiled at his vehement accusations, until one morning he set himself to stalk José upon his occasions, and succeeded in taking a photograph of him feeding the pig from the saloon teapot.

In the horse latitudes we unbent our No. 2 suit of sails, which had been good enough for the trade winds, and replaced it by our best suit in readiness for the strong westerly winds. The operation of changing sails lasted several days owing to the inexperience of the crew, and one morning some one let go the wrong rope with the result that our best lower topsail went over the side and sank before our eyes. This was a severe blow, but it would have been pointless to make a fuss about it.

At lunch-time Donnelly came on to the poop.

" It is the wish of the watch," he said, " that I should apologise on their behalf for losing the lower topsail. If you will allow us to make good the . . ." etc.

What a remarkable ship we were. It must have been the first time in the history of square-rigged vessels that the bosun had been sent aft to apologise for the loss of a sail. As a matter of fact that lower topsail was the only important sail we ever lost.

Very soon it was evident that Roper's scientific mind was too deliberate and precise for a ship's cook, so Willie Marsh took over from him. Willie had never done any cooking before, but he had one invaluable theory.

" Don't matter what it is so long as it's hot and there's plenty of it."

Strangely enough Willie was more fussy than anyone else about his food; that is to say, he hated anything that was not solid or simple. He loathed curry and couldn't drink coffee, but he was a very hard-working and punctual cook, and there was no lack of good simple food while he was in charge of the galley.

As we drew nearer to the Tristan islands, the weather clouded over, and for three days on end we were unable to take observations of the sun or stars.

At the end of this time we could only tell roughly where

we were, and to make matters worse, on the morning of the 30th of January, when we reckoned we were within fifteen miles of the islands, the dawn crept unwillingly upon us through a blanket of thick white fog.

With the wind light sou'-westerly we stood on through the dripping forenoon, straining our eyes for a glimpse of breakers, or the dark shadow behind the mist, which might be an island.

I tried hard to make up my mind to alter course until the horizon should clear; but I was also very anxious not to throw away what might be our only chance for a week or more of making Tristan in calm weather. There is no shelter and no safe anchorage for a sailing ship at Tristan, so all the stores would have to be discharged in open boats with the ship under sail. Furthermore, there is a gigantic surf running in on the beach in all except the calmest weather, and it is not very often that a boat can put to sea at all.

At last came the time when a decision could no longer be delayed, and the watch were called to the braces. We were on the point of bearing away due north when, as if by magic, there was a sudden lift over the eastern horizon, and at the same time a thin sliver of black grew out of the sea ahead. It was no more than the suggestion of harder black in a world of murky grey; but it was enough to give us our position. No sooner had we taken our bearings than the fog swept down again thicker than before.

But now we knew where we were. We had established the land as Inaccessible Island, the westernmost of the Tristan group. The daylight faded without any change in the weather, and we held on through the fog and darkness of a night without a moon.

There must have been a benign genius watching over us just then, because at dawn there was another sudden lift, showing a high black wall of rock stretching right across our path, and no more than four miles away.

At 6 o'clock we were almost becalmed, so one of our dories was lowered, and manned by the starboard watch. They looked like the crew of some old vessel of discovery as they stocked the boat with water, a day's rations, compass, fog-horn, oil-bag (in case of rough seas), and life-belts. They pulled away for the northern end of the island, and before they were well clear of the ship the mist rolled down once more and swallowed them. All you could hear was the steady thump of oars on thole-pins growing gradually fainter.

All through the forenoon the *Cap Pilar* drifted lazily before occasional puffs of wind, rolling in the long swells with slatting canvas and the boom creaking against the masts. The fog condensed like silver dust on cheek and beard. Occasionally the wavering scream of an albatross marked the loneliness of a deserted ocean, or a penguin's harsh cry rang like the despairing challenge of a soul in purgatory. The sense of desolation was complete; yet we knew, although we could not see it, that only a mile or two away was a snug little British village with 180 inhabitants.

As Tristan-in-the-mist we had always thought of these mysterious islands—hidden from the world, and often even from passing ships—aloof and untroubled by the querulous nonsense of modern life. In the old days of sail the Tristaners used to do a flourishing trade in fresh provisions with passing ships; now the island has become the very last place on earth, and each time another sailing ship leaves the sea Tristan loses one more possible link with the outside world.

At noon the wind freshened, and within an hour the land loomed close to starboard. This time we stood straight in and soon we could make out the cluster of little cottages on Herald Point. About a mile off shore we hove-to and lowered another dory, filled this time with mail-bags.

As we pulled away from the *Cap Pilar* we saw her for the first time in our lives under sail; with her high green

sides and orange canvas, she looked like an illustration out
of an old story book; we could almost imagine the cannon
poking their ugly mouths over her rail. As we drew nearer
the island it stood up more black and forbidding than
before; the high land in the centre was still covered with
cloud, but all along the coast, as far as we could see, grim
black cliffs fell sheer into a boiling surf, save right ahead,
where a vivid green tongue of grassland threw out a wel-
coming hand towards us.

Suddenly José, who was pulling the bow oar, started
jabbering excitedly and pointing towards the settlement.
We followed his gaze, and there, sure enough, was a tiny
white triangle of sail creeping along the coast. We sat for
a while and watched it in silence.

To me this was the most thrilling moment of the voyage.
Three years before Lars and I had first seen Tristan; and
our longing to see it again had brought us back in an old-
time sailing ship, carrying the mail as they used to years
ago. Out at sea lay the *Cap Pilar*, nodding and bowing in
the swell, and from the shore came a boat pulled by men
who had had no news from the world for over a year—men
to whom the stores we brought represented the very means
of life.

We wondered what sort of folk they would be. How
would they dress? Would we be able to understand their
speech? How would they receive us?

We pulled on again, and in another ten minutes we were
within hail of the other boat. In her stern sheets was a
wild looking figure in a cassock and wearing a long black
beard. We knew that this must be the Reverend Harold
Wilde, who had spent the past three years on the island.
The others were sturdy looking men of uncertain age, who
now lay on their oars, and stared at us with expressionless
faces. They were dressed in clothes of all types and colours.
One of them had a straw hat with a hat-band in the colours
of a well-known public school, another wore a pair of

striped cashmere trousers, which must have spent their early years at a city desk. Quite a number of them wore stewards' jackets with brass buttons, and one also had a steward's peaked cap.

The two boats lay bobbing, while the occupants stared at each other in silence for several minutes. Willie Marsh was the first to break the ice.

"Can you tell us the way to Tristan da Cunha," he shouted suddenly.

Jane and I accompanied the Tristan boat out to the ship, while one of the islanders agreed to pilot the dory. The following description of their landing comes from George :

We set off at a brisk pace, and soon we were pulling through the beds of *kelp* which fringe the shore; the pilot then told us to lie on our oars while he waited his chance. For a few minutes he sat watching the rollers smashing upon the reef farther out. Suddenly he turned : "Lie back on it now. Pull all you know !" The oar-blades dug deep, the dory leaped ahead. Using every ounce of our strength we hurled her towards the beach. I've never felt a boat travel so fast. We could see a huge comber lifting astern of us; we could hear the one before it thundering upon the shingle. At all costs we must reach the shore on the crest of a wave; we swung out together, and pulled with all our might. Suddenly a thole-pin snapped, then another, and two of us fell head over heels into the bottom of the boat. The boat lost steerage way. The wave picked her up, and flung her broadside in a welter of foam upon the beach, rolling her over. We arrived at Tristan on our ears beneath a shower of mail-bags.

Luckily none of us was hurt, and as we were soundly kissed on the spot by over fifty women and girls, we soon forgot our discomfort in the excitement of our first hours in a new world.

CHAPTER XIV
THE ISLANDS OF OPPORTUNITY

ON THE WAY OUT to the ship the Reverend Harold Wilde held Jane and I in animated conversation, while the islanders continued to stare and smile shyly; we took it in turns to answer the padre's eager questions, and, between whiles, we tried to become acquainted with the others. I offered the nearest Tristaner a cigarette; when it was lit, he drew two or three puffs, and then passed it to the man behind him, who did the same until the whole crew had had a go at it; then the first man finished it off.

The boat was one of the most remarkable examples of the Tristaners' ingenuity. The frames and keel were made of driftwood, lashed together with twine and wire. This skeleton was covered with canvas upon which had been laid coat after coat of paint until it was completely water-tight. There are seventeen of these home-made boats on the island; the largest are about thirty-five feet long, but very light for their size, and though undoubtedly frail, they are so handy in the surf that they are very rarely damaged.

Alongside the ship we loaded the boat with stores and then set off again for the beach. When we reached the *kelp* they hauled a long streamer of this seaweed aboard, and we lay there virtually at anchor, while half our cargo was transhipped into a second boat.

When the *kelp* had been cast off again the men stood up at their oars, and the boat literally leaped forward. We caught a wave at precisely the right moment; in came the oars, and on the back of a breaking roller we went charging up the beach, almost to the high-water mark; then the Tristaners jumped out, and helped by others from the shore, they pulled us bodily out of reach of the sea.

When Jane and I climbed out we were immediately surrounded by over fifty women with their children, and we kissed and were kissed by every one of them—it took more than twenty minutes. These women wore long cotton dresses with embroidered bodices, and girdles or sashes about their waists. On their heads the younger ones all wore kerchiefs, the older ones shawls. But what interested us most was the fact that there was hardly one among all those women without a baby in her arms.

Both men and women were exceedingly courteous. Every man removed his cap and bowed as he shook hands; every woman curtsied before she kissed us. They seemed genuinely excited to see us, and some of the older ones had tears in their eyes as they wrung our hands.

The stores were now put on to large wooden sledges and wagons drawn by oxen. For the lighter loads the islanders used donkeys.

The whole population followed us up the track to the settlement, the children dancing on ahead. A hundred yards up from the beach, we came out on to a meadow of rich green grass upon which were dotted two or three dozen houses, little low stone crofts with thatched roofs. The meadow sloped gently up to the foot of the cliffs, and went rolling away to the westward, where one or two small green cones marked ancient volcanic vents; beyond these lay the islanders' potato patches. It looked a pitiable little apron of land upon which nearly two hundred people must depend entirely for their livelihood; but actually the soil is so rich that it would support nearly twice that number.

In the vicinity of the houses the meadow was strewn with flocks of geese, pigs and chickens. This was our first big surprise on Tristan; we had always imagined that the community was in a state of semi-starvation; yet the village appeared to be overrun with live-stock, and in the distance we could see sheep and cattle.

In the middle of the village was a slightly larger cottage

with a corrugated iron roof and a cross upon it. This was the chapel, school and meeting-house. We all repaired at once to the chapel, where the padre was to hold a service of thanksgiving for our arrival.

It was easy to see that their religion was of first importance to the Tristaners, and on this particular occasion their emotion was extreme. Nearly fifteen months had passed since the last stores had reached the island; winter was not far distant, and the small stock of flour, sugar and tea was running very low; some of the older people, who remembered other winters of famine, had become anxious and depressed. Now suddenly, with the arrival of the *Cap Pilar*, their whole outlook had changed overnight.

There was no organ in the chapel, but a portable gramophone, with a few worn records, did duty instead; so during the interval before the service began we all sat, gravely listening first to " The Funeral March of the Marionettes ", by Gounod, and then to the sweetly melodious fox-trot " Polly " of 1925 vintage.

After the service the men returned to their boats to continue the discharging of stores, while the women helped the padre to distribute their mail. We had brought, in all, nineteen sacks of letters and parcels to the islands, and by far the largest number of both were addressed to Agnes Rogers, who is the solitary Roman Catholic in the community. She must have received nearly one-quarter of all the mail.

I asked Mrs. Repetto, the headwoman, what Agnes would do with all those clothes and shoes.

" Oh ! What she doesn't want she'll give to me for the poorer ones. No, we don't do no trading on the island; there's nothing we want of each other, really."

The padre was doing more work than anyone during the mail-sorting, and with great self-control he refrained from opening any of his own letters until all the others were distributed. This must have required a prodigious effort of will, after spending about three years away from civilisation.

At last the job was done, and the Reverend Harold could turn to his own little pile of letters. On top lay a buff-coloured envelope with O.H.M.S. upon it.

The padre sighed as he picked it up. "Business before pleasure," he said; "that's always the way when you're a representative of the Government." The envelope contained a demand for the payment of arrears of income-tax.

We left them all to their mail and wandered off to the highest point of the meadowland. We lay upon the grass above a beach of jet-black sand, to watch the rollers galloping in. The turf was soft and springy, and the air was full of the scent of thyme; below us the little cluster of houses looked very friendly. On the horizon we saw the *Cap Pilar* go about, and stand in once more towards the land. As she came nearer, the Tristaners on the beach below launched two boats into the surf, and went crawling on their wooden legs to meet the ship. Beside us a large beetle was clambering patiently through the forest of grass. How little it concerned him that there lay 1,500 miles of wintry ocean between him and Africa. We listened idly to the barking of dogs, the gaggling of geese, and the wavering thunder of the South Atlantic. After a while we fell asleep.

In the afternoon we went with the padre to call on some of the islanders in their homes. We were received everywhere with smiles and usually with home-made gifts. There were beautifully worked woollen mats, cowhide moccasins (the Tristaners wear these all the year round), table-centres and caps made of penguin skins, socks and stockings made of home-spun wool. One woman gave Jane a whole set of baby clothes. The Green family entertained us to a feast of roast mutton followed by a huge potato pudding made in the shape of a bomb. This potato pudding was a very rare luxury owing to the risk of a potato famine; and anybody who wished to make one was obliged by law to apply to Mr. Wilde for permission to do so.

There is little or no timber on the island, so the walls of the houses are lined with any odd bits and pieces of packing-case that can be found. Larger timber for beams, tables and beds is rarer still, and the islanders have to rely for this upon the wreckage which occasionally comes ashore on the western beaches. We found one bed made out of the poop rail and stanchions of an old sailing ship which had struck on Inaccessible Island nearly a hundred years before.

For pictures to cover their walls the islanders use the pages of newspapers, which they paste all over the wood-work. One bedroom wall was covered with sheet after sheet of the *Daily Mail*, including the " Situations Vacant " page and the " City Stock Prices ". In other rooms the occupants had taken the trouble to cut out photographs of actresses, race-horses and railway engines; and one girl had beside her bed a full-page portrait of a famous debutante, wearing her Court gown.

We asked several people what interested them most about the outside world. One of them said he would like most to see a horse; another was looking forward to his first sight of a woman with red hair.

In the evening there was a dance in the meeting-house, and until nine o'clock at night we stamped about the tiny floor in the orange gloom produced by the two or three inches of precious candle that could be spared. One of the islanders played an accordion, and the few remaining gramophone records supplied the rest of the music. Of course the Tristaners have no idea of dancing as it is under-stood in England, and strangely enough they appear to have very little sense of rhythm. Tristan dancing consists of " one-two-one " to the left, and then " one-two-one " to the right; but you don't dance in time to the music, you set your own time and the music is incidental. The islanders also have one or two simple folk-dances, which we enjoyed much more. The high spot of the evening was reached when our Mr. Sanson, dressed in kilts, demonstrated the Highland fling.

That night the shore party remained on the island, and Jane and I slept in the hospital. In the morning we were called by a boy scout with a cup of hot tea; and found a wonderful breakfast waiting for us in the kitchen.

Whilst we were still standing by the fire, Mr. Wilde burst in, full of high spirits.

"Good morning, my boy," he shouted, and struck me sharply in the stomach with his fist. I staggered against the wall, and on the rebound retaliated with a hearty punch to the reverend gentleman's breast-bone, whereupon he in turn overbalanced and sat down heavily upon a chair.

"Ha! ha! ha!" roared the padre, and turning to the two astonished boy scouts, who were waiting to serve breakfast, he said: "We're Englishmen, you see. We Englishmen often fool around like this, don't we, my boy? Come on now, let's show them what an Englishman's made of," and before I could reply he had leapt out of the chair and landed me a telling blow in the solar-plexus; it hurt rather, and I hit back as hard as I could. For the next five minutes we pranced round the tiny kitchen accompanied by a running commentary from the padre; it went something like this:

"Here we go"—*bang!*—"We're Englishmen you"—*ouch!*—"see. We can"—*thump!*—"take punishment like men. We don't"—*ouch!*—"mind a good mill"—*crash!*—"do we, my boy?"—*bang!*

The scouts watched us open-mouthed. I felt horribly embarrassed. At last the padre's wind gave out, and we were allowed to sit down to breakfast, which we ate in a strained and breathless silence.

After breakfast all the children were summoned to

school, and we went to watch them at their lessons. The children enjoyed themselves immensely; George, a schoolmaster himself, was very impressed with the way in which Mr. Wilde maintained their interest in such things as spelling and simple arithmetic. With the children he showed an unlimited fund of kindly patience; but the older people sometimes received firmer treatment. We heard him go among them like a lion. " I tell you *what* ! " he roared, and at the word " *what* " we all jumped, while the islanders smiled and looked happy. We heard him deliver quite a number of harangues, full of rhetorical questions, to which he always insisted upon an answer.

" This is the Island of Opportunity," he said. " It is untrue to say that we are starving. Isn't that so ? " Pause, silence. " Isn't that so, I say? Answer me, men. Are we starving ? "

Chorus : " No, Father."

" Of course, we aren't. We'll show these people from England we're not starving. I want every man out in the boats fishing to-morrow. I tell you *what* !

" In the last three years we've repaired all the houses, built a lighthouse and a hospital, and built bridges over the streams. We've also built a house on Inaccessible Island, and in the summer our young men go there to till the land. In five years we'll be self-supporting on Tristan. That's what we want, we want to be self-supporting, don't we ? "

" Yes, Father ! "

" All we need is clothes, tools, and a large boat for inter-island communication. In return for those we'll make one of the finest colonies in the Empire on this very island, won't we ? "

" Yes, Father ! "

" Now I want these young men from England to see how well we look after ourselves. To-morrow I want every man on his potato patch. Every man, d'you hear me ? "

" Yes, Father ! "

" I tell you *what* ! "

The Tristaners are a simple, kindly folk, though they undoubtedly lack energy and ambition. Their philosophy would be admirably suited to the inhabitants of a South Sea island; but in the cold stormy regions in which they live any lack of determination leads straight to starvation. The Tristaners have developed the habit of only eating one meal a day, but in spite of this there have been times, before Mr. Wilde took charge, when the whole community did actually starve. Freedom from the risk of starvation is the greatest blessing that the padre has bestowed on the people of Tristan. He husbands their provisions, regulates the consumption of potatoes, and is continually spurring them to greater efforts on land and sea. Moreover, he sets them a good example in self-support; he told us that he always tilled his own potato patch and caught his own fish.

In spite of their one meal a day the islanders have wonderful health. They all have flawless teeth, and in build they are distinctly "hefty"—no other word describes them so well. During the three years before our visit there had only been one death (due to an accident) and twelve babies had been born. A miscarried child is unknown.

It is one of the most remarkable facts about the Tristan settlement that its constitution has no trace of enforced Communism. There are rich and poor on the island, some families owning a great many more beasts than others; but this state appears to have arisen by chance, and there is no attempt on anybody's part either to alter or maintain it. Each family produces as much as it can be bothered to work for; and inheritance, such as it is, has little effect on the future of a young Tristaner; because within a few years of inheriting his father's flocks, he will only have maintained as much of his inheritance as he would have amassed on his own had he started poorer. In any case it is of no importance to anyone else whether he owns many sheep or few. He may raise a thousand sheep if he likes, or fill his storehouse with potatoes; but the potatoes will sprout through the roof before he can eat them, and most of his sheep will die of old age.

They live calmly on Tristan. We never heard an islander's voice raised, nor the note of urgency in a command. Having been brought up from childhood to handle their boats in mountainous rollers, they appear to need no commands; although, when we watched them bring their craft tearing in through the surf, we wondered how they ever managed to escape what looked like certain death. Tristan men and women have become, throughout four generations, so accustomed to quiet that they are now actually *unable* to shout. When we met that first boat-load of islanders on our way ashore they answered our hail so softly that it was impossible to hear what they said. On another occasion when we were waiting at dusk outside the surf for a chance to run in, we heard the islanders, only a hundred yards away, trying to shout advice; but even at that distance we could hear no more than a high-pitched crying, like the mewing of a colony of seagulls.

The Tristaners' idea of relative values is peculiar. One of them exchanged a beautifully worked mat of penguin feathers, with Cyril Money, for an old cap; then, turning to Roach, he offered him another mat for the fo'c'sle gramophone. Another man was telling me about the fresh-water lake that lies in the crater at the peak of the island. This peak is 7,600 feet above sea-level, so we could not help asking what it was that ever took them up there. "Oh, just to look, ye know; and sometimes we has a picnic up there," was the answer. We tried to imagine an English yokel climbing to the top of a peak twice as high as Snowdon for a picnic.

One morning an old lady said to her husband:

"Don't go down to the patches or you'll get rheumatics for sure, Bob. It's blowing feather-white to-day."

We followed her eyes to where the white bundles of

cloud were torn to shreds by the peak of Tristan, and high above them streaks of cirrus lay like goose feathers in the sky.

"They must be a race of poets," we thought, "these picnickers on mountain-tops."

The Tristaners have all a poet's care-free philosophy. Time means nothing to them. "What you don't do to-day," they said, "you may perhaps do one day next week, so why worry?"

It is far easier on Tristan to live exclusively on potatoes, because the "patches" are only two miles from the settlement; so potatoes form the staple diet of the whole community, and one of the padre's hardest tasks is to make the islanders vary their menus sufficiently to avoid a potato famine in the winter. The sea within a hundred yards of the beach is swarming with fish, but it is only occasionally that the weather will allow a boat to be launched, and when it does there is the business of collecting a crew, besides which the Tristaners for some reason or another do not care for fish. They do not much like beef or mutton either; out of a herd of over 150 head of cattle nearly half are bulls, but these cattle live on another part of the island which can only be reached by boat, and the islanders would rather eat potatoes than go to the trouble of killing and carrying home a few of the surplus bulls.

Tristan da Cunha was first discovered in 1506 by a Portuguese Admiral of approximately the same name. Attempts to colonise it were made by the Dutch and the British East India Company, but the first permanent inhabitant was an Englishman named Thomas Currie, who landed there in 1810. In 1816, owing to its use by American cruisers as a base from which to raid British shipping, the island was formally annexed to Britain, and a temporary garrison was placed there. When this garrison departed, Sergeant William Glass, his wife and two children as well as two masons were left behind. These people were the founders

of the settlement, and to this day there are only seven sur-
names amongst the 180 inhabitants; they are: Glass,
Swain, Green, Rogers, Hodges, Lavarello, and Repetto,
the two last being the names of two Italian sailors who
managed to swim ashore from a shipwreck. We were told
that, except for the original Mrs. Glass, the wives of the
first male population were all brought from the Cape and
St. Helena.

Sam Swain is the oldest inhabitant, but he still pulls his
weight in a boat as heartily as any of his strapping grandsons. He has never been off the island and nothing, he said,
would ever persuade him to leave it.

" But I would like a good set of false teeth," he added.

" What's that, Sam? " said a voice from behind our
backs, " false teeth at your age? Don't talk nonsense,
man, you've got one foot in the grave already. You'd die
before you had time to get used to them."

This sounded horribly cruel to us; but it made the old
man roar with laughter. " That's right," he said at last,
" what do I want with false teeth? I'll soon be dead anyway," and off he went, chuckling.

Mrs. Repetto is the Chief Woman of the community and
the most remarkable personality on Tristan. She was only
61 when we saw her, but she had twenty grandchildren and
one great-grand-daughter. We had already been amazed
by the quiet dignity of all the islanders, by their deep, untroubled philosophy, their patience and their genuine
kindliness towards each other. But Mrs. Repetto stood out
from among them; she bore herself with the unassailable
graciousness of a queen. All the Tristaners go to Mrs.
Repetto for advice, and one evening Jane and I visited her
in her house. The dull candle-light shone on her weather-
beaten face as she talked to us. She told us about grim years
of famine and dark winters spent on Tristan. She spoke of
her childhood and the days when there was no " Society "
to send them stores, and of that terrible morning when half

the male population of the island had been lost in a capsized boat. Then she asked about us, and soon we were pouring out to her our own troubles, as eagerly as though this wonderful old lady, who had never in her life left the shores of Tristan, were the wisest prophetess in the world.

CHAPTER XV
CRISIS IN CAPETOWN

FOR FOUR DAYS the *Cap Pilar* stood off and on the northern coast of Tristan. During those four days the ship was tacked fifty-three times.

Just before sunset on the second day a heavy squall came up from the westward and we had to cast the boats adrift in a hurry, and stand out to sea. Half a dozen of the islanders were left with us, and the others in the boats just succeeded in reaching the shore before the wind came.

On the fourth day, the wind freshened from the nor'-west, and we knew we must leave before the gale which was on its way made further boat-work impossible.

We bowled down to the Cape in twelve days with a steady westerly wind behind us.

We raised the mountains of the Cape Peninsula on the morning of Monday, 15th of February. The weather was fine and clear, and the *Cap Pilar* slipped along under all plain sail at seven or eight knots.

At midday we were off the Lion's Head, almost becalmed; and at 3 o'clock the pilot cutter met us near the harbour breakwater.

One of the strong south-easterly gales, for which the Cape is notorious, was just beginning to blow, and the cutter parted three of our hawsers while trying to tow us inside. Eventually we were picked up by the most powerful tug available—a vessel nearly as large as the *Cap Pilar* herself.

The day after we arrived in Capetown, the whole crew went off for a week's holiday, whilst we busied ourselves with the despatching of articles and cables about Tristan to the *News Chronicle*.

At Capetown we went through the worst period of crisis in the whole voyage. There were three reasons for this. First, in spite of the efforts of all on board, the *Cap Pilar* was still in very bad condition aloft. We had taught the whole crew the elements of sailmaking, but they were still far from proficient, and we had only managed as yet to make one sail. Secondly, we had no money. Before leaving England I had spent every penny I had—over £3,500—on the ship, and we had been forced to borrow another £1,400 for stores and equipment. Since then we had spent about £200 in various ports, so it was soon quite clear that the revenue from journalism would never bring us in enough money to continue the voyage.

These two problems alone were difficult enough to solve. We had sufficient stores aboard to carry us in safety to Australia, but before we could venture into the Southern Ocean westerlies we *must* have a reliable suit of sails; if we lay in Capetown for several weeks while we made the sails we should certainly have to buy fresh provisions, and also pay heavy harbour dues.

At first we decided to play for time by sailing up the coast to Saldanah Bay, where we could anchor free of charge and make our sails in peace; but the most difficult problem of all was still unsolved, Jane was not well.

We had first known about this on the way to Rio, and both George and I had done our best to persuade her to go home from there. She had refused, but her sufferings on the voyage to Capetown had made us realise that either she must go home or the whole voyage would have to be abandoned. Life in a fishing schooner is hard enough on a woman in any case, but when she is feeling ill it becomes terrible; constant rolling, coarse food, leaky decks and the smell of bilge water—no woman who has never experienced this sort of life can begin to understand the conditions under which Jane had had to live.

It was decided that she would return to England by

steamer, but when we arrived in Capetown and were confronted with the imminent dissolution of our partnership we were unable to face it.

However, we dragged ourselves disconsolately to one or two shipping firms. In the Union Castle offices they told us that all their ships were full until the end of May; we tried several other firms without success—some ships were too expensive, in others there was only steerage accommodation available. In the end, with a feeling of temporary reprieve, we scuttled off and bought ourselves an expensive dinner with wine. We felt very happy that evening, because we had put off the evil hour of parting.

After another two or three days ashore Jane was feeling quite well again, so we decided to shelve the problem of her future in favour of the more pressing need of finding a quiet berth for the ship.

The Navy had been very kind to us ever since our arrival—the base of the Africa station is at Simon's Town; so we decided to sail round to False Bay and do our sailmaking there. When the Admiral heard of our plans he immediately suggested that we should take with us his midshipmen "and give them a taste of sail training". Accordingly, on Thursday, the 25th of February, nine midshipmen, each with a suitcase and a hammock, came aboard and reported themselves politely to Lars. Jane went off to stay with friends who had very kindly offered to take care of her until we reached Simon's Town, and at 3 o'clock on that Thursday afternoon we towed out to sea.

The white cloud, known as the tablecloth, was already pouring over the edge of the mountain when we left. This was a certain warning of a south-easter, and if we had had our own way we should probably have remained in harbour; but the Admiral's secretary had sounded appallingly efficient over the telephone. "The midshipmen will be aboard you at 1100 on Thursday," he had said. This meant 11 A.M., and I had rashly replied that the *Cap Pilar* would put to sea at 1500. So at 1500 precisely—that is, at 3 P.M.—off we went with the wind already piping across Cape Flats, and the ships in the harbour laying out extra moorings in preparation for a blow.

The gale caught us suddenly just before sunset, and the *Cap Pilar* heeled over before the first violent blast as though she would lie upon her side. One or two light sails blew out at once, and there was a great deal of shouting and rushing to and fro in which the midshipmen took part with immense gusto, galloping about the deck in eager groups to lend a hand wherever it was wanted.

It was a dead headwind for us, and soon a high sea started to hurl us about, so we furled all except the essential canvas and settled down to ride it out. During the next twenty-four hours the *Cap Pilar* fought a hard battle; the waves were like small cliffs, and she pounded into them, one after another, with sickening shocks. Soon most of the midshipmen and half our crew were ill, and before morning the rest of us were so weary that we could do little more than lie on deck and wait for the weather to moderate.

The gale continued out of a brilliant cloudless sky until midnight on Friday 26th February; then left us as suddenly as it had sprung up. On Saturday morning we were becalmed, and our forenoon sights put us 120 miles due west of Cape Point.

For the next two days all hands, including the midshipmen, were busy repairing the sails that had been blown out. We reached False Bay on Tuesday morning, five days out from Capetown.

The journey from Capetown to Simon's Town takes less than one hour by train.

In Simon's Town our troubles descended upon us more heavily than before. We were beset by doubts and indecision.

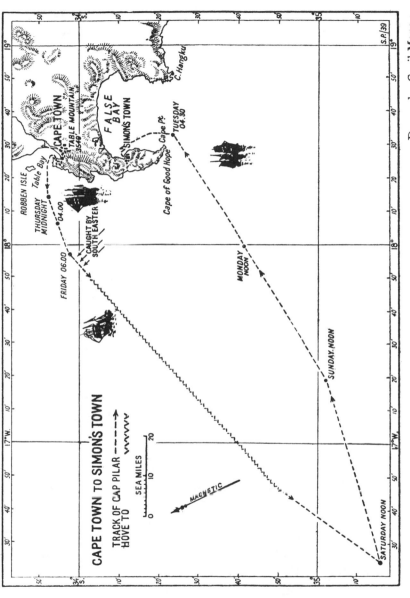

CAPE TOWN TO SIMON'S TOWN

TRACK OF CAP PILAR ----→
HOVE TO VVVVVVV

SEA MILES

MAGNETIC

CAPE TOWN
TABLE MOUNTAIN
3549
ROBBEN ISLE
Table Bay
THURSDAY MIDNIGHT
04.00
CAUGHT BY SOUTH EASTER
FRIDAY 06.00

FALSE BAY
SIMON'S TOWN
Cape of Good Hope
Cape Pt.
TUESDAY 04.30
C. Hangku

MONDAY NOON

SUNDAY NOON

SATURDAY NOON

S.P/39

Drawn by Cyril Money

Jane must go home—we could not separate . . . the ship must be sold—we couldn't admit defeat . . . we must stay in South Africa till the baby came—the crew were getting fed-up with the delay . . . we must build new accommodation—we had no money. From week to week our plans were changed. At one time I definitely decided to send the *Cap Pilar*, in charge of Lars, up the coast to Zanzibar and back to Durban, whilst I found a temporary job to keep Jane and me going until after the baby was born. A week later four young South Africans agreed to join the ship and contribute £75 each; so we made plans for an ox-waggon trek across the Karroo Desert to fill in time while new accommodation was being built.

So it went on. Every day some fresh problem presented itself, and we were forced to alter our plans. The crew, who were busy on the new sails, began to grow listless and discontented at the delay. Soon we saw the whole enterprise beginning to break up before our eyes. The Doc, who ought really to have gone home from Rio to sit for further examinations, agreed to stay with us until the ship reached Durban; but our future was so uncertain that we had to advise him to waste no more time. Soon after he had gone Roper disappeared for two days, and when he returned he announced that he had found himself a job on a fruit-farm.

In all we spent nearly nine weeks in the Cape, and seven of them in Simon's Town. Jane and I first stayed at the Lord Nelson hotel; but unfortunately one night a riotous party, which included some of our crew, removed a picture from the wall of the lounge. When we heard about this escapade next day, we sent Newell, who has a way with hotelkeepers, to return the picture and apologise for his shipmates. He did this so thoroughly that on the way back he fell into the sea, and had to be fished out on the end of a boat-fall. Next morning Jane and I were politely asked to leave; so we established ourselves at the British Hotel.

Our room, overlooking the harbour, had a large airy balcony, where we used to have breakfast in the morning sunshine. For one hour of the day only, between seven o'clock and eight o'clock in the morning, Jane and I used to sit alone together—talking about our baby, or about the little house we would some day live in, or the dinner we would eat together in our favourite restaurant in London. We no longer thought about seeing the world; we felt that we had been fools ever to attempt such a voyage; but, for this one hour of the day, we thought resolutely of happier times.

From where we sat we could see the whole of False Bay spread before us, and beyond it the Hottentots Holland mountains, standing like fortresses to protect our little peninsula from the continent of Africa; the air was fresh and laden with the memory of last night's flowers; the south-easter came skipping across the water, and the whole bay trembled into winking life like a field of snowdrops. For that one hour we felt happy and at peace, as though the whole beautiful world were our own to play in.

At eight o'clock the bugler on the training ship *General Botha* sounded "Still!" and all the ships in the harbour made their colours. Another day had begun.

As the weeks went by we felt more and more at home in the Cape; we all made many good friends, and our list of acquaintances became almost unmanageable. At the Admiral's garden-party Jane was nearly run over by the Governor-General's car; she was saved by the presence of mind of the naval officer on duty at the gates, who picked her up bodily and thrust her behind his back with one hand, while he saluted smartly with the other.

Some of the crew fell deeply in love. This was hardly surprising, because there is no doubt that South African girls are very beautiful, and very charming; although this comment sounds like the answer to an interviewer over the radio, it is none the less true, and must stand for what it is worth.

Suddenly one day a letter arrived from England. It brought a reply to our urgent report upon the difficulties which confronted us. It told us that at all costs the voyage must go on!

From this moment the voyage assumed for me a new complexion, and a very much more interesting one. Our honeymoon was over; the whole enterprise now belonged to someone else, and my job was only to make sure that it should succeed.

Our first act was to dump the ship's paraffin-stove into the sea and replace it by a coal range. Jane booked a passage to Sydney in a cargo steamer that was due to leave in three weeks' time. The rest of us, fired by a new enthusiasm, went to work with a will, and in a few more days the *Cap Pilar* was ready for sea.

We were now a company of nineteen, of whom six were new to the ship.

CLAUDE MAGGS, an Englishman of 34, who looked very much younger, was now the eldest of the crew. After leaving school he had been a fruit farmer in Kent, and later was sent out to take charge of the Government botanical gardens at Rangoon. When we met him he was working at the Kirstenbosch gardens near Capetown. He joined us as official photographer, and the illustrations in this book make further comment unnecessary; but here is an extract from *The Caterpillar*, the forecastle magazine, whose affectionate irreverence none the less gives one a very good idea of Claude's many remarkable qualities:

OUR BOOK CORNER

Safaris I have Led, by CLAUDE MAGGS.

Able-bodied seaman, scientist, photographer, scout-master, St. John Ambulance Claude Maggs (we got the idea from *Time*) has made a big name for himself as an intrepid leader of safari. "Claude is on safari"—the words have a familiar ring.

Claude has felt the call, and is off again; but this time within the covers of a handsome volume (20s., *Back-woods*), and we are privileged, from our comfortable chair in the forepeak, to follow in the footsteps of the great leader through the Arctic wastes of Iceland, across the sun-baked veldt of South Africa, and deep into the eerie jungles of mysterious Malaya. Often will danger beset us, but always our leader's wide experience as a boy scout saves the day.

The sands of time are running out, but Claude is still game. He hopes to lead yet another safari before finally putting aside the thumb-stick.

CHARLES JAMES CARMICHAEL had a passion for the sea and all its traditions. His home was near Capetown, but he had just returned from a world cruise, as a cadet under A. J. Villiers, in the ship *Joseph Conrad*. This two years' experience of a sailing ship made him a very welcome ally at that time.

DOUGLAS LOW was a chartered accountant, and the son of the mayor of Capetown. He had a cheerful, friendly face; he was very quiet and hardworking.

The fact that, in spite of the activities mentioned in a further extract from the book reviews of *The Cater-pillar*, he remained for a year and a half one of the most popular members of the crew, testifies to his imperturbable good nature:

My Struggle, by MR. LOW.

This is a true story with a moral. "If at first you don't succeed, try again," says Mr. Low, who has spent the major part of a lifetime at the pianoforte in the 'tween decks in an endeavour to master the popular classic "When I Grow too old to Dream". Friends of Mr. Low had for many years been deeply impressed by his dogged perseverance, and it was at their suggestion that the book was written.

WELSLEY MURISON worked as a clerk in the office of the *Cape Times*; he was also an expert musician, and spent his evenings as the leader of a dance band. When he joined us in Simon's Town he was obviously in urgent need of a holiday.

> If, during a conversation, you suddenly hear a high-pitched cry of "listen 'ere—listen 'ere, mun—listen 'ere" don't get alarmed. It isn't a battle-cry, nor yet the song of the Fuzzy-Wurzel. It is merely a South African asking if he may say a few words.—*The Caterpillar*.

GEORGE SMITH was 58 years old and a pensioned chief petty officer, R.N. He had first gone to sea at the age of 15 in one of the training brigs used by the Navy in those days. Shortly after the Great War he received his pension, and then became seamanship instructor in the South African training ship *General Botha*. When Smithy grinned, and he was always grinning, his round red face seemed to ripen and burst in the sunshine of his good spirits. He was only with us on the passage from the Cape to Sydney—the coldest, stormiest passage of the voyage—but, although he was more than twice as old as most of us, he never made a murmur of complaint during those arduous weeks, and we have always looked upon Smithy as one of the best shipmates we ever had.

The last of the South African contingent to join us was JACK OVENSTONE. He was a 17 years old schoolboy, very shy and youthful even for his years. In his quiet way he was tremendously enthusiastic about the voyage; but when he mentioned that he had always been prone to sea-sickness we began to fear that a winter passage through the westerlies would prove too much for him. However, there was no disputing his keenness. He used to come down to the ship every day in a large and expensive car driven by a chauffeur. All day he worked aboard, and in the evening the car called for him again to drive him home, covered in the grime of honest toil.

We were leaving the Cape nearly a fortnight before Jane; but kind friends had asked her to live at their house at Kirstenbosch until her steamer sailed.

On Saturday, 17th of April, the harbour launch towed us out of Simon's Town basin. On the quay stood Jane waving her pocket handkerchief; she looked a tiny pathetic figure—waving—waving—waving, until we were too far away to see her any more.

There was once again that terrible feeling of desolation in many of our hearts as we called good-bye. We had been too long in port; we had become almost part of the community that lived there. Somehow we had not realised, until the last moment, how hard it would be to say good-bye to all our friends; now suddenly there was deep water between us, and we should probably never see any of them again.

PART III

THE SOUTHERN OCEAN

CHAPTER XVI

RUNNING THE EASTING DOWN

THERE WAS NO WIND on that Saturday morning; the tug dropped us, like a wet rag, in the middle of False Bay. All through the night we were dead becalmed. The full moon clambered over the mountains, and hung above us like a fat old man holding his breath. Sunday morning found us still inside the bay with only the lightest of airs to stir our sails. All Sunday we lay becalmed.

East and west of us the mountains squatted like a gallery of gnomes peering over each other's shoulders. The Simonsberg looked clear and close at hand, yet we knew that we were too far off for our friends on shore to be able to see us; we were as completely cut off from them as though we had already been tumbling across the southern ocean a thousand miles away. The sun shone strongly upon us, as we lay about the decks in attitudes of ease and mental apathy. The gramophone was played; some sang, some washed and sewed. But a few were out of tune with their surroundings; their conversation was filled with retrospective melancholy:

She was so perfect. The first evening I met her I got a bit sentimental; she said it would be silly to go and fall in love if we had to be parted in a week or two, so we never talked about it again. One day I asked her to come back to England and marry me. We both felt a little awkward then, and she told me to be careful or she might say "Yes".

Then the night before last, coming back from the party, it was so hot that we had to bathe. She looked so white and beautiful in the moonlight. We walked home together. She cried when I had to go; her hair was full of moonlight. I suppose I shall never see her again.

I listened to the talk with a heavy heart. On our last morning together Jane and I had sat as usual upon our sunny balcony, talking very deliberately of ordinary things. At eight o'clock I walked down to the ship, and at ten o'clock Jane had come down to see us off. It was the first time we had been parted; in our efforts to avoid emotionalism we had spoken almost gruffly to each other.

At moonrise on Sunday evening dark boulders of cloud gathered in the nor'-west, and stepped, on legs of lightning, over the hills. We could hear the hiss of wind upon the water; soon the first sharp puffs came whipping across the bay. The ship steadied upon her course; on either hand the horizon grew, as the rocky headlands came abeam. The wind increased, the headlands fell astern, and once more we were out upon the ocean.

Now the sky became overcast, and the wind freshened quickly. Before it was quite dark the *Cap Pilar* was striding along under a press of sail at over nine knots. The mountains faded into the gloom behind us; the night closed round us full of the rush of wind, like a host of vultures falling upon us out of an inky sky. Slowly the glass began to fall; it was time to shorten sail. In came the gaff-topsail, main-topmast-staysail and flying jib.

In the eight to midnight watch the barometer fell in a series of ominous jerks. From windward a wall of black cloud, slashed and shattered by vivid streaks of lightning, came racing down upon the ship. We called all hands, and as fast as we could we stowed the lighter canvas. The moon had held his breath too long; at midnight it burst from him, and under a reefed topsail and close-reefed spanker, the little *Cap Pilar* fled south and east before a growing gale.

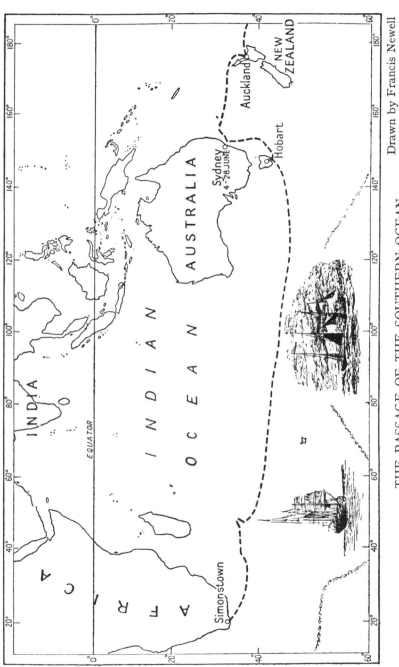

THE PASSAGE OF THE SOUTHERN OCEAN

Drawn by Francis Newell

During the next three days we ran before the hardest blow that any of us had experienced. At dawn on Monday morning the glass was still falling, while the wind continued to increase in ugly slashing squalls. The sky was no longer overcast, and the sun broke through with a hard, unearthly brilliance upon a seething ocean. The sea was smoking white; the *Cap Pilar* lay over, hard pressed and straining. At the wheel the helmsman struggled with all his might to keep her head away before the wind.

Throughout Monday the gale grew stronger. By nightfall there was a heavy sea running; we could feel the ship being lifted by each foaming crest, which carried her like a surf-boat before it. During the night she began to stagger under the weight of weather; sea after sea came clawing over the lee rail; the foredeck was awash; a big wave lifted the pig-sty into the scuppers; another stove in Murison's racing dinghy, which was lashed on the maindeck. All through Tuesday it blew between force nine and ten without a lull. Although only four of the crew were badly ill, the effort of keeping upright in a labouring ship soon began to tell on all of us.

Any attempt at organised cooking had by now become impossible. Claude Maggs, realising that all the other hands were badly needed on deck, volunteered in true scouting spirit to take over the galley work. By means of gallons of cocoa, hot milk drinks and stews, he kept the spirits of the whole ship's company well above normal.

Soon after dark on Tuesday evening a terrific squall came shrieking after us. The ship seemed to cower into the sea beneath it, then gather herself and leap forward as though in terror of her life; she quivered from stem to stern as a big sea exploded upon her, sending clouds of spray as high as the main top. We worked like mad to close-reef the mainsail and get the foresail in. But still she laboured, and the sea was now rising fast; so we hauled down the mainsail and furled the upper topsail.

The *Cap Pilar,* under her lower topsail and fore-top-mast-staysail only, still made eight knots.

All through the night we stood in a silent group aft, clinging to the rail or sitting upon the skylight. It was blowing so hard now that one felt as though at any moment he might be lifted bodily on to the main deck. My hands grew numb with cold, my thoughts wandered from one incongruous mental picture to another; yet always they circled back to the same unanswerable question: "What would happen if anything went wrong now?" But the *Cap Pilar* ran on without faltering. Wave after wave towered above her; to each one our little ship lifted smartly, just in time to shake herself free.

The pandemonium of wind and sea made conversation almost impossible.

"Got a light, Lars?"

"Yes."

"Got a light?"

"What?"

"*I said, 'Have you got a light?'*"

"Oh! I thought you said, 'What a night.'"

"What?"

"I thought you said . . ."

We gave it up, and took a fresh hold of the rail. There we clung, our eyes wandering from the sails to the sea ahead, over to windward and back to the sails again.

My thoughts went galloping, like the ship, through a wild sea of imagination. What was the name of that fellow in Moreton's? Frith, wasn't it? His father had a yacht. He said they sailed to the Azores in three days—that's impossible. Nothing's impossible; King Lobengula suckled thirty-three of his children.

Eight bells. Newell comes on now till four o'clock. What's the glass doing? Fallen three-hundredths. Newell was in the Navy; he doesn't feel cold. Do these chaps sleep at all when they turn in? That was a big one; I wonder if it smashed those skylights forward? I ought to go and see. It's all right, Newell's gone to see. The moon's very bright when it comes through. If a steamer saw us she would think we were an iceberg. What ought we to do if we ran into ice now?

Two bells of the middle watch. The sea's still getting up; we shall have to stream the oilbags soon. What's the glass doing? Fallen two-hundredths. How long has it been blowing? About two days. What's two days out of a lifetime? Only forty-eight hours. In the trenches men had to be on their feet for eight days sometimes.

Four bells. It isn't blowing any harder. I wonder if Potter'll get the primus going for cocoa this watch? Potter never fails. Willie was a gardener; I wonder what he thinks of this? We'll have a garden round our cottage —there'll be hollyhocks and roses. We'll have tea there on hot summer afternoons.

Six bells. The glass is steadying up—the wind's going more westerly. It won't blow much harder than this. Jane won't leave Capetown for another ten days.

Eight bells. Lars comes on again. The glass is steady now. It'll be light in another hour. I think the wind's taking off a bit. The sea's still running; if the wind dies now she'll roll her guts out.

Two bells of the morning watch. Lars is manning the pumps; that's the beginning of the day's routine. I feel as grey as the sea. Soon the sun will be up, and the sea will turn blue.

Four bells. Brilliant sunshine: the ship is plunging straight at the sun—clouds of spray go smoking through the fore rigging, shot with rainbows. I can't see properly; the horizon is jumping up and down. Good heavens! There's a steamer. No it isn't, it's a bird—there are thousands of birds and butterflies; wherever I look they seem to gather—little clouds of tumbling brown and red butterflies. I can go below now—Lars 'll look after the ship.

That was Wednesday morning. By the evening the gale had blown itself out, and the *Cap Pilar* was once more ambling along under all plain sail, with a steady south-westerly breeze on her quarter.

For four days there was very little wind; but we knew that the respite would only be temporary. Between us and our next port lay six thousand miles of cold, grey ocean, and we must get well down into the Forties to find the steady west winds which would carry us across it. So we made all secure and waited for the wind to come back to us.

On the second Sunday out we spent an exciting day catching albatross. The great birds swam so close to us that we were able to drop an improvised lasso over their heads; and soon we had six, looking as awkward as farm-yard geese, upon our main deck. Drummond Sanson attached to their feet brass tabs on which he had scratched the name of the ship, her position and the date; then we launched them over the side, and away they flew.

Gradually we worked our way south. In latitude 37°S. we picked up the west winds once again, and away went the *Cap Pilar* with a bone in her teeth; after another week we had entered the Roaring Forties.

From now on it seemed as though nothing could stop our little ship. Day after day she thundered along; week after week she battled across the gloomy desert of the southern ocean, peopled only by penguins and whales and countless sea-birds. Down came the gales with snow and sleet, the look-out cowered shivering upon the forecastle-head, the mate on watch went stamping up and down the poop. Sometimes the nights were steely clear; Orion and the Southern Cross blazed with a fierce splendour, fading at dawn to delicate patterns in lace and tinsel; individual stars glittered like needle-points of ice. Every day the sun sank lower over the northern horizon. From the Antarctic ice-packs the Aurora Australis lit the midnight sky with its ghostly wavering fingers. The *Cap Pilar* raced on through the dim watery light of southern winter.

Here is what one of the crew has written about a Saturday in the westerlies:

Day is breaking. There is a cold wind from the south-west, a clear sky, but a low grey bank of clouds to give warning of an approaching squall. The mate is busy with his sextant taking sights of the rapidly vanishing stars. The helmsman shivers in the biting dawn wind, and strikes four bells.

At the sound of the bells the port watch stumble out of the galley, where they have been sheltering from the spray; work on a sailing ship begins officially at six in the morning and never really ends. Yawning and heavy-eyed from eight hours' sleep, the cook comes up from below to put the porridge on for breakfast. He works from 6 A.M. to 9 P.M. feeding driblets of hungry men. In the westerlies the cook is one of the most popular men in the ship. Hot food must be prepared even though the ship is heeled over so far that he is obliged to hold the pots on the galley stove, and risk scalding from a flying kettle of water.

At 7.30 breakfast is taken down for the watch below. The starboard watch have been sleeping only since 4 o'clock; but they know very well that, if they do not tumble out, they will go hungry; for at 8 o'clock both watches gather at the break of the poop, and the mate shouts "Relieve the wheel; port watch below!"

"Strike me!" snarls Willie Marsh, the carpenter, scuttling on the deck with the last huge slice of bread and butter in his fist. "The blighters never wake a man at all."

The morning watch lasts from 8 till 1. Everyone is busy—a man, perched like a fly in the rigging, is splicing a parted buntline; there are two more in the 'tween decks sewing a fore-topmast-staysail, and "Chips", in his shop, still chewing the remains of his pathetic breakfast, is repairing a block. On the poop the second mate and the skipper are making plans for new lifeboat davits.

The navigator is waiting patiently for the sun to emerge from behind a heavy bank of cloud, his beard and jersey are full of flour and little barnacles of dough; he has just been making the day's supply of bread, as he now does the job of ship's steward as well as his own.

All the time the *Cap Pilar* is bowling along at a brisk seven knots under upper and lower topsails, foresail and reefed mainsail . . . riding the following seas like a gull.

The morning is soon gone with a hundred unconsidered jobs below and aloft. At 1 o'clock the port watch come up to take over, and the starboard watch disappear below to a dinner of fried corned beef, potatoes and sago.

As it is Saturday afternoon there is no more work for the watch on deck, other than the essentials of taking turns at the wheel, and trimming the sails whenever necessary. The wintry sun has come out, and blankets are brought on deck to dry. The bos'n sits patiently darning his socks, while the ship's cat plays with the ball of wool. One of the crew is laboriously writing up his diary, another is sitting on the windlass reading, another gazing dreamily at the spray clouds and the wheeling gulls. It is noticeable that all have their oilskins on, ready for anything that the weather may bring. The starboard watch straggle on deck to fill their buckets at the pump, and wash before going below for "the best sleep of the week". The wind dies down, and the following white-tops flatten.

Two shrill whistles . . . the watch on deck turns to. Mending and reading and dreaming are left. . . .

"Set the t'gallant and shake the reef out of the mainsail," shouts the mate. A man climbs dizzily to the highest yard to loose the t'gallant gaskets. The rest go to the mainsail; the mate shouts the time as they haul.

At 6.30 there is supper of pea-soup and spotted dog for the watch below. At seven the watches are changed once more. Potter, the ship's stalwart donkeyman, takes over the wheel, buttoning his oilskin and pulling down his sou'-wester. The lookout on the forecastle-head shivers as a slapping wave sends a shower bath of icy spray over him . . . the wind is rising, and it is bitterly cold.

The second mate comes aft, and reads the barometer anxiously with a flashlamp.

" What's it doing ? " calls the skipper, coming up from below.

" Falling fast. . . ."

The skipper dives down again for his sweaters and oilskins.

Meanwhile the three remaining members of the watch are huddled in the warmth of the galley, sitting on flour-tins. A tiny hurricane lantern throws out a thin, encouraging beam of light.

" Wonder what Australian beer's like ? " asks a wistful voice.

" Ruddy pubs close at 6," mutters the pessimist . . .

Two bells are struck.

A man stumbles out into the darkness to relieve the half-frozen helmsman, but the latter's troubles are not over; he looks sadly into the galley as he passes on his way forward to take over the lookout.

From the forecastle-head Carmichael, of Capetown, used to South African sunshine, staggers aft, blue with cold. He stops for a moment to warm his salt-cracked hands at the galley stove. " Blowing up for a gale," he says gloomily.

They sit silent, listening to the thrum in the rigging —wondering how long it will be before the order comes to shorten sail.

Not long. The two whistles shrill out. The men hurry stiffly aft, tying the wet cords of their sou'-westers.

" In t'gallant," shouts the second mate above the increasing roar of the wind. They run to the down-hauls.

"Aloft and make fast!" Potter and Carmichael leap into the fore rigging. The ship lurches and rolls violently as a heavy sea strikes her. Aloft they worm out along the yard, grasping at wet, tossing folds of canvas. Far below them they can see the white line of the bow-wave, as the ship drives her nose in deep. . . .

At midnight the starboard watch goes below to snatch a few hours' sleep. At four they are back on deck again, leaving warm, steaming bunks to find the wind now blowing half a gale.

The watch on deck is struggling to put a reef in the mainsail, with the half-frozen rain lashing their faces. Both watches hoist the sail together, then a big sea sweeps the main deck, and washes the unwary into the scuppers.

The dawn of Sunday breaks to reveal the starboard watch aloft, clinging to the upper topsail yard, taking yet another reef—a job that requires a cool nerve, with both hands full of canvas and the wind screaming like a demon and wrenching you back. . . . Another windjammer day has begun—the first of a week's work.

On this passage the *Cap Pilar's* best day's run, from noon to noon, was 221 miles; but, running eastwards in high latitudes, the actual time elapsing between one solar noon and the next is only about $23\frac{1}{2}$ hours; consequently, on that particular day, *Cap Pilar* averaged over nine knots. But the most remarkable illustration of the persistently favourable winds we encountered, was the fact that for over a month on end we averaged 170 miles a day.

Gale after gale came howling after us as we edged every day deep into the Forties. The forecastle became a damp, reeking hole. The crew got used to snatching what sleep they could, fully dressed in oilskins and sea-boots. Their bunks were soaking wet, and after any two consecutive days of heavy weather, there wasn't a stitch of dry clothing left in the ship. There was no room in the galley for more than one pair of socks per man to be dried, so if anyone wanted a dry shirt, he had to sleep on it and hope that the warmth of his body would make it worth changing for the one he had worn the watch before.

Young Ovenstone from South Africa, suffered from chronic seasickness of such a violent nature that at one time we seriously considered altering course for Albany in South Australia. But before we were far enough east for a decision to be necessary his condition improved and we continued on our way to Sydney round the south of Tasmania.

Poor Burgess, the ventilating engineer from Birmingham, never got over his seasickness either, but he found that in the comparative warmth of the galley, he was able to keep just well enough to work. So Burgess took over the cooking and did it remarkably well. In this he showed exceptional fortitude, since it would be difficult to imagine more disagreeable surroundings in which to feel ill, than the galley of a deep-water sailing vessel in heavy weather.

But a remarkable change had come over all the crew. At the lee fore brace and sheet, when sails had to be trimmed, the green water poured over the rail, like a mixture of ice and broken glass, on to hands already scarred and split by long exposure to the weather; but despite frozen hands and sodden bunks they all stuck grimly to their work. Grumbling and quarrelling ceased; at last they were face to face with the sea, and they took up the challenge eagerly. Only a few weeks before they had still been a miscellaneous collection of landsmen; now they had suddenly become sailors.

CHAPTER XVII
ATTEMPT AT HOBART

On the 12th of May, in latitude 44°S. and longitude 85°E., we celebrated the Coronation by declaring a holiday. Unfortunately the West Winds appeared not to have been informed of events in England, so our holiday differed very little from the Saturday and Sunday described in the last chapter. However, we were able, during a lull, to collect in the saloon, where we drank their Majesties' health in a bumper of rum punch. "Smithy" draped the saloon table with an immense Red Ensign, which he had brought for that purpose, and Murison played the national anthem on his fiddle, with a saxophone accompaniment by Sanson.

The 20th of May was the aniversary of my wedding. This time we drank South African wine, and thought of Jane all alone in her steamer. The wine had been her parting present to us, but as we toasted her we thanked God that she had not been obliged to make this passage with us.

Except for Burgess and Ovenstone, I think José, the cabin-boy, was the only one of us who heartily disliked this part of the voyage. His seafaring had never before carried him farther than to Rio de Janeiro. He was such a simple fellow that it was doubtful whether he had even been aware of the existence of such sunless regions as the one he was now crossing. José was still unable to speak more than three or four words of English. He still referred to every meal as "breakfast", and announced it, without ceremony, by giving a shrill whistle and poking two fingers down his widely opened mouth.

As the weeks went by José got more and more

depressed. For two hours every day he stood miserably at the wheel, cowering before the icy wind, and no doubt dreaming about his sunny Madeiran home. One afternoon he suddenly spoke to me for the first time since leaving Capetown.

"English ship—no good 'comida,' " he said. I tried to smile encouragingly.

"Portuguese ship very plenty . . ." he resorted to pantomime by means of which he depicted the skylight beside us heaped high with luxuries. With one hand he helped himself to this imaginary feast, while with the other he outlined a huge paunch and bloated cheeks. When he had finished he pretended to throw large quantities of surplus food over the side. As an afterthought he added: "Plenty *vino*—all time *vino*," and then staggered off in the direction of the galley.

On account of those two months in the hot dry atmosphere of the Cape, the *Cap Pilar's* decks had shrunk and opened badly, so that during the first gale a great deal of water had poured in upon our stores. We thought that most of them must be ruined, since they were almost afloat before we were able to spread old sails under the deck-head to lead the water off. However, when we inspected them, we found to our amazement that, in spite of the deluge, we had lost nothing but seven tins of flour, which had made holes in each other through being badly stowed. On the other hand our self-raising flour, though only packed in wooden boxes lined with waterproof paper, came through the storm unspoilt.

Our precious cocoa had become so wet that the weight of each tin had been doubled. We found, however, that after draining and drying it as much as possible, it was still as good as ever, and cocoa became our staple beverage throughout the voyage.

Before Capetown we had never been able to make a

decent pea-soup. The yellow peas, as hard as bullets, had resisted every effort of soaking and boiling, to make them edible; but now after a week awash in sea-water, their first line of resistance appeared to have been broken, and we were able to have pea-soup twice a week in weather which made it the most acceptable dish on the menu.

Our sugar, which was packed in hundredweight sacks, lay in a pool of salt-water treacle; but this again was quite unharmed in anything but appearance; we simply changed the sacks and cleared up the mess. The dried fruit had become wet fruit, but tasted just as good after the salt had been rinsed away. Our safety matches had never been so safe in their lives, so we dried them in the oven; after that they frequently went off in one's pocket.

At last, towards the end of May, we drew near to the coast of Tasmania. Through all the wet and cold and discomfort of the Westerlies, one thought had sustained us all—we were making such a good passage, due to the succession of following gales, that we should have time to put into Hobart, and spend a week in Tasmania before going on to Sydney. On the 28th of May, just forty days after leaving Capetown, we sighted Eddystone Rock off the entrance to Storm Bay and Hobart. The passage of the Southern Ocean was over.

The morning of the 29th of May was clear and warm, with the lightest northerly breeze hardly stirring a ripple upon the sea. We stood in close to the thickly wooded headlands; as we approached them, we felt like old-time explorers who had sighted an unknown country. Tasman and Entrecasteaux must have felt as we did, when they first sailed into this bay. It is doubtful, too, whether the appearance of the Tasmanian coast has in any way altered since those times; we sailed past rugged cliffs, fjords and mile upon mile of forest, unrelieved by a single clearing or sign of human habitation. We saw neither ships nor boats, nor any evidence of civilisation.

In the afternoon it blew fresher, but still the wind came from the north, and we soon found that a strong current was holding us out to sea. During the whole of that day we made no ground; towards evening the glass began to fall, and the wind freshened quickly from the nor'-west.

Suddenly a violent squall whistled down from the mountains. Newell flew to the fore-topsail halliards, and cast them off. I eased the peak of the mainsail. Even so the *Cap Pilar* was struck down helpless. Fortunately the rigging held, and as soon as the ship gathered enough way, George was able to steer her off the wind.

For an hour we flew before it, shortening sail as fast as we could, and when we finally had the ship snugged down, the land was almost out of sight. It was with heavy hearts that we abandoned the attempt on Hobart.

With the wind now set in the nor'-west, and freshening, we squared away past the cape called Pillar, after which our ship may have been named. For the next few days we worked slowly up the east coast of Tasmania.

We had now been six weeks at sea—six weeks of storm and bitter cold—many of the crew were suffering from salt-water boils and badly split hands and fingers; we were all growing tired of the eternal gloom of high latitudes; we longed for port and sunshine and the leisure in which to enjoy them.

To the South African recruits especially, the westerly passage must have been particularly trying. Not only was it; for some of them, their first experience of seafaring, but they had also spent the greatest part of their lives in the torrid climate of the Cape; so the cold, wet weather of the Southern Ocean must have been very hard for them to bear. Murison changed more than any of them during that voyage. He had joined the ship a thin, pale and exceedingly neurotic city boy; but by the time we reached Australia he was already quite plump and full of confidence. Music was still an all consuming passion with Murison; one day he asked leave to repair our piano. This unfortunate instrument had all but been abandoned. During the first part of the voyage it had suffered with all our stores from the badly leaking deck. We had decided that if we were unable to sell it in Sydney, we might as well give it away. Murison, however, worked upon it for a few hours, and then triumphantly pronounced it as good as new. Thereafter the piano was continually in use, and there is no doubt that the music of Murison, and several others in the crew, contributed very largely to the ultimate success of our voyage.

At 9 A.M. on Wednesday, 2nd of June, land was sighted fine on the weather bow. Almost immediately the sky cleared and the wind moderated, and for the rest of that day we went swinging up the coast of New South Wales in brilliant glowing sunshine—the first real sunshine we had felt for a month and a half.

The sun put new life into the whole ship's company. Every stitch of clothing, every blanket, sea-boot, suit-case, bag, every article of gear that anyone possessed was dragged up from the stinking depths and laid out upon the deck to dry; skylights, that had been screwed down, were now opened wide, and from one end of the ship to the other there was an almighty scrubbing and sweeping and turning out.

In the afternoon we all congregated on deck to bask in the sun; we leaned on the rail to watch the hilly coast-line crawling by. Murison got out his fiddle, and there was a great deal of singing and playing of gramophones. We must have looked like a party of day-trippers on a pleasure boat.

In the afternoon of the 3rd of June, a strangely regu-

lar hump of a hill appeared in the distance. The tele-
scope revealed that the hill was made of iron girders;
it was, in fact, the top of Sydney Harbour Bridge, seen
from a distance of nearly thirty miles.

It was soon obvious that we would not reach Sydney
Heads before dark; but we were determined, if possible,
to get in that night. In the morning the wind might
shift, or a sudden squall force us out to sea again, as it
had at Hobart.

Night fell, and the innumerable lights of the great
city shone out in rows and avenues of yellow points.
Sydney looked like a magnificent Christmas cake decorated with a million candles, over which the beam of
the South Head lighthouse went sweeping like a
magician's wand.

To the stranger, Sydney is a very confusing harbour
to enter at night. There is only one lighthouse, and the red
and green leading lights on shore are rendered practically
useless to anyone unacquainted with the topography of
the city, by being almost indistinguishable from the many
bright neon signs outside cinemas and public-houses.

The result was that though we knew our direction from
the lighthouse, we could not, at first, be quite certain of
our distance off shore; and we actually sailed past the
harbour entrance still looking for the elusive leading
lights, and had to spend two hours beating back again.

The wind was S.S.W. and cold, with an overcast sky
which threatened drizzle and poor visibility; so when at
midnight we once more regained the harbour entrance
we decided to sail right in to meet the pilot, who, we felt
certain, must have seen our flares and be waiting for us
in the narrows.

We entered the harbour, close-hauled upon the port
tack; but there was no pilot to welcome us. A wallowing
ground swell began to send us careening as we got into

the shoaler water, and there was a danger of the ship missing stays; so we stood in still further in the hope of getting under the lee of South Head. At the same time, Lars made all the preparations for letting go the starboard anchor, in case the ship failed to tack. When we had approached Middle Head as near as we dared we eased the helm a-lee, and without a moment's hesitation *Cap Pilar* rounded up to the wind and fell off upon the other tack.

Encouraged by the success of this manœuvre we decided to work right in to the port on the making tide. But a few moments later a winking light from South Head told us that we had at last been seen, and we were instructed to stand off again until the pilot reached us. We hove-to outside, and the pilot eventually came aboard about 2 A.M. At 6 A.M. a tug arrived, and we were towed ignominiously in to the quarantine anchorage.

It was a cold grey morning, with mist and rain; but the weather did not in any way detract from our feeling of relief and satisfaction at having crossed the Southern Ocean. Now at last we were in the Pacific, with only a few hundred miles of blue and sparkling water between us and the South Sea Islands.

As we went slowly up the great harbour, with the red and yellow houses coming down to the water's edge, the peaceful calm of the scene seemed quite unreal. For the first time for nearly two months we no longer had to battle against the forces of nature. But the arrival of two launches, full of newspaper reporters, quickly reminded us of the fact that there were other forces that still had to be reckoned with.

The reporters clambered on board, and the interviewing began:

" Have you had any storms ? " asked a business-like

looking young man in a mackintosh and a green hat.

"Yes. Can you tell me any news of my wife?"

"No. Didn't know you had one. Were you ever in danger of being wrecked?"

"No; but are you sure my wife isn't in Sydney?"

Here another reporter in horn-rimmed spectacles broke in with: "Yes, she's about here somewhere, she came in in the *Tricolor* a few days ago. Now can you tell me, Mr. Seligman, what exactly is the purpose of this voyage?"

I hurriedly referred him to George, and went off in search of a more neutral source of information.

After breakfast Jane arrived alongside, looking bonnier than we had ever seen her. Our reunion was accompanied by the rattle of photographic artillery; but we were so genuinely relieved at being together again that nothing mattered much—not even the excited camera-man who had missed our first greeting, and wanted it repeated for the benefit of the great Australian public.

CHAPTER XVIII
AUSTRALIA FAIR

BEFORE I COULD GO ASHORE with Jane there were as usual a great many things to be settled on board. Papers had to be filled in and signed, the crew's shore leave to be arranged for, the catering arrangements settled with George, and the customs officers interviewed. With regard to the latter, one must in all fairness admit that, although the Australian customs regulations involve the inexperienced in about three full days of clerical work, the officers themselves are extraordinarily kind and helpful.

Before we left the ship also, we had to entertain the crew of the tug which brought us in. They were a very remarkable company composed of three generations of the same family. The grandfather was the engineer, the father was the skipper, and the son was the deck-hand.

The old grandfather, while having a glass of rum in our saloon, was very interested to see the little wooden crucifix which adorned the forward end of the *Cap Pilar's* skylight; then turning round he saw the figure of the Virgin Mary at the after end of the skylight. "You're backed both ways, I see," was his dry comment.

The day after we arrived in Sydney there were headlines and photographs in most of the newspapers; and a good deal of friendly interest was taken in ourselves and the ship. We received a very genuine and hearty welcome from all sorts of people, many of whom had no connection with the sea; so we all immediately felt at our ease. The publicity we received, however, so much infuriated one gentleman that he subsequently wrote a very embittered article, entitled: "Yo! ho! ho! and a Bottle of Raspberry Syrup", in which he professed himself disgusted with the fuss that was made of voyages such as ours. He poured scorn on our "French fishing vessel (probably softwood), and as for her appearance, the less said about that the better."

He was right about the *Cap Pilar's* appearance. She might have been the inspiration of those lines from Kipling's "The Merchantmen":

> *By Sport of bitter weather*
> *We're walty, strained and scarred*
> *From the kentledge on the kelson*
> *To the slings upon the yard.*

She looked a very rugged figure among all the dainty yachts and magnificent steamers in Sydney Harbour; her green topsides were faded and flaked and streaked with rust from the anchor cables; her white paintwork was foul with black and brown stains; her brasswork was a brilliant bluish-green, and aloft she was as whiskery as an old seal.

But we were very proud of our little ship, no matter what she looked like; and perhaps if her critic had ever made the passage she had just completed he would have been proud of her too. At any rate, it was more important just then that the crew should have an opportunity of seeing Australia than that they should spend all their harbour time in painting ship. So during our stay in Sydney we concerned ourselves only with a final re-arrangement of the ballast.

Sydney is too important and too fine a city to be dismissed here without comment.

The first question which a visitor to Sydney must be prepared to answer is: "What do you think of our harbour?" Everyone you meet in Sydney comes out with this time-honoured formula, and fortunately you

In a few moments, we were out of earshot and bowling down the river . . .

Outward bound for Rio and Tristan da Cunha . . .

The boys changing sails in the Trade Winds . . .

Once more, the sky
began to breathe . . .

Roping a new lower topsail . . .

Colin Potter at the wheel in the Southern Ocean . . . .

Lars snapping a sight . . .

Found him feeding Dennis from the saloon teapot . . .

Anchored in Tai-o-Hae . . .

The lagoon of Hao in the
Tuamotu Islands . . .

Through the pass
into Hao . . .

A pretty South Sea islander . . .

Cap Pilar entering New York . . .

Family Life . . . .

Homeward from Halifax . . .

We were home again . . .

can reply with truth and conviction that you think it is one of the finest in the world. In fact, if you have never been to Vancouver, Rio, Hong Kong, Auckland, Halifax or Queenstown, you can unhesitatingly reply that you consider it the finest harbour you have ever seen.

The harbour bridge also merits unstinted praise, and so, I gather, does the weather as a rule; but while we were there it was cold and very rainy. However, we were assured that this was so exceptional as to be almost a phenomenon, which assertion we gladly accepted; and were thankful to escape from further inquisition upon subjects about which our hosts appeared to be unduly sensitive.

In all the material things of life the Australians are assiduous copiers of Americans, and Sydney itself reflects this very clearly. It is far more like an American than an English city. The American products, both engineering and otherwise, are more efficient, up to date, and often cheaper than English goods, besides being more suited to Australia, which is geographically a similar country to the U.S.A. Furthermore, the American manufacturer takes far more trouble to study his customer's requirements than the English. So it is scarcely to be wondered at that an Australian " buys American " whenever he can.

But in every Australian's heart there lies a very real affection for England, the Old Country or " Home ", as it is usually called. Every Australian wants one day to visit England, and what is happening " at home " is of the greatest interest and concern to him. This love of England, however, does not necessarily extend to Englishmen, who are, more often than not, referred to as " bloody poms ". This is usually more a term of derision than anything else, " pom " or " pommy " referring to the supposedly " rosy apple " complexion of all Englishmen. But working-class Australians certainly have some cause for complaint, since Englishmen in the colonies are notoriously willing to work long hours for low wages, thereby jeopardising the Australian working man's exceedingly high standard of living; and no Australian is really happy unless he is in a position to tell his employer to go to hell whenever he feels like it.

But we ourselves found the Australians a most genuine, hospitable, energetic and thoroughly friendly race. True, we became involved in a great many furious arguments about the relative merits of our respective countries; but we always made a point of being as dogmatically partisan as our opponents; of matching their most outrageous assertions with even more indefensible counter-charges; and we soon found that in this way we made many excellent friends.

In Sydney, Jane and I spent the happiest three weeks of our lives. We were the guests of the George Bryants, who insisted upon our making their home our own during the whole of our stay; nor would they hear of our leaving them, even though our visit dragged on into nearly a month. Jane was in glowing health the whole time, and it seemed, for the moment, as though most of our troubles were over. I had, as usual, to spend a large part of the day in the city, where there were always matters requiring urgent attention; but Jane and I often met in the evenings at an oyster bar. Sydney oysters are the most delicious in the world, and even if they were not, one would enjoy them more than any others, if only for the fact that they may be had for 1s. a dozen.

George Bryant was nothing if not a typical Australian —kind-hearted to a fault, and tremendously keen that we should get to know Australia, while being at the same time ferociously critical of the English and English methods; but his criticisms were always downright and genuine rather than malicious. He took no trouble to conceal his opinion of the average Englishman, although he *had* taken the trouble to pay more than one visit to England, and he was extremely proud of some good English furniture he had in his house.

We were very happy with the Bryants and all their friends, who sometimes paid us the doubtful compliment of calling us "very un-English"; perhaps it was George's flowing black beard, effectively concealing any trace of "pomegranate" complexion, which won their hearts. The fact remains that the time spent with the Bryants was one of the most enjoyable episodes of the whole voyage. Not even when our George committed the absurd indiscretion of asking George Bryant what he thought of Shakespeare was the harmony of our relations seriously impaired. Our host curtly retorted: "When I was at school we had to wade through the hound," and George wisely let the matter drop.

Through the Bryants we met a great many interesting people, among them a certain jovial Dr. Fitzharding, who took us out in his car to spend a week-end on his son's sheep-farm, about 200 miles inland from Sydney.

We had to cross the Blue mountains on the way, and here the scenery was certainly very beautiful. Beyond Bathurst, however, it became mile after mile of undulating grassland, sparsely dotted with gaunt dead trees. In Australia, and in some parts of New Zealand, they kill the commercially valueless gum-trees by "ringing" them. The lifeless trunks are left standing, and the grass flourishes in the abundant sunshine to which it then has access. This custom gives to large tracts of New South Wales the desolate appearance of a modern battlefield; though to the Australian-born it still has a grim beauty.

But New South Wales is not by any means a desert. There are, of course, the sheep.

During our week-end on the sheep station we were introduced to the art of working sheep-dogs. At first sight it appeared very simple: a shout from their master, and the dogs immediately set the mob of sheep in motion—a whistle, and the flock was wheeled round; another, and they stopped, and so on. One morning when Jane and I were out for a walk with the dogs we saw a small mob of sheep on a neighbouring hillside and decided to try a little sheep droving on our own account.

" Go back ! " I shouted, and like flashes both dogs disappeared in the direction of the sheep. A moment later we saw the mob cluster together as the dogs approached. I gave a loud whistle, and they gathered way, and came trotting down the hillside towards us. They came on faster and faster, and when they had nearly reached us I suddenly realised that I did not know the signal for " stop ".

In desperation I gave two whistles, and away went the flock to the right, followed by the dogs, who were by now yelping with excitement. I tried every combination of whistles and shouts I could think of, but these merely seemed to goad the dogs into a greater frenzy. I started to run, but they were already half a mile away, and a moment later they disappeared over the horizon.

As I pounded after them in an agony of terror, I imagined the maddened dogs hounding our host's sheep all round the estate, probably collecting others as they went, and eventually driving the entire valuable flock into the bush, where they would no doubt disappear without trace.

I verily believe that this would have occurred, had not our host, by sheer good fortune, been there to intercept them in the next valley. We were careful never to whistle again until we got back to Sydney.

George's beard was a constant source of pleasure to the inhabitants of Sydney; but he was determined not to be bullied into shaving. However, when he was invited to a fancy-dress ball, he refused to go in fancy dress, for fear that someone would think that he was wearing a false beard, and try to pull it off, so he went in a borrowed dinner jacket.

At the dance he was introduced as a professor from Cambridge University. He felt, therefore, that a little eccentricity of conduct would not be out of place, so he removed his borrowed shoes, which were far too tight, and thereafter danced in his socks.

From Sydney, Ovenstone, the young South African who had been so seasick, went home; and "Smithy", his departure deeply regretted by all of us, went on by steamer to Canada. José also left us on account of illness, so we had to get another cabin-boy. We decided to try a paid galley-boy as well. Roy Walker and Jack Riordan were eventually taken on to fill these two posts. Riordan left the ship in Auckland, but Walker, who very soon became known as "Scanty" from the fact of his having worked in a ladies underwear factory, stayed with us for the rest of the voyage, and was to become one of the great characters of the ship's company. We also culled one contributing member in the person of Sydney Marshall, probably best described as a young Australian yachtsman and crack Sydney Harbour dinghy racer.

At first we had considered the idea of remaining in Sydney until the baby was born; but after a week or two in port we began once more to feel impatient, so it was decided that Jane and George should travel on by steamer to New Zealand, while we would follow with the first fair wind. Accordingly, on Friday, 25th of June, they left in the American passenger steamer *Monterey*.

Episode on Board an American Liner.

It is 9 A.M. The navigator of the *Cap Pilar* opens his eyes and yawns, then leans over and lifts the receiver from the telephone beside his bunk.

"Will you connect me with the bridge, please?"

" Hallo. Is that the officer of the watch? Good morning. Where's the wind this morning? Sou'-sou'-west—
strong? Rough sea? Thanks."

Replaces receiver — yawns — turns over and goes to
sleep.

On Monday, 28th of June, the *Cap Pilar* picked up her
anchor and sailed out of Sydney Heads. The passage to
Auckland was uneventful. For nine days on end we were
close-hauled to light sou'-sou'-easterly winds, and picked
up North Cape, New Zealand, on the twelfth day out of
Sydney. The thirteenth and fourteenth days we spent in
running down the east coast of North Island in beautiful
clear weather and a moderate northerly breeze, and at
dawn on the fifteenth day we sailed into Auckland Harbour with every sail set.

CHAPTER XIX
AUCKLAND AND JESSICA JANE

As THE DAYS of the Sydney-Auckland passage dragged by, I had become more and more anxious about Jane; but when we arrived in Auckland she and George were there to meet us, and it transpired that they had found what it is no exaggeration to say was the most attractive small house in the whole district. It was a four-roomed cottage made of wood, and surrounded by a beautiful little garden full of bright flowers and fantastic-looking tree-ferns. Here they had been living, doing all their own housework and cooking. They had also fitted in a five-days' visit to the famous thermal district of Rotorua, so there had not been much need for anxiety on their account.

The *Cap Pilar* eventually arrived on Tuesday, 13th July, and on Friday, the day the baby was expected, we decided to ask a few friends in to supper by way of creating a diversion. But Jane had only just begun to cut the sandwiches when she had to hurry off to the nursing-home. The party still took place, and I was hovering about in the background, like Banquo's ghost, adding very little gaiety to the proceedings, when, soon after 8 P.M., the telephone rang to inform us that Jessica Jane had arrived. At once the tension relaxed and the party soon developed into a hilarious carouse, while I dashed off to see my eldest unmarried daughter. It was four in the morning before the party finally dispersed. This was the first, but by no means the last time that baby Jessica was made the excuse for a night of revelry.

For the next few days the excitement of becoming a father drove all other thoughts from my mind, and I found a temporary, though rather ostrich-like, respite from numerous worries.

Jessica was undoubtedly a sweet baby, with wide open indigo eyes, long eyelashes and beautiful soft brown hair. I still wonder how so delicate and pretty a little creature could have been formed in the crude, comfortless surroundings of a deep-water sailing ship.

As soon as Jane was strong enough, they both came to live at our little house in Mount Eden, Auckland. A very kind friend lent us a magnificent Ford V8; so at every week-end we packed Jessica Jane in her basket and made long expeditions into the wilds. These drives provided the most enjoyable of any New Zealand memories. We always cooked and ate our meals by the wayside—sometimes in a *kauri* forest, or on a mountain side or, most beautiful spot of all, in a grove of pine-trees beside a galloping mountain torrent.

But very soon we were faced with a crisis that looked even more difficult to solve than the one in Capetown— namely : '' What was to be done with Jane and Jessica ? ''

Doc Atkinson who had been with us as far as Capetown, had left little doubt that, in his opinion, it would be tantamount to infanticide to take a new-born baby to sea in the *Cap Pilar*; but although we could not honestly contradict this opinion, we could not help feeling that his outlook had become somewhat embittered by an unfortunate leak in his cabin deck-head, which caused a steady drip of water to splash on his nose whenever the weather was very rough or rainy. However, there were plenty of others who, knowing nothing of the ship (or any other ship), were full of the gloomiest forebodings. When Jane pointed out that a century ago babies not only survived the roughest passages, but were sometimes actually born on board sailing ships, they would shake their heads and say: '' Ah, it might have been all right in the old days, but it's very different now. Babies can't stand what they used to.''

I must say that I held this view myself; but Jane was quite determined to stay with the ship, and when one of the most eminent doctors in New Zealand backed her up, I had to give way. It appeared that modern tinned foods had made the diet problem quite easy, and that the only risk was that some serious complaint might develop when we were hundreds of miles from land; but this, of course, applied equally to grown-ups and babies. Furthermore, the risk of picking up any serious infection at sea was very slight.

So Jane and Jessica were to continue the cruise, and, after all, who could say that they had less right than anyone else in the ship's company to be considered? The voyage had been originally intended as a sort of honeymoon cruise for Jane.

But now there was the problem of making suitable accommodation for them both. The cramped, leaky and often malodorous hutch, in which we had existed up to now, was quite obviously out of the question for a young mother and her baby; so we began estimating the cost of building a new, properly lighted, ventilated and appointed cabin and bathroom.

We found that it would cost about £60, so we decided to advertise for additional contributing members of the crew. Unfortunately this would necessitate the enlarging of the crew's accommodation as well; we should therefore need a few more recruits still to pay for that job. But if we were going to increase our numbers, we must also have another lifeboat and proper davits, etc., and then the galley must be altered. And so it went on, until we found that in order to balance our budget we must find at least ten recruits.

As it turned out, the whole scheme was financially unsound, chiefly because we found it quite impossible to keep to our originally estimated expenditure; but on looking back I do not for an instant regret the fact that we added several hearty young New Zealanders to our company, for they proved themselves in every way the most excellent shipmates.

But, just as in the early days in England, when we had to start fitting out the ship before we had found our crew, now also there was no question of waiting until we had sufficient money before we put the alterations in hand. The delay would have been disastrous; even the seven weeks we were forced to remain in Auckland taxed everybody's patience to the utmost. So we wasted no time in getting the shipwrights aboard, while the existing crew went off for a three weeks' tour of the country. I very much hoped to be able to get all the work on board finished during those three weeks, so that everything would once more be clean and tidy by the time the crew returned.

Applications to join the ship came in very slowly at first, and the strain of financial worries was as great as it had ever been before, with expenses rapidly mounting, and only an occasional £50 or so coming in to keep things going.

Meanwhile the crew, some hitch-hiking and some on bicycles, had scattered all over New Zealand. Burgess, Low and Donnelly got as far as the snow-covered mountains of the South Island. They brought back stories of glaciers, mountaineering and ski-ing, which made us all envious. Others made expeditions to the thermal districts, where the Maori villages are situated beside the warm springs. Strangely enough the constant hot baths in which they indulge, and the damp warm climate in those parts, has not in any way impaired the Maori people's magnificent physique. The Maori women require no cooking fires, they put their pots into any convenient steaming hole in the ground. There are hundreds of these vents, and they are by no means all at the same temperature; so Mrs. Every-maori has her dishes for the midday meal dotted about all over the " village green ", under bushes or stones or in the open, according to where the best " steamers " happen to be situated. The warm water also solves the good lady's nursery problems, because, as soon as breakfast is over, she undresses all the children and pops them into the nearest pool. There they remain contentedly for the rest of the morning, the soft embrace of the warm mineral-impregnated water being far more effective in keeping them quiet than the bars of a play-pen.

Other phenomena of the thermal districts are the mighty " geysers ", which erupt with an awesome thundering and huge columns of boiling water at precisely regular intervals, and the morasses of spitting, bubbling mud—that resemble vats of boiling chocolate. The latter lie like horrid monsters all about the valleys; and we shuddered at the thought of slipping, on a dark night, into one of them—belching sulphur, scalding and bottomless.

But more sinister were the deep pools filled with crystal clear sulphuretted water, which, though not boiling, were at a temperature almost as high as, or maybe higher than, the boiling-point of pure water. The still green depths of these pools were almost irresistibly inviting, and we imagined some unfortunate traveller plunging unawares into their depths.

While we were in New Zealand a Maori woman did fall into one of these, and her husband heroically plunged in after her. Both were killed.

The Cap Pilarians found hitch-hiking the ideal mode of progression in New Zealand, and I must record (quite objectively) two distinct methods adopted by the *Cap Pilar's* brotherhood of hitch-hikers. Low and Burgess preferred to swing briskly along the road with a cheery smile and a wave for any motorist who chanced to pass. They found this method very successful, being helped upon their way at different times by a lorry full of pigs, a huntsman on the way to a meet, a Salvation Army officer and a ladies' basket-ball team.

Murison and Roach, on the other hand, tried sitting down by the roadside until they heard an approaching car; they then got to their feet and started sloping wearily along the road. Just before they were overtaken they used to hold up a hand appealingly, trying to look as though they could hardly totter another step. If the response was negative they would merely sit down again and wait for the next car. No doubt this method is a good one, but their technique must have needed a little polishing, for, after several blanks, a young farmer pulled up beside them:

"Don't like to see a couple of healthy young fellows doing nothing," he shouted. "Hop in and I'll find you some work to do."

This was the last thing Roach and Murison wanted; nevertheless, to gain time, they asked him what the work might be.

"Help me look after the cows, and I'll give you each five quid a week," answered the farmer.

Being hard up they temporarily abandoned further hitch-hiking, but after a fortnight's grinding work on the farm they both swore that the very sight of milk made them feel ill, so they took to the road again with deep relief.

There is little more to tell of our wanderings in New Zealand; we found the New Zealanders the kindest and most democratic people, and their country as beautiful as any we visited. George called at a police-station, where he was allotted a free night's lodging in an unemployed shelter. Potter and Money ran short of food in the bush, and were taken in by friendly Maoris at a native village. Willie Marsh got a lift and a night's lodging from two ladies, one of whom was 60 and the other 87; the latter drove the car. Low and Burgess spent one night, upon what pretext I cannot imagine, in a home for the aged; another night they spent in the open, and were lucky enough to meet a cow which they promptly milked.

CHAPTER XX
DISCONTENT

ONE OF OUR GREATEST hopes had always been to avoid, if possible, any of that " trouble " which has so often marred the success of similar enterprises. It would be very remarkable indeed if a voyage in a sailing ship lasting two years were completed without a single difference of opinion between the various factions on board. But I was confident that if everyone were given an opportunity to voice their complaints, whenever they occurred, there would never be any serious dissensions.

But during the enforced inactivity of our long stay in Auckland the small dissatisfactions and disillusions, which almost everyone was bound to feel on a voyage of this sort, gradually combined to cause an oppressive atmosphere of grievance.

The first outward sign was the failure of nearly half the crew to return from their hiking expeditions on the day we had fixed. This made me angry at first, because there was a great deal of work to be got through before the ship would be ready for sea. But I put it down to the fact that most of them were depending on getting lifts from cars during their wanderings, so that it was quite understandable that a few of them would be late. In any case, it was a blessing in disguise, because, although we had hoped to get the shipwrights ashore before the crew came back, this aim had by no means been achieved; and at the very time when the crew were returning the ship was actually in her most filthy uninhabitable state.

Let me hasten to assure our very good friends Messrs. Bailey and Sons, shipwrights, that the responsibility for this in no way rests upon their shoulders. We found them, in every way, the most friendly, generous and reliable firm; in fact, in a commercial age, a very shining light among contractors. The delay was entirely due to the repeated modifications we had to make in our original plans for alterations, according to the ever varying number of additional crew we expected to carry. But there it was, and the unfortunate Cap Pilarians came aboard to find the decks of their ship piled several feet deep in loose timber, coal, ashes, wreckage from the gutted accommodation and every imaginable sort of litter; while their own quarters, where the most extensive reconstructions were in progress, looked as though they had suffered a direct hit.

This state of affairs seemed like the last straw to the already dissatisfied crew, and it soon became obvious to all the people aft that a very deep and rapidly widening rift existed between them and the forecastle crowd. However, obsessed by financial and family worries, as well as the work of collecting new hands, I completely failed, at first, to notice the mutterings and surly glances; but a trivial incident that occurred one evening—namely, the crew's refusal to eat the food provided for supper—suddenly opened our eyes to the dangers of the situation, and we realised that something must be done at once.

Accordingly a meeting of all the ship's company was called, and a very solemn gathering took place in the saloon aft. All were present, and each one was asked in turn to voice his grievances. Practically all of them put forward some complaint; but, greatly to my bewilderment, they were all on different and mostly quite trivial matters, which concerned each individual only. It was therefore quite obvious, either that they had in mind no special or even very tangible grievances, or that the discontent was even more deep-seated than even the crew themselves cared to indicate. After everyone had had his say, and most of the problems had been settled on the spot, the meeting dissolved without our having actually got at the root of the matter.

At the time I felt indignant and very depressed that they should complain about insignificant things, when they must know that we were already faced with such terrific problems. Surely, I thought, we had fulfilled our obligations to the letter. Here we were, in spite of everything, at the other side of the world, with the South Sea Islands as our next port of call.

But as I turned the matter over and over in my mind, I began gradually to see the whole thing in a truer perspective. One of the crew had complained that their opinions were never asked upon matters of policy or upon the actual route which the *Cap Pilar* was to take round the world. Here was the real clue to the trouble. They felt that plans were made and discarded without their having had any say in the matter at all, in spite of the fact that each of them had contributed his £100 towards expenses. This had certainly been the case; with a group of men of such very diverse tastes and opinions, none of whom was really in a position to understand fully the various difficulties, both navigational and material, with which we were continually faced, I had felt that there was no alternative. Another obvious source of "bloody-mindedness" was that the voyage had not turned out as any of us had expected. The long stays in port, particularly, had been unpopular with everybody. A week or ten days would in every case have given people ample time to see all they wanted, and to spend a good deal more money than they had intended.

Once the true cause of the trouble was understood, the remedy was obvious. We would avoid all further long stays in port, and a vote would always be taken by the whole ship's company upon every important decision. In return the crew, on their part, must undertake to bring every smallest complaint to me as soon as it arose, so as to minimise the risk of any serious dissatisfaction brewing in the dim recesses of the forecastle. We adhered to this policy for the rest of the voyage; and although, under the new system, modifications of the crew's wishes were sometimes unavoidable for practical reasons, their opinion was always considered, and the experiment was an unqualified success.

The general meeting certainly achieved its immediate object, because after that there were no further symptoms of unrest, and everyone set to work with a will.

With Jane and Jessica Jane aboard we were very keen to have a doctor with us once more; but it seemed almost impossible to find one who could give up his practice or make the necessary arrangements in time to accompany us. We had almost given up hope of ever getting one when a letter arrived from a certain Dr. Stenhouse, who described himself as a man in the early fifties, who had done a great deal of sailing all his life and would be very glad to join us as ship's surgeon. This he eventually did just before the ship sailed.

We had naturally been prepared to take a doctor for nothing, or even pay him a small salary; but Dr. Stenhouse insisted on signing on on the same basis as everyone else, and contributing his share to our expenses. He also brought a good wireless set with him, and presented the ship with 1,200 best New Zealand eggs. It seemed almost too good to be true, but *there* was Doctor Stenhouse—cheery, red-faced and full of confidence, and *there* were the eggs, all ready to put into water-glass.

On the 13th of September we went into dry-dock on the other side of the harbour, where we found, to our joy and relief, that the zinc sheathing was intact and still in good condition.

On Friday, 17th September, we were once more ready for sea, and since a fresh off-shore breeze was blowing, we hurried through the formalities of departure, and 3 P.M. found us with our moorings singled up and the gangway coming aboard.

By this time the *Cap Pilar* had become almost part of the Auckland water-front, so the news that she was about to leave brought a large gathering down to the Western Viaduct wharf. The ship herself was crowded with friends, including most of the crew's New Zealand girls. George's little friend Joan was the last to leave; but just as the gangway was coming in, a shout was heard, and Alan Burgess came rushing up on deck from the forecastle, carrying a sea-bag, several bulky brown-paper parcels and an odd assortment of shoes, oilskins, and sea-boots tucked under both arms.

At the last minute Burgess had been offered a job as mountaineering guide on the Fox Glacier in the South Island, so he had gladly taken the opportunity to give up the grim battle with chronic seasickness which he had been waging so courageously for nearly a year.

When he appeared on deck the gangway was hastily run out again, although the ship already lay nearly two fathoms from the quayside. As Burgess was gingerly crossing it, the cords of his sea-bag came adrift, and the whole contents began pouring out into the sea. A pair of brilliant pyjamas and some hair brushes remained floating jauntily beside us, while the rest of his possessions sank without a trace. A roar of laughter went up from the onlookers, while Burgess blushingly salvaged the few articles which still lay upon the gangway, and in doing so nearly lost one of his enormous brown-paper parcels. At last he was safely across, and his sea-boots, which he had left aboard, were thrown after him.

In came the bow-line; the *Cap Pilar*, held only by a slip rope aft, fell away from the wharf with her head pointing out into the harbour. We made sail on the foremast, the *Cap Pilar* strained at the leash. When all was ready, we slipped the stern mooring, and the little ship surged away from the quay. The good-byes and bursts of cheering were flung back and forth between ship and shore, until we were well beyond earshot.

A small motor-launch followed us down the harbour, and our last sight of New Zealand life was a picture of the gay Alan Burgess sitting on the launch's deck-house, engaged in animated conversation with sweet little Joan; apparently quite oblivious of the gloomy, suspicious gaze of poor George from the poop of the *Cap Pilar*.

When we reached the bend of the channel we made all plain sail, and were soon scuttling past Rangitoto Island, and out into the open Pacific.

CHAPTER XXI
THE ROAD TO THE ISLES

SAYINGS OF THE GREAT:

> " I put the apples through the mincer to get rid of
> the —— weevils, but some of the ——s seem to have
> got through."

> " It's a bloody good pudding—there's an egg in
> it. The egg was a bit rotten, but I don't think you'll
> taste it."

The fair breeze held, and next morning we found ourselves well clear of the land. We were bound for the
Gambier Islands, which lay upon the tropic of Capricorn,
about 3,000 miles east-north-east of Auckland, and quite
near the famous island of Pitcairn. But owing, as always,
to the limitations of a sailing ship, our first courses were
south of east towards latitude 40°S, where we might expect
the westerly winds.

On the second evening out we were having supper in the
saloon, when the bos'n's legs were seen coming down the
companion, followed in due course by his head; he brought
with him a very dirty and dishevelled individual who
grinned cheerfully at us all, but offered no explanation for
his presence in the ship.

" Er—excuse me," Donnelly began, " but this person
was found in the fore-peak. I rather fancy he is a stow-
away."

There was very little doubt about that, but there was
also very little to be done about it, so we signed him on the
ship's articles under the name of Jim Grant. He remained
with us for the rest of the voyage, and proved himself one
of the most skilled and hardworking craftsmen in the ship.

At this stage the total ship's company was twenty-eight, including Jessica, who had signed on as assistant stewardess.

The new hands were as varied a collection as the old; we had another solicitor in BEVAN SUTHERLAND, who was about twenty-four years of age, six-foot tall, and big in proportion. " Big Biff " was, I believe, a first-class Rugby footballer, but he was also very quiet and easy-going in character, and soon became the unofficial father of the New Zealand gang. STEWART TALBOYS, on the other hand, was exactly what he looked—a healthy young schoolboy of seventeen, rather frail in physique at first, but, by the time he had been with us a month or two, he had filled out and developed into a very strong and active young seaman. For the first fortnight of the voyage Talboys was continually seasick; then he suddenly recovered, and, as far as I know, he never suffered from seasickness again.

KEN CLAYTON was in the early twenties, although he looked much younger. He was very small, with a perky, good-humoured face which was never known to wear a frown. He was desperately keen on the sea, and the greatest disappointment of his life had been when they turned him down for the Navy on account of his size. He was always referred to aboard the *Cap Pilar* as Nobby, Nobby Nelson, or just Young Nose, by everyone, both younger and older than himself.

> Mr. Kenneth (" Nose ") Clayton, who has just arrived from the Dominions, informs me that his hippies, which were covered with cocky's joy, are still good-o, from which I gather that his bathing shorts, which were covered with golden syrup (can't think how it happened), are still in good condition.—Gossip column of *The Caterpillar*.

DON ALEXANDER was Nobby's pal; he was a sturdy,

kind-hearted fellow, with very blond hair and huge muscles. He had been a woodworker by trade.

ALEX MACMASTER was definitely the funny man of the party. He was small and active, with bristly red hair, on account of which, for some obscure reason of their own, the crew gave him the nickname of " Blue ". He was very independent and inclined to suspect the whole world of attempting to do him down, in the absence of proof to the contrary. However, he never allowed himself to become embittered by this wholly unjustified suspicion; but, being abnormally sharp-witted, he embarked upon a relentless anti-encirclement policy, much to the amusement and secret admiration of us all.

The two remaining recruits were both Englishmen. JACK POWER was the son of a manufacturer from the Midlands, LESLIE LETHBRIDGE the heir to a prosperous grocery business in Bristol.

Jim brought the number of new hands up to eight, so we thought we might as well take advantage of this happy state of affairs by putting the crew into three watches instead of two. Accordingly C. J. Carmichael, the young South African, was appointed third mate and put in charge of the extra watch. But a watch aboard the *Cap Pilar* only consisted of five men, so we still had three men over; we were therefore able to have a forecastle orderly and two cooks on permanent day work. The crew took it in turns to do a week each at these three jobs.

The changing of cooks every week may appear to have been a risky experiment, but since working ten hours a day in an overheated galley and being sworn at by the forecastle because the puddings were not cooked at the end of it all, was not a cynosure of a job, the even distribution of this labour amongst the whole crew seemed the only fair way of arranging things.

One of the complaints, made at the historic general meeting in Auckland, had been about the "terribly low standard of cooking". "I'm certain that, after a little practice, I could produce something more appetising than what we've been having lately," McDonald had declared. The answer had been obvious; as soon as the ship was once more at sea it was up to McDonald to vindicate his boast.

On his first day in the galley he was kept under constant observation from a network of spies sent out from both ends of the ship. We were, not unnaturally, though perhaps unfairly, sceptical; and our misgivings deepened considerably with the first reports which filtered in from the scene of battle. One trustworthy agent reported having seen McDonald earnestly studying the cookery books for instructions on how to boil potatoes; while another had been asked by him whether one-third of a pint was more or less than half a pint.

After two or three days the outcome of the experiment was a complete triumph for McDonald (and incidentally for Mrs. Beeton). He was more than just a good cook; he put his very heart and soul into the job, and an extremely fertile imagination as well. Not only was McDonald's cooking the best we had ever tasted, hot spicy curries being his speciality; but, for the first time since the beginning of the cruise, the bread was consistently recognisable as such. In point of fact McDonald had discovered that Colin Potter was the son of a baker, so Mac had persuaded him to give a few demonstrations in the art. How Potter had managed to put up with the sort of bread we had been used to for a year without disclosing this secret is still a mystery to us all.

McDonald set a standard of cooking which roused the competitive instincts of all the rest. "Blue" and Jim later proved worthy rivals to him; but as a matter of fact the whole crew became good cooks, with one exception; and

he was such a charming fellow that we received his con-
coctions with a friendly smile, even though we could not
always bring ourselves to eat them.

I must, in any case, make it clear that cooking (as
opposed to making "something hot" on a primus) in a
small galley at sea, is an experience so heart-breaking that
no one who has not actually tried it can possibly understand the difficulties involved. You are probably holding
a frying-pan with one hand, trying to stir a pot with the
other, and, at the same time, struggling to keep your
balance on a slippery deck. If you relax your vigilance for
one moment a large saucepan is likely to go shooting off
the stove, carrying all the others with it. Roach, when
cook on one occasion in the westerlies, was reported to have
stood by the forecastle table, watching to see how his pea-
-soup went down. Sanson made some remark about the
stove being a more proper place for lumps of coal than the
soup, but on the whole it got a fairly favourable reception.

"Glad you liked it," said Roach, turning to go, with a
look of melancholy satisfaction upon his face, "the whole
bleedin' pot upset, and I had to ladle the bloody stuff off
the galley deck."

On this passage we experienced excellent sailing
weather, with only two sharp gales to vary the daily
routine. The New Zealanders, after the first few days of
seasickness, took fairly well to their new life; but the conditions at the beginning of this second part of the voyage
were very different from those upon our first putting to sea
from England. We now had a well-found ship and a year's
experience of running her, and, above all, a good nucleus
of trained seamen to show the newcomers where and how
to pull.

At first the New Zealanders, though not unwilling to play
their part, showed clearly that they did not appreciate the
trials and hardships which had marked the first year of the
cruise; they were apt to take things easy about the decks,

and leave a great deal to the older hands. This was quite understandable, and did not greatly affect the working of the ship; but, by contrast, the Englishmen and even the South Africans, who had been with us barely six months, stood out like tried and seasoned veterans. In fact the old hands settled down at once to a general standard of smart and conscientious seamanship, of which even they had probably never thought themselves capable.

McDonald was an extreme example of this new professional pride which had suddenly been born. During the first part of the voyage he had been a somewhat lukewarm sailor, a fact which he is always the first to admit. He put it down to lack of encouragement from me, and I in my turn must agree that he received no special coaxing. However, from the moment that he made such a success of the cooking, he became a different man overnight, and subsequently developed into as keen and energetic a seaman as any on board.

It was not long before the newcomers found their feet, and within three months of leaving Auckland we felt smart enough to exchange signals with any merchant ship afloat, or to have sailed tack for tack into harbour with one of the famous South Sea Island brigs of last century.

"Scanty", by the way, already considered himself an old hand, although he had only joined us in Sydney; but even he showed a grudging respect for the strength and efficiency of men like Potter and Money. "Cor! I always thought all 'poms' was bleedin' washouts," was his characteristic way of admitting the fact. Scanty was an irrepressibly cheery soul, and, in spite of his very unpolished performance as a cabin-boy, we all grew fond of him. He had a disconcerting habit of butting unceremoniously into our conversations round the saloon table. On one occasion this occurred when we were trying to entertain some rather formal guests. Somehow or other we had got on to the subject of whether or not tigers purred, when suddenly a raucous Australian voice burst in from behind our backs:

"Of course they do—up against trees like dogs; I seen 'em in Sydney zoo."

We smiled wanly, and lit a mental Abdulla; while Scanty, who sensed his mistake, tried to make amends by picking up the whisky decanter and pouring drinks all round, at the same time repeating to each frigid visitor what he imagined to be the "correct" English formula for such occasions: "Jolly ole whisky, what?" and "Awfully jolly soda with it, eh?"

Half-way through the passage to the Gambiers we had another general meeting; this time to decide what route we should take across the Pacific. Owing to the fact that we were about a month behind schedule it was decided to remain in south latitude and to approach Panama by way of the South American coast, which would give us plenty of time to reach the Caribbean before the hurricane season. If we were not unduly delayed, we hoped to include a visit to the Galapagos Islands as well. Unfortunately, we had no charts of the Peruvian coast; but we felt confident of being able to obtain a pilot outside Callao should the need arise.

In view of Jessica's age (six weeks when she first joined the ship) it was not surprising that she took to sea life quicker than any of the new hands.

Jane writes:

I never felt very much doubt about Jessica Jane's ability to stand up to the supposed strain of sailing ship life; despite her diminutive size, her wobbly head, and a tendency to hiccoughs, she seemed so excessively healthy. But most people were inclined to be rather damping, and kept asking what I would do if such and such a calamity occurred. At any rate I was in this way prompted to provide for quite a number of eventualities which otherwise I should never have foreseen.

While I had been ashore in Auckland the most marvellous transformation had taken place in what had been our cabin in the *Cap Pilar*. Formerly it had always been leaky, and consequently rather smelly, so a water-tight lining had been put under the deck-head and along the ship's side. Then a luxurious spring bed had been substituted for the 2-ft. wide boxes in which we had slept before, and over it dangled a little canvas bassinet for Jessica.

But the greatest thrills were in the bathroom. It had been enlarged and fitted with wardrobes, chests of drawers, a linen cupboard, and even a full-length mirror. After a great deal of debating as to the shape of the wash-basin, we decided to have an ordinary enamel sink, which made a very good baby's bath. There was also hot water for the big bath, provided by a chip heater—a very simple form of geyser, obtainable for as little as 17s. 6d., in which the water was warmed by the burning of a few handfuls of paper and shavings instead of by gas.

We made use of every corner in the new cabin. In one of them we had a "Primus" stove, which could be converted into a radiator for drying clothes, so that at sea I could have an ironing day once a week. I had an electric iron, but I always had to warn Potter before using it, otherwise all the lights in the ship would go dim, and I would be roundly cursed.

Owing to inevitable last-minute delays, we lived aboard the ship for nearly two weeks before she sailed, and I had to spend a lot of time ashore collecting the necessary stores and equipment for Jessica. While I was away, one of the crew would always keep an eye on the baby, who usually slept quite peacefully. One evening I returned, however, to find the first and third mates in great distress, and Jessica yelling the roof off. She had apparently woken up, and not knowing what to do, the officer of the watch had uncovered her and put her on her tummy, which had, of course, annoyed her intensely.

When we got to sea I was surprised to find how easy it was to manage a tiny baby on board. I confess that I was often unable to air her nappies and clothes; but, as she never got a chill of any sort until she reached England, this did not appear to have done any harm.

Nor was Jessica very much trouble to anyone else in the ship; in fact, during those early days, a more or less permanent string of nappies on the poop was about the only evidence of her existence.

Jessica never showed any symptoms of sea-sickness. As a matter of fact we were very lucky with the weather on her first passage, and there were only two days upon which I was totally unable to bath her. There were several days when it was rather an arduous task, but the baby herself never seemed in the least ruffled.

Her routine was very much the same as that of any baby of her age on shore. We used to bring her on deck whenever the wind was not too strong or the spray coming over the rail. She appeared to be thriving, and I looked forward to being able to weigh her when we arrived at our first anchorage.

After about a fortnight's sailing we reached the longitude of Rapa in the Austral Islands, and it was time for us to turn *slowly* northwards towards the Gambiers. We were making a fast passage, so it required the utmost self-control not to steer directly for our objective, in spite of the risk of easterly winds as we neared the tropics.

On Saturday, 9th October, when we reckoned, after two days of cloudy weather, that we were about forty miles south-south-east of the Gambiers, the glass began to fall rapidly, and the wind flew round to the north-west; then freshened quickly to half a gale with blinding torrents of rain.

It was as though the heavens had enveloped us in a dense grey curtain. We hove-to, and set ourselves to wait patiently for it to lift and reveal those brilliant palm-covered islands waiting for us in the tropical seas beyond.

PART IV

THE PACIFIC ISLANDS

THE PACIFIC ISLANDS

CHAPTER XXII
PALM TREES AND CORAL

On Sunday morning the sky cleared and a soft west wind filled our sails. The *Cap Pilar* slipped merrily northward—away from the cold grey west wind seas—away from the gales and rain and fog—northward towards the edge of the tropics. The wind gained strength; the white-caps danced joyously upon the sparkling wavelets; aloft the creamy castles of sail stood stiff and round and full.

Everyone was in the highest spirits. For more than a year we had been voyaging across twenty-thousand miles of sea. Now at last we were within a short distance of the islands; at any moment we might see them. Hour by hour the air grew warmer, several of the crew removed their shirts to get the full benefit of the sunshine. At 10 A.M. Cyril Money made the hail of "Land ho!" from the fore t'gallant yard.

This was the most dramatic moment of the whole cruise —our first sight of the South Sea Islands. For many minutes we gazed at them in silence. Looking back in our minds, we realised for the first time that these islands had been our only true objective since leaving London; almost from the time that we had first thought of making the voyage.

The islands rose steadily higher out of the sea before us. The song of the wind in the rigging made a descant for the deep thunder of our bow wave, growing to leeward.

At first we could only make out the misty outline of the two main peaks of Mangareva, the largest of the Gambiers; but, as we drew nearer, other humps and hillocks lifted above the horizon. Soon we could see the palm-trees upon the barrier reef itself.

The Gambiers are a group of small volcanic islands enclosed within a coral reef, half of which is submerged to a depth of several fathoms. The other half of this reef lies three or four feet above sea-level and forms a horse-shoe of land, protecting the islands from the west, north and east. Long stretches of the reef are covered with palms, and the lagoon formed by it is about ten miles in diameter.

By 2 P.M. we were near the south-west passage into the lagoon. On either hand, where the swell was breaking upon the submerged part of the reef, a continuous ribbon of gleaming surf stretched as far as the horizon; immediately before us lay a narrow band of brilliant green, where the absence of surf showed that the water was deeper. We made for this gap. George was busy taking cross bearings so as to determine our position every few minutes, and, from this series of positions, to make sure that the course we were steering would take us across the deepest part of the reef. The rest of us, with the exception of the helmsman, were still gazing ahead.

When we had almost reached the pass I went aloft. From the foretopsail yard I could make out every detail of the reef upon which the little ship seemed to be charging so determinedly. It seemed, as I looked down, that the *Cap Pilar* had never moved so fast. She drove her long jib-boom, like a harpoon, across the sea, and split the ocean with her sturdy bows.

The last correction on our chart had been made in 1906; I wondered, in a vaguely fatalistic way, how quickly coral would grow; and strained my eyes ahead to pick out a place where the green was perhaps a little darker, and therefore, the water a little deeper than the rest.

"Port fifteen!"

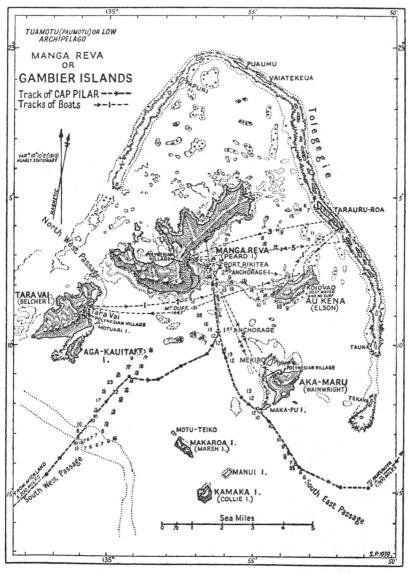

MANGA REVA
OR
GAMBIER ISLANDS

Drawn by Cyril Money

"Port fifteen!" shouted Syd Marshall in answer, as he spun the wheel. Slowly the *Cap Pilar* began to swing up to the wind.

"Midships!—Starboard five!—Steady!"

"Steada-a-ay!" sang Marshall. We bore up again, straight for the pass.

Suddenly the water beneath us turned from blue to brilliant green, and *there* was the coral, seemingly so near the surface, that one could have waded upon it; red, yellow, orange and white, the individual "heads" showed through the crystal water like monstrous cauliflowers. I felt a thrill of terror; suppose our chart were wrong—it was, after all, thirty years out of date; in imagination I felt the sudden grinding shock as the ship struck; saw the chaos which followed. I had never seen coral before. What if this reef were really as shallow as it appeared?

It was too late to do anything now. I shot an agonised glance at the deck. All in that brief moment I saw the crew, standing at their stations, ready to haul; George, on the poop, clearing the lead line; Doctor Stenhouse levelling his binoculars at the land; Jane peering over the rail, and in her arms, young Jessica crowing excitedly at the glittering sea. I saw Newell scratching the back of his left calf with the stem of his pipe; Donnelly making a humorous gesture at somebody's large behind doubled over the rail; Scanty tying a ropeyarn on to the cat's tail.

Next moment George had made a cast of the lead, and began to call the soundings.

"By the deep nine!"

Nine fathoms—fifty-four feet! It seemed impossible: I had expected three fathoms at the very most.

"By the deep eight," called George, in the traditional sing-song voice of the leadsman, and a little later, "By the mark seven."

There was plenty of water after all, and our chart was still accurate; with a sigh of relief I sat down upon the yard to enjoy the view.

We were now in the very middle of the pass. A few hundred yards away on either beam I could see and hear the rollers, ten or fifteen feet high, thundering upon the shoaler parts of the reef. The spray rose smoking to the height of our masts. Ahead of us the lagoon lay blue and placid as a lake. The coral flashed past beneath us; then, as suddenly as it had come, it slipped astern and disappeared.

"No bottom!" sang George, heaving the lead for the last time, and we were inside the lagoon.

The nearest of the islands was no more than a mile or two away, and as we sailed past them, beautiful bays, with gleaming white beaches, opened before us. Each one was backed by a dense grove of palms and bread-fruit, and here and there a wisp of smoke told of a collection of native dwellings.

Late in the afternoon we anchored in twenty-eight fathoms. As the sun went down the wind died away, and through the dusk the full sweet scent of tropical flowers and the rich tang of sun-baked rocks stole out to us. None but those who have taken the long road South will be able to understand how we felt as we stood that evening upon the motionless deck—drinking in the smell of the land, gazing at the distant line of spray-drenched, palm-dotted reef, and at the twisted crags of the main islands, brushed with the colours of sunset. Now indeed we were true romantics, every one of us. In this moment we cared nothing for the world from which we had come. If the masts of our ship had dissolved into the air and left us cast away here, we should not have cared. And yet many of us, each in his own way, tried to hide his feelings from himself, tried to arm himself with scepticism against an imaginary disappointment: facetious comments dropped like vulgar little bits of orange-peel into the stream of genuine emotion which flowed among us.

Willie Marsh was, as usual, the most genuinely excited.

" D'you think there's pearls in this lagoon ? " he asked a little breathlessly. "We ought to dive down and get some."

"You ought to take a basket with you to bring them back in, Willie," said someone.

" A piece of string to thread them on would be better," said another.

And all the time we knew that there *were* pearls in this lagoon—any number of them.

In the evening a bright half-moon shone down upon the gently lapping water, and sprinkled a powdery brilliance upon the shoulders of the hills. Far into the night we still sat talking and watching the land, loath to lose sight of the islands, lest they should disappear while we slept.

Next morning we launched the lifeboat and gig and put into them a few small mark buoys, which we had brought with us from St. Malo. There was another reef between us and the native village of Rikitea, and it was unlikely that the channel through it would be adequately marked; so we decided to make good this probable deficiency before taking the *Cap Pilar* any further. We worked away throughout the morning with lead-line and buoys. We saw the white triangular sails of several native outrigger canoes skimming across the lagoon; but to our surprise none of them came near us. When we got back to the ship we found out the reason for this apparent indifference on the part of the Mangarevans : waiting for us on board, was a tall, fine looking native in the uniform of a French gendarme.

He informed us that, only a few weeks previously, the port of Rikitea had been closed to vessels from "foreign", and that we must at once weigh anchor and depart!

At first we were so overcome with dismay that we could say nothing. I looked round at the faces of the crew who were standing near—at Willie Marsh, who had slaved and sweated for the means to accompany us to the South Seas—at Murison, who had changed, during that long passage through the westerlies, from a "city lad" into a robust and determined sailor—at Lethbridge, whose only ambition it was to see the South Sea Islands before settling down to become a respectable grocer in Bristol. To turn away now when we were actually in sight of the promised land was unthinkable; it would have been better to sink the ship where she lay, and swim ashore. I told the gendarme that I would come to see the administrator, and when he had gone off with my message we all gathered on the main deck.

"Well, of all the sour-faced, narrow-gutted, silly-born . . ." began Willie.

"Why don't we go ashore and capture the island?" suggested someone else. But most people were in no mood for talk, they felt that the voyage was virtually over; that the sooner they could get home the better.

After a little consideration we realised that our case was not yet hopeless: we had a clearance for Mangareva, given us by the French Consul in Auckland. Besides, we had counted upon calling at these islands and upon being able to obtain water and fresh provisions; they could not possibly send us to sea without stores and water.

When I went ashore I begged the young Tahitian administrator to wireless to the Governor of the Tuamotu Islands. This he agreed to do; so I returned aboard fairly confident that the reply would be favourable.

Next morning, when I came on deck at dawn I found Willie already there.

"Any boats from the shore yet?" I asked.

"No, that's what I'm waiting for," he answered grimly. "Gawd! If those devils don't let us in I'll jump overboard."

My confidence of the night before began to evaporate. Suppose they did refuse us? If the port had been closed by order of the French Government would they bother to show any special lenience to a British yacht?

Newell came out of the chart-house, and "Blue", who was cook of the day, strolled aft from the galley. One by one others came on deck to join the group. For some time we stood in silence, watching the land.

"What'll we do if they turn us down?"

"What can we do?"

"Go home, I suppose."

"Go home!" cried Willie. "What! After sweatin' an' slavin' all this bleedin' way round the world—an' curry twice a week for breakfast?"

Willie had spoken for all of us. We endorsed his view with a gloomy silence. I personally felt that something desperate must be done; that almost any risk would be justified in order to save the situation.

Suddenly a thought struck me. Why wait out here for the Governor's reply? What was there to prevent us from sailing straight into the inner harbour before we were formally forbidden to do so? Once we were inside it would probably be a good deal easier to find an excuse for staying there.

No sooner was the idea born than we set about acting upon it. We were anchored in thirty fathoms, within three hundred yards of the reef; and it was blowing from the south-east, rather fresher than we would have liked. It was lucky that the channel was now marked by our buoys; but everything would depend upon our being able to keep sufficient way upon the ship and yet heave the anchor home before reaching the shallow water in the pass. This pass was only one ship's length wide, and

very tortuous; so we took the precaution of having a
kedge anchor handy aft in case of accidents.

When all was ready we set the two fore-topsails, two
jibs and the mainsail, and then manned the windlass.

With only those three hundred yards between us and
the reef it was essential that the ship should pay off and

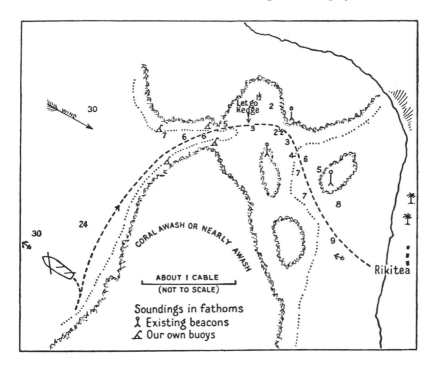

gather way the moment her anchor left the bottom, otherwise she might drive astern on to the coral. Twice, before
the anchor was a-trip, she began to cast to port—the
wrong direction; we stopped heaving and held our
breath. Suddenly she began to pay off fast to starboard;
from then on, everything seemed to happen at once.

Round flew the yards, the sails filled, and in less than
a minute the ship was heading along the reef. Two-thirds
of the crew still hove desperately at the windlass, the

rest were setting and trimming sails for all they were worth.

We made a great deal of lee-way; soon we were only fifty yards from the coral. At the wheel, Potter had to exercise the utmost self-control to keep the sails well full —if she once came too near the wind, the anchor, still hanging at her bow, would drag her round and she would drive ignominiously ashore. We weathered the first buoy with a yard or two to spare, and put the helm hard up.

So far, so good—the anchor was nearly home, and the ship steering well. Then suddenly the windlass jammed, and before anything could be done to clear it the anchor once more took the ground—right in the narrowest part of the pass!

At once the ship's head began to snub up to port, and it looked as though she would run straight on to the reef. Don Alexander was standing by the kedge lashing with an axe; the moment the ship's head began to swing— down came his axe, and the kedge splashed into the water. There followed a terrible moment of suspense; then, just in the nick of time, the kedge got a grip and held.

As soon as the windlass was cleared, we hove the anchor up; then cut the kedge adrift, and sailed without further trouble into the inner harbour, where we anchored in eleven fathoms, half a ship's length from the shore.

When the administrator's cutter came alongside after breakfast, we already had stern moorings made fast to the palm trees.

" The Governor's orders are that you must take water and stores and depart immediately," he said firmly.

" Very good," I answered. " We will not remain here a moment longer than we must—we will leave with the first fair wind." As I spoke, we both glanced at the precipitous hillside above us, and at the unbroken semi-circle of mountains which enclosed the bay, effectively screening it from that direction.

The administrator nodded gravely; then suddenly he smiled:

" The auxiliary schooner *Mouette* will be calling here in twelve days' time," he said. " She will tow you out. It's lucky for you we haven't a warship handy."

CHAPTER XXIII
AMONG THE ISLANDS

THE GAMBIER ISLANDS lie in the "horse latitudes", the belt of variable winds between the trades and the westerlies. For this reason they are liable to great and sudden changes of weather. It was just this variety and uncertainty about the weather which made the islands so interesting to live in.

We spent almost every day in our boats, sailing from island to island, sleeping round the camp-fire or in disused huts; fishing, swimming, climbing or just sitting beneath the palm-trees.

One day Tioni, the native policeman, accompanied us to the barrier reef. As we approached it we had to pick a tortuous way through a forest of coral heads. They grew out of the sandy bottom like clumps of trees and bushes, with brown, yellow and pink-tipped branches, just below the surface of the water. Between the coral heads the sea was only two or three fathoms deep and a brilliant swimming-pool blue; the palms were vivid green.

The islet upon which we landed was entirely formed of broken shells and coral debris, which lay no more than a few feet above the surface of the sea. The beaches were glaring white. Among the trees flitted hundreds of dainty little terns; and even they were white all over—so dazzling white that it hurt the eyes to look at them.

Early in the afternoon a jet-black cloud began to grow across the northern horizon. Out of the lifeboat sail we made a shelter among the palms and no sooner were Jane and her baby safely beneath it, than the squall hit us.

The rain lashed down, the furious gusts of wind bent the palm trees like bows.

"Nor'-easterly wind," said Doctor Stenhouse gloomily. "It usually keeps up all night when it comes on like this in New Zealand."

Vaguely I wondered whether Jane and Jessica would survive a night of this should we be unable to find more substantial shelter. However, for the time being Jessica seemed quite satisfied with her rather diluted lunch and Jane was too busy shielding her baby from the rain and wind to bother much about the future.

Half an hour went by without any sign of a change in the weather. All round us the sky was black as ink, and the rain fell in icy torrents. I tried to light a fire by pouring methylated spirits into a hollow log; it looked rather clever, but was really quite futile, and called down a great deal of facetious comment from George. The others sheltered where they could among the scrub; but soon they began to feel cold; so, with one accord, they dashed headlong, like the Gadarene swine, into the sea. Here they remained, fully clothed, their sun-hats still upon their heads, up to their necks in soft, warm water.

Suddenly the storm passed, trailing its inky skirts across the reef and out to sea; the sun shone down brilliantly as before, and the lagoon flashed serenely blue between the islands. Once more we felt warm and happy.

That evening at sunset we reached an island called Au Kena. Another dark rain-cloud was driving down towards us, so we resolved to get ashore as quickly as possible and ask for shelter at the native village.

When the boat grounded I grabbed Jessica's cot and made for the trees, Jane following with the baby in her arms. It was pitch-dark in the forest as we set off, half-running, in the general direction of the village. The palms moaned dismally with the first gusts of wind from the approaching squall; a few large drops of rain splashed in our faces; Jessica began to whimper with hunger. We missed the track, but went struggling on through the tropical undergrowth.

At last we had to admit that we were lost, so Jane sat down at the foot of a large plantain, whose broad leaves might offer some shelter, and next moment Jessica was hard at work over her supper.

After a while Tioni came to look for us. He led us back to a small clearing by the beach, in which stood three deserted huts made entirely of palm-fronds. Here we found the rest of the party gathered round a fire of coconut husks. Upon the embers Tioni had laid four or five breadfruits and also two enormous fish, speared by himself earlier in the day.

After supper three natives appeared silently out of the trees. One brought a guitar, and far into the night we sat round the fire, listening to their songs.

Not a breath stirred the palm-tops now. High above us their fronds caught the moonlight, like bright scimitars against the stars. When the singing died away only the occasional call of a night-bird broke the stillness. Then the sweet, heavy scent of the palm-groves poured softly in, like the spirit of the islands settling upon us.

At 8 o'clock next morning the sun was well up; a gentle easterly breeze made the air cool and fresh, and set the wavelets leaping about the coral just awash in the lagoon. Within the shore reef not a ripple stirred upon the china-blue water. Myriads of gaily coloured fishes chased each other, in and out, through the flowers and branches of the coral.

The sea was in her gentlest mood; idling and eddying through the shore reef, gurgling among the stones, and softly kissing the gleaming beaches, which lay creamy white as a maiden's cheek.

From Au Kena we steered west, and lay basking in the sun as our little boat went scuttling across the lagoon with every sail set. When we arrived at Taravai, the second largest island within the atoll, the natives leaped into the surf to meet us and haul our boats ashore. Wreaths of *Tiaré Tahiti*, a waxy white flower with a beautiful scent, were hung round our necks, and we were escorted in triumph up to the village.

The natives of the Gambiers have the appearance of being fairly civilised. Many of the women wear dresses and even hats, but no shoes; most of them, however, are clad only in a single length of cloth, called a *pareu*, which reaches from under the armpits to a little below the knees. Almost all of the men also wear *pareus* in the form of a loin-cloth or skirt, and both sexes carry their civilisation as lightly as their garments: one feels that even a few months of freedom from government organisation would be sufficient for them to revert to a state of ecstatic barbarity.

On each of the four inhabited islands of the Gambiers there is an exotic-looking church. The one on Mangareva was built to accommodate a congregation of 1,200; the other three could hold 700 each. Now there are only a few score of inhabitants in each island, and the total population of the whole group is only 650. In all the villages there are a great many tenantless houses, and in one or two more than half the houses appeared to be empty. It seems that, if the population of these islands continues to dwindle at the present rate, they will become virtually uninhabited in about fifty years.

We visited each of the islands in turn, and everywhere the natives would welcome us with an overwhelming display of hospitality. In the evenings they gathered in the moonlight to sing age-old Polynesian songs and to dance in the traditional grass skirts, which swung and rustled fascinatingly about their swaying hips. Every day they brought us freshly speared fish, and were always willing to pilot our boats or accompany us upon our expeditions ashore.

Their skill at spearing fish was uncanny. We often watched them as they stood, keen-eyed and motionless, like fierce sea-eagles, in the surf. Their harpoons consisted of a slender shaft about twelve feet long, with four or five unbarbed prongs lashed to one end. Sometimes a harpooner, standing with one foot on the outrigger of his canoe, would spear a fish at fifteen or twenty yards, before we, in the canoe, had even seen it.

The natives said there were no large sharks in the lagoon, although a few tales were told of lone fishermen who had mysteriously disappeared.

One day Lars, Newell, Money, and Potter set off in our dinghy for a day on the barrier reef. On their way home the wind fell light, and moonrise found them still two miles from the ship. For some time they lay at their ease in the bottom of the boat, gazing down the yellow moon-path to where the rollers broke in fiery splendour upon the reef. Tufts of palm-trees stood out dimly through a haze of silvery spindrift.

All at once a grey fin cut swiftly through the moon-glitter astern, and disappeared into the darkness beyond. Once again the fin slipped across the light, then turning, followed steadily in the dinghy's wake. Soon they could make out the shape of the brute; Newell was all for trying to catch it with Lars's hat lashed for bait to the boathook; but since the shark appeared to be nearly twice as long as their boat, this course did not recommend itself very strongly to the others, in fact they were considerably relieved when it eventually sheered off and disappeared.

We never saw another shark of any size while we were in the Gambiers; but the lagoon was infested with large rays (first cousins to the common skate), some of them measuring more than six feet across. These fish were apparently quite harmless, but they were responsible for several false shark alarms, and we all soon lost the desire to bathe anywhere but on the island beaches.

CHAPTER XXIV
TO NUKUHIVA IN THE MARQUESAS ISLANDS

ON WEDNESDAY, the 20th of October, the *Mouette* arrived. She was a white-painted schooner of about 100 tons, and her captain was a very immaculate Tahitian with the Scandinavian name of Karlson. He smiled when he was asked to tow us out of the basin.

"The day of sailing ships is past," he said. "I never use my sails except when the wind is fair, and even then I keep my motor running. As for sailing through the reefs—the idea, in these days, is ridiculous!"

"Surely hundreds of ships sailed in here before the days of motors?" I said.

"Perhaps," he admitted, "but, in any case, sailing ships are cumbersome, useless, and out of date."

There is no convincing answer to this argument, so I let it go.

The *Mouette* towed us without any difficulty to the outer anchorage, where we lay for a few more days.

Then, one morning, we once again weighed anchor and sailed out of the lagoon. On reaching the open sea we headed northwards towards the Equator.

The Marquesas Islands lie in about latitude 8° South, a little over a thousand miles north of the Gambiers. We reached them after twelve days of idyllic trade-wind sailing.

Every day the sun climbed higher into the heavens and beat more fiercely upon us. On this passage we rigged awnings for the first time—one over the forecastle-head and one on the poop. Since the wind blew steadily day and night, it was always pleasantly cool under the awnings, and they also served as a protection from the squalls of rain which usually found us two or three times each day. Thick clothes were discarded for good. Some of the more devouted sun-worshippers, such as Cyril Money and Don Alexander, literally grilled themselves black. In the evenings almost everyone brought their mattresses on deck; in fact the accommodation was no longer used, except at meal-times.

On Wednesday, the 3rd of November, we sighted the easternmost island of the Marquesas group, and next morning, at dawn, the unnaturally jagged pile of Nuku-hiva lay before us. The island is over 3,000 feet high, and in the slanting sunlight, each headland threw a hard, black shadow upon the next, giving the impression of a bewildering number of ridges and pinnacles.

Tai-o-hae Bay, for which we were making, is a deep U-shaped indentation which goes back nearly a mile into the land, on the southern side of the island, and is completely surrounded by high mountains. Our first attempt to reach the anchorage at the head of this bay was a failure; as soon as we got under the lee of the cliffs we were becalmed, and had great difficulty in working clear for a second attempt. Next time, under all plain sail, we literally hurled the *Cap Pilar* at the entrance. She dashed on into the calm water, after which we were able to work her from puff to puff, until we finally reached the shallows near the village where we could anchor.

We now lay a few hundred yards from the shore upon an unwrinkled sheet of water, like quicksilver, held in the bowl of the mountains. Except for the continuous booming of the surf outside we might have fancied ourselves upon the placid surface of an Alpine lake.

The first boat that came off to us was a four-oared outrigger containing five natives, one of whom was the dispenser of the island, a Tahitian with a rudimentary medical training. The administrator of the Marquesas was absent in Tahiti, so the dispenser examined our papers and gave us permission "to communicate freely with the shore".

By this time "the shore" had come out in large numbers to the ship. We were particularly interested to see the natives of the Marquesas Islands, because we knew that some of them were actually the grandsons of cannibals. In appearance they resembled the other Polynesians we had seen, but in size and physique they were truly remarkable. Most of them were over six feet in height, with huge arms, and barrel-like chests; but their faces wore an unaccountably kind, almost melancholy expression.

From Tai-o-hae we could wander at will across the mountains. Most of the crew made long expeditions on horseback to the bays and villages upon the other side of the island. Some of these villages were almost untouched by civilisation.

When Newell and Lars arrived at the village of Atiheu, they saw a man dragging a heavy bundle up the main street. When they got closer they saw that the bundle was a buxom young woman. The man had her by the hair, and was dragging her over the ground on her back. She made no resistance, but contented herself with a stream of shrill invective at which everyone, including the man, was laughing heartily.

Newell sought some explanation from the guide who was accompanying them.

"Oh, he's just found his wife!" answered the guide, still grinning. "She ran away into the mountains a week ago to live with another man!"

There are a few convicts on Nukuhiva, nominally in charge of the dispenser, but they live a comparatively happy life. One evening we met one of them running back from the village just before sunset; he was a huge fellow of about thirty, with a perpetually friendly, smiling face; he had often been of service to us, and we all liked him. On this occasion we stopped to ask him why he was in such a hurry.

"If I don't get back to the prison before they close at six," he panted, "they'll lock me up for two days," and off he ran as fast as he could go. This man was serving a sentence of fourteen years for having killed his wife by holding her head in a stream till she drowned.

There were two other murderers among the prisoners, and half a dozen who had committed lesser crimes. They worked a few hours a day for the administration and spent the rest of their time sitting aimlessly on the beach. Once a fortnight the prisoners were taken into the mountains to hunt. There was no game on Nukuhiva, but there were several herds of cattle, sheep and pigs, which ran wild in the remoter parts of the island, and also a great many chickens, who had reverted completely to their natural state, and were as strong on the wing as pheasants. All these animals were descendants of the domestic stock brought by the original settlers. The normal method of killing the cattle was to stalk them and cut them down with knives lashed to the ends of long sticks; but on hearing that we had rifles and ammunition on the *Cap Pilar*, the dispenser asked some of the crew to go with them on one of their hunting expeditions. Duncan McDonald was the best shot on board, so he automatically took charge of the armoury and all "shikari" work.

I personally have an unnatural horror of killing things; but on one occasion, when it was absolutely necessary to procure a little fresh meat, George and I accompanied McDonald and one native to the top of a near-by hill. We were "out after" domestic fowls and goats.

It was about 2 A.M. and pitch-dark when McDonald called us to get ready for the chase. An hour before dawn the rugged skyline, 2,000 feet above us, hardened against the east. From the galley forward the blue wood-smoke grew straight as the masts—higher than the trucks, then wavered and mingled with the dawn. The air was so still that we could hear them talking aboard the Government cutter, which was anchored half a mile away. We drank our coffee and waited. Presently our native guides came out to us in a canoe, and we all clambered aboard and made for the shore.

It was now nearly 4 A.M.; in the jungle it was so stiflingly hot that we sweated abominably even before we had started to climb. Half-way up the hill McDonald and I sat down, while George and the native went off after a rooster that had crowed at us in an insolent manner from a near-by tree. As we sat waiting two chestnut-red cockerels, with scarlet crests and shimmering green tail-feathers, sailed out over the valley below us. They were of the ordinary farmyard variety, but in flight they seemed to be the most beautiful birds we had ever seen.

A little later George returned empty handed.

" He must have heard us coming and sneaked off," he said, in the scornful tone with which one refers to a cowardly opponent. This remark was immediately answered by a prolonged and derisive crow from the same tree as before. George turned angrily to requite this further insult; but we restrained him and set off again up the mountain.

A little higher we came out of the trees on to a bare grassy hillside, and looking up we saw a ring of goats, watching us with interest from the surrounding cliffs. We pretended not to see them and plodded on.

Eventually we reached a point immediately below the ridge where the goats had been. On hands and knees, with infinite caution, we wriggled our way towards the summit. George knelt on a stone, but was immediately "shushed" into indignant silence; he continued with his legs straight, and I think that his behind must have broken the skyline nearly a minute before anything else. When at last we reached the top and peered over, the goats were still patiently watching us from a further hilltop. We plodded on.

After a little it was decided that we ought to try a new strategy, so we split up with the intention of each striking out in a different direction. As we set off again, the head goat, with a sneering chuckle, led his whole flock up a vertical cliff face on to a completely inaccessible pinnacle; so we left them to it, and plodded on—and on—and on—and on.

About an hour later a report rang out from the other side of the hill on which I was plodding, and when I reached the pre-arranged rendezvous I found that McDonald had shot a goat. It was certainly a fine animal, weighing about one hundred and fifty pounds, with long horns and a great bristling mane and beard—in fact, the same one that had recently sneered at us. The native was tremendously pleased and excited.

"It is the finest goat on the island," he cried. "The Administrator himself brought him here two years ago, in order to improve the breed. He cost two thousand francs in Tahiti!"

The Marquesas Islands were first discovered in 1595, but were never properly explored until the end of the eighteenth century. In 1813 America tried to found a colony there, but failed, and it was not until 1842 that the French took formal possession of the group. In about 1865 the colony was virtually abandoned; and civilisation was not finally imposed upon the islands until nearly twenty years later.

Before the first settlers arrived there, the Marquesas are said to have supported a population of about 100,000 sturdy Polynesians, physically the finest of all South Sea islanders—eating each other whenever they got the chance, and settling all their troubles in one way only. To-day there are less than 2,000 people in the whole group. For Polynesians freedom is the necessary complement to existence; the mere atmosphere of restraint, or even routine, is sufficient to deprive them of the desire to live; and once they no longer enjoy living they very quickly die; they are even able, like wild animals, to lie down and will themselves to die.

The Queen of Tai-o-hae is a very old woman. No one, not even she herself, knows how long ago she was born; but, as far back as anyone in the valley can remember, she has sat all day upon the verandah of her little house, made of palm-frond thatch. Beside her dwelling is a small shed, with open slatted sides, where a fire of coconut husks smoulders all day; upon it a cast-iron pot, containing taro and breadfruit, is kept simmering continuously, tended from time to time by one of the great-grandchildren of the Queen.

One day a Tahitian friend of ours took us to see the Queen; and translated for us the gist of what she said.

" Why have you brought these white people to see me? " she asked. Her voice was sad, but her eyes glowed fiercely from her yellow, shrivelled old face.

" They would hear tales of the days when you were young," said our friend.

Her smouldering eyes left our faces and gazed down the valley. When she spoke again her voice was heavy and dull.

" In the days when I was young there were men on the island. Each valley was the home of one tribe only, and never, without many armed companions, could a man venture on foot beyond his tribal border.

" The women used to fish round the rocks, and the old women were always sent to fish upon the furthermost points; so that when the war canoes from another tribe

came in search of food, they would catch the old crones
first, and carry them off to be eaten.

" The Chief of Tai-o-hae was a great man—great in
strength, and great in cunning. Woe to any man who
turned his back upon the chief; for, as surely as you husk
a coconut, would his skull be split and his body be hung
to ripen for the next tribal banquet."

Her voice began to rise from the monotonous crooning
with which she had begun her tale. Her eyes blazed.

" A wedding in those days was the greatest moment in a
woman's life. There was dancing and fighting—shouting
and madness. No woman knew whether the man who
dragged her before the priest would be the one she would
sleep beside that night, or just one of those she would help
to eat at the banquet afterwards. But she *did* know that
the man who would eventually protect her during child-
bearing was strong and ferocious and very crafty in
battle."

The old lady got to her feet. Her voice rose to a cracked
crescendo.

" Those were the days ! " she cried. " Those were the
days when men were strong, when the tribes came over the
hilltops to destroy, to plunder, and to rape !

" Those were the days," she went on more quietly, " before we were completely subdued, before the white people
came with their dirt and their disease, before the yellow
man brought opium, before the drinking turned our heads
to madness and our bodies to skin and ashes.

" The white people found us strong and fierce for freedom "—the Queen of Tai-o-hae flung out an arm towards
the sea—" look at us now ! Look at us, I say ! Down by
the water a few still live, but every valley is a burial-
ground, the hills look down upon a wilderness that once
rang with the shouting and the screams of battle. In the
lifetime of one man the forest has grown over the signs
of all our glory."

The old lady shot us a final withering glance and sat down.

More about Jessica. Written by her Mother.

During the three months we spent in the islands Jessica lived the life of the tropics, in fact she achieved a greater freedom than even the native babies. At night she wore the very minimum of clothing, in the daytime none at all.

The natives were horrified at the way Jessica was treated; their own babies were always wrapped in blankets, and usually wore bonnets as well. At times I wondered whether perhaps the natives knew better than I, but Jessica seemed so contented, and her little body was getting such a lovely golden colour, that I stuck to my original principles.

I was also surprised to find that most of the native babies were bottle-fed; some of them lived on coconut " milk ", made from the juice of the nut mixed with the white kernel, very finely ground into a creamy paste. This milk certainly tasted delicious, and was said to be more nourishing even than cow's milk.

Of course Jessica had to go, willy-nilly, wherever I went; and we soon got used to carting her little basket, which was waterproof lined, in and out of the lifeboats and dories, and ashore through the surf. Occasionally I left her on board for an hour or two, and always came back to find her quite contented, either asleep, or playing in somebody's bunk.

CHAPTER XXV
MARQUESAN MOMENTS

THREE MILES WEST OF Tai-o-hae is the canyon of Hak-aui. It lies almost hidden from the sea by high cliffs that curve round, leaving a narrow entrance through which the long Pacific rollers follow one another, like regiments of soldiers, to smash against the ramparts of rock and coral; then running on, they spend themselves upon the quiet surface of the bay within.

One morning we took passage to Hakaui in the Government cutter. Jessica Jane's pram was slung from the awning spar amidships. In the galloping swells the boat rolled her gunwales under, the spray flew over her, but Jessica slept peacefully all the way.

As we approached the cliffs off the mouth of Hakaui the rollers lifted in the shoaler water, and picking up the cutter, they carried her like a surf-board upon their backs. The cliffs towered vertically above us, black and sheer to two thousand feet; against the foot of them the surf exploded with a noise like thunder, and huge fountains of water spouted high into the air. Suddenly we came to the gap in the cliffs. The cutter turned in, and a moment later we were chugging across the motionless blue water of the bay.

This bay had two arms divided by a headland; one of them had a beach of black sand, while the other was a spotless yellow. We made for a solitary hut, surrounded by palms, upon the yellow beach, where the sea lapped peacefully against the shore, and the water was crystal clear.

Jane, Jessica and I were landed here, while the cutter continued on her way to the other side of the island.

We had been warned that the wilder parts of Nukuhiva were infested with little black flies called *nonos*; these flies had a very painful bite which turned, on most people, into an ugly sore within a few days. So, the first thing we did was to light a fire, and upon it we piled green leaves to make it smoke. Then we threw off our clothes and plunged into the sea, leaving Jessica asleep in the hut under her mosquito-net.

After a bit, Jessica woke up and began to cry for her lunch, so Jane waded ashore and sat down in the hut to feed her. The meal had hardly begun when Jane gave a scream, and I rushed up the beach to find her surrounded by a cloud of tiny insects, about the size of midges; our wet bodies had proved so great a temptation to the *nonos*, that they had braved the smoke to get at us. I whipped the mosquito-net off Jessica's pram, and Jane with her baby immediately climbed right into it. It was made in the form of a sack, but unfortunately the mouth was not *nono*-proof, and for the next ten minutes I had to stand holding the neck of the bag, naked to an onslaught of upward of a thousand voracious flies, while Jessica dined in comfort within.

" Do they hurt much ? " asked Jane, interested.

" Only at first; after a bit you go numb, and then you don't feel it any more."

" I'll bet there are a hundred on you. You can't see the ones on your back."

" Never mind. Thanks for telling me they're there."

" You will look funny to-morrow."

As soon as possible we packed our things and made our way to the next bay. Here we found a small group of grass-thatched native dwellings, standing in a palm-grove upon the delta of a good-sized stream. There are rivers in most of the valleys in the Marquesas. All of them are full of crayfish and large conger-eels.

The Chief of Hakaui received us with bewildering

courtesy, and offered us refreshment in the form of coco-nut-milk and fruit on the verandah of his house. After the meal the chief sent for three ponies, and we all rode off up the canyon to see the cascade at the head of the valley.

The path led through dense jungle in which grew occasional clumps of breadfruit, plantains and orange-trees. These fruits had once been cultivated; they marked the native gardens of fifty years ago; now they were completely engulfed by jungle. A great deal of fruit still grew on the trees, so that anyone who lost their way in these forests would run no risk of starvation. Every-where, among the undergrowth were platforms about twenty feet square and three feet high, built on huge boulders, cunningly fitted and shaped.

The chief pointed to these, and said:

"On every one of those *paepaes* was a house, with orange-trees and plantains near by. In those days there were five thousand men and women in the tribe of Hakaui. Now there are only twenty people in the whole valley."

He also spoke of the days when there was perpetual war between the tribes. He pointed at a pinnacle of rock, a thousand feet high, which had detached itself from the cliffs to lean outwards, like the tower of Pisa.

"Behind that rock," he said, "is a hidden valley; the entrance to it is only a few yards wide, and easily defended from within. Our ancestors planted it with breadfruit and plantains, which still grow there. When-ever the tribe was attacked by its neighbours, the women and children would take refuge in it. If our tribe were defeated, all of them would retire to the valley and live there—perhaps even for a whole year."

A little farther on the chief showed us a tiny cave, high up in the cliff face.

"The most honoured woman in the tribe lived in that

cave," he said, "her name was 'Tête de Lune'; her whole life was devoted to watching the pass for marauders from the next valley. Once she had taken her post, she never again returned to the tribe. The people used to carry the best food up to her every day. When she died, her successor would eat her remains, so as to become gifted with the same powers of vision and ceaseless vigilance."

As we climbed farther up the valley the path became more tortuous and steep. The stream, across which we forded at frequent intervals, grew narrower and swifter, until it developed into a series of falls and rapids. The old chief, who spoke perfect French, rode ahead of us, entertaining us all the way with tales of the olden times.

"When Tête de Lune gave the alarm the men formed up in lines across the valley. In the first line were the orphans, next came the old men and boys, and last of all the married men. Even the old women used to go into the battle to help in any way they could. It was only the mothers and their children who hid themselves."

Eventually we left the track and picked our way through the jungle itself. Soon we heard a low thundering which grew steadily louder, until we emerged from the trees at the brink of a deep pool. We now stood in the twilight, at the bottom of a rift in the black wall of the canyon. From the edge of the cliff, fifteen hundred feet above us, and nearly three thousand feet above sealevel, a bright ribbon of water fell vertically into the pool, and the spray went steaming up again over the trees.

"This is the most beautiful waterfall in the world," said the chief firmly. "It is also the highest."

He led us back into the forest. Here, deep among the trees, overgrown by the undergrowth, was an ancient stone figure upon a pedestal of rock. This was one of the "tikis" for which the Marquesas are famous. It was very crudely carved, with barely recognisable features; farther on were others like it, all overgrown and green with moss. Some of them had fallen from their foundations, and lay half-buried in dead leaves and slime.

"These were our gods," said the chief, leading us on up the hill. He stopped in a clearing from which we could look down the whole length of the canyon above the trees.

"At one time we believed in our own gods," he went on. "Our ancestors worshipped them in magnificent temples. Now those temples are destroyed, and in their place have been built a few wooden chapels with corrugated iron roofs. Maybe our gods were false; but at least we believed in them. Now——" he paused to look down upon the rank and fœtid jungle that once had been a fertile vale, "—now we believe in nothing."

One evening Scanty and I had an argument—over some fruit he had been told to fetch, as far as I remember. The result was that Scanty went ashore and failed to turn up to lay the table for supper. We ate our meal and washed up but still there was no sign of young Australia, and after a little while I began to feel a bit worried. Had he possibly been so hurt by my rebukes that he had swum ashore in a rage and been eaten by a shark? It seemed unlikely that a Sydney boy would take a risk of that sort; but he might have walked off into the jungle and got lost.

Just when we had decided to go and find him, there came the bump of a native canoe alongside and next minute Scanty himself hopped over the rail. He came up to me with a bonny smile all over his face.

"Sorry I didn't come back to get yer supper," he said. "I've brought that fruit aboard. Bli! I didn't 'arf 'ave a time getting it, too! Thought I was goin' to get eaten alive in the jungle there—flies as big as bleeding elephants buzzing all round me . . ."

I let him rattle on a bit, but I could see that there was something at the back of his mind.

"What's the matter?" I said.

"Nothing's the matter. I'm all right. Well—well, you see the fact is well—well the fact is, you see—I've decided to stop on this island!"

For the moment I was too surprised to make any comment.

"What are you going to live on?" I asked eventually.

"Well, yer see Skippy, the natives 'ere 'ave been very decent to me. They want me to stop 'ere. They're going to give me a house and a plot of land and a wife and all that sort of thing. You see, the fact is they want to make me sort of king of the island."

"Heavens! You must have impressed them. Why do they want you for king?"

"Well, this evenin' while they was showin' us their 'hula-hula', I joined in; and when they finished I went on and showed 'em a bit of good old Australian tap-dancin'"—he rattled off a lively tattoo upon the deck by way of illustration—"and they was so took with it they asked me to stop here and teach them how to tap!"

This looked like the romance of a lifetime. I saw the headlines in the Sydney papers: "Local lad makes good", "Crowned king of South Sea Island", etc. In the end, however, Scanty agreed to remain with us until the ship sailed. Luckily, within a week, the Marquesans had grown tired of tap dancing; and the wives offered for selection, though all of them robust and well-built women, proved, upon closer acquaintance, to lack that ability for sparkling conversation which had always been the very food of life for Scanty.

It was difficult to obtain sea stores in the islands; potatoes had to be sent by schooner from Tahiti; tinned and dry goods were prohibitively expensive and could only be procured in small quantities. Pigs, chickens, fish, fruit, and also vegetables such as "taro", breadfruit and "manioc", were very plentiful; but none of the livestock could be carried in large enough quantities to feed us all upon a long sea passage, and the tropical-grown vegetables went bad very quickly.

Whilst we were in the island we naturally ate a great deal of fruit. Limes were sixpence a hundred, oranges ninepence a hundred, bananas tenpence a stem, pine-apples a penny each. There were also paw-paws, avocado pears, mangoes, and other tropical fruits; most of which we found rather uninteresting.

Water in the Marquesas was plentiful, but difficult to procure. We had to collect it ashore in metal drums and carry it to the ship in our boats.

On Wednesday, 10th of November, the French naval schooner *Zelée* entered Tai-o-hae bay. She was a very fast ship, having formerly been an American trading schooner with several record runs between San Francisco and Tahiti to her credit. Now she was marconi-rigged, with auxiliary power, and armed with one point-75 gun on her foredeck.

She was the watch-ship of the South Seas station, and was making a two months' cruise of the Islands in charge of Lieutenant-Commander Peaucellier.

The *nonos* of Nukuhiva were a very formidable pest. Luckily they did not occur on any other island we visited. I myself was fortunate not to be very much affected by them; but many of the crew found it impossible to make long expeditions inland because of the *nonos*, and soon we all began to grow tired of Nukuhiva. It was undoubtedly one of the most beautiful countries we visited, but the climate was very hot, and, because of the heat and the insects, we found it very difficult properly to appreciate the beauty of our surroundings.

Apart from this there were the bogies of leprosy and elephantiasis lurking in the native villages, so that most of us were unwilling to risk a very close interest in Marquesan home life.

There is not, as a matter of fact, very much leprosy among the Marquesans to-day; and it has been found that if the patient is treated in the early stages of the disease its growth can definitely be controlled. Anyway, the natives do not appear to have very much fear of it.

In the village of Motopu we asked the two pleasant-looking girls, who showed us round, whether it was true that there was leprosy in the village.

"Oh, yes!" they answered cheerfully. "We both have it."

From Nukuhiva we went to Hiva-Oa, the largest island in the Marquesas group, lying about sixty miles east-south-east from Tai-o-hae. This passage was a dead-beat to windward between Nukuhiva and the neighbouring island of Ua-Pou. . . . Full, warm trade-wind blowing; sunset, and the cliffs of Nukuhiva turning black astern; then growing upwards and outwards into the night, blending with the darkness. No moon, stars shining dimly through a haze. Our little ship plunging at the short seas, splitting and turning them; heeling a little to the full warm trade-wind blowing.

Dawn. Ua-Pou quite close upon the weather bow. A white halo of cloud upon the island; huge pinnacles of basalt piercing the cloud, like monstrous symbols of a prehistoric worship. Sunset again. The cliffs of Nukuhiva turning black. So, for five days; beating to windward over glittering sun-blue seas, and through the moonless cavern of the night, with the full warm trade-wind blowing. . . .

CHAPTER XXVI
HIVA-OA

In the early hours of the morning on the 29th of November we stood in upon the coast of Hiva-Oa, about four miles east of Atuona. We lay-to under the cliffs to wait for daylight.

Just before dawn the trade-wind failed, and the land breeze crept out to us in tiny puffs and cat's-paws upon the water. The air was charged with the overpowering scent of *Tiaré Tahiti*; there was something wicked, almost repulsive in this heavy exotic perfume. One snuffed at it avidly, and felt like a man drowning in a bath of syrup.

As soon as it was light enough to see we squared away, and ran down towards the bay of Taa Hu Ku. Unfortunately we arrived there about twenty minutes too soon; with the land-breeze still blowing we were unable to work into the anchorage. There was a heavy following swell, making manœuvring difficult, and just as we reached a point a few hundred yards beyond the entrance, the sea-breeze came flying in and pinned us to the lee shore—embayed between the island and Noire Point. We made one half-hearted attempt to tack, but the swell was too much for the *Cap Pilar*; so, without more ado, we let go the starboard anchor and forty fathoms of cable.

That day the breeze blew freshly till an hour before sunset, and a nasty sea ran into the bay; but the anchor had a good grip, and we were in no danger of dragging. In the evening, however, we lashed two boats together, and carried the other anchor well out into the fairway; next morning we kedged the ship clear of Noire Point and cast her on to the port tack as soon as the sea-breeze came. We sailed about a mile clear of the island, then went about, and laid fair into the mouth of Taa Hu Ku Bay, anchoring this time in the spot for which we had been aiming.

In general appearance Hiva-Oa is exactly like Nuku-hiva; but the valley of Atuona is very different from that of Tai-o-hae. A mountain peak, with a cliff face more than 3,000 feet high, overlooks Atuona, and the bed of the valley is watered by a beautiful little river, reminiscent of one of the tributaries of the Thames.

Hiva-Oa was the last island in the Marquesas to submit to French rule; so we were amused to find by the foot-path leading up from the beach one of those Citröen road-signs which you see dotted about all over the French highways. It bore the information:

> *" Atuona, ½ km."*

and underneath:

> *" Don de Citröen "*.

It stood like the triumphant seal of French sovereignty upon the Marquesans, and we wondered how many of them understood what it represented. We asked a little boy.

"It is a memorial," he said, "to the captain of a Spanish frigate who was slain here by our forefathers."

In Tai-o-hae and Atuona the natives do very little harpoon throwing because it is only possible to do this in the shallows where the fish can be impaled against the bottom; most of the Marquesas coastline is steep. Instead the natives dive and prong the fish under water with a single-tined spear. Often they remain below the surface and transfix two or three fish, one after the other, like a common-keeper collecting pieces of paper with his stick. They also go out at night to catch flying fish. It is done from a *pirogue*; one man holds a flaring palm-frond above his head, which attracts the fish, and the other man catches them in a long-shafted net as they fly past.

At 10 o'clock one morning Carmichael and I went ashore in the dory. At the head of Taa Hu Ku Bay are a few native dwellings, clustered round a small fresh-

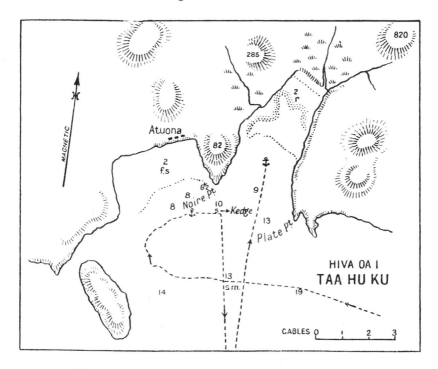

water lagoon, formed by a stream before it flows out over the beach into the sea. We used to drag our boats up this stream out of reach of the tide; but this morning the tide was out, and we found the dory too heavy for the two of us to shift.

We called to some children, bathing naked in the lagoon, but they laughed at us and ran away. Next we tried an old Chinaman, who was lying upon his verandah in philosophic contemplation of the roof of his house.

" Eenglish son-of-a-beech," he said simply, without turning his head. So we passed on to the next house.

Here our hail was answered by an immense Negress about 6 ft. 3 in. in height, and probably weighing more than twenty stone. She came out grinning from ear to ear, and, picking up the dory by the bow, dragged it bodily on to the sandbank. We shuddered, and set off up the hillside as fast as we could.

The track led us through a plantation of coconut palms, then zig-zagged up a precipitous hillside until the trees lay like a green sea below us; then out to where the ridge ended in a cliff one thousand feet above the ocean. Below us a huge surf thundered on the rocks, and the trade-wind blew fresh and cool in our faces.

We tramped on throughout the morning, across ridge after ridge—down into the sombre jungles of the valleys between, across the dry beds of streams, and up the other side under a scorching sun. In every valley there were deserted *paepaes* and groves of palm-trees, breadfruit and oranges, all overgrown by the jungle and deserted. We strode on through the noon-day heat, and far into the afternoon. Before sunset we lost count of the valleys we had crossed, and found it impossible to estimate the distance we still must cover to reach our destination, the village of Otatehe.

Each time we crossed another spur of the mountains we told ourselves that the next valley would be the one for which we were looking; but each time we found only the ancient remains of human habitation, or a solitary hut from which the dogs came howling at our approach.

Just before sunset we came to a larger valley than the rest; and here, at last, we found a village. There were half a dozen houses, and about a score of natives living in them; a healthy mountain stream went bickering through the clearing. What interested us most was the fact that every house had a well-kept flower garden—

roughly fenced off against the cattle; and in the middle of the clearing was a fresh-looking patch of grass upon which the children played beside the river.

As we walked up a woman was washing clothes in the stream, two babies lay in the water near by; upon the steps of the largest house sat an old man, smoking a pipe of enormous length. As he rose to greet us, we noticed that his legs were covered with an intricate maze of blue tattooing.

This tattooing, we learned, was another relic from olden times. Apparently it was applied to both men and women by means of a very painful process; the amount of tattooing upon his or her body indicated the Marquesan's social position. The bodies of some of the chiefs of those times were tattooed from head to foot.

The old man invited us to spend the night in his house, but we were deterred by the sight of another figure sitting in the background. This fellow's legs were swollen by elephantiasis till they looked like two giant cucumbers. Elephantiasis, like malaria, is transmitted by mosquitoes; so we decided to push on, hoping to reach Otatehe before nightfall.

We had not been very long upon our way when it grew suddenly dark and we were obliged to stop for the night beside the nearest tree. Since we had thought it better not to fill our water-bottles from the stream which ran through the village we now unfortunately found ourselves without any water. We climbed a palm-tree and threw down half a dozen likely looking nuts.

We spent a very uncomfortable night: there were just enough mosquitoes to prevent us from sleeping, and the tepid, sickly sweet coconut milk drove us nearly frantic with thirst. In the middle of the night there was a great commotion in the bushes near by, and a herd of pigs came stumbling almost on top of us. We were still awake when the first grey whisper of daylight stole across the hills, and the forest woke to the sound of cocks crowing—shouting to each other across a jungle-carpeted valley. In these surroundings their raucous challenges sounded wild and unearthly, like the trumpets of God at the Day of Judgment. Then the doves began to coo softly in the trees; from below us came the grunting of pigs and the lowing of cattle; far away in the mountains a solitary goat bleated. All the dawn-music of a European countryside rang out about us in this exotic wilderness—gruesome as laughter at a warrior's funeral.

We had brought with us only ship's biscuits and chocolate to eat, but we were now too thirsty for this sort of fare, so we set off again as soon as it was light enough to find the path. The sea-breeze had not yet come in, and it was oppressively hot among the trees; we sweated and panted for water, but struggled on. Suddenly we came upon a mossy rock, and beneath it we found an ice-cold pool into which the water tinkled drop by drop. Each drop was a tiny jewel to us, and we drank as we had never drunk before.

Then we tramped on again through the still, hot air—into dim glades strung across with spiders' webs—down into dark valleys, full of ruins and the screaming silence of dead places—across dry water-courses and over the ridges, till at last we came out upon a lofty headland, where the turf was springy and the sea-breeze whistled through a clump of native pines. Far, far below us the bright sea trembled, and, on our left, ran in upon a yellow beach.

This at last was the valley of Otatehe; at its head we could make out the vertical white streak which marked the cascade by which it could be recognised. We ran down the zig-zag path, scattering a flock of wild goats; then through the palm-grove below, and straight into the sea, where we lay for many minutes without even exerting ourselves to swim.

Otatehe was a very beautiful little valley, but it was inhabited by only one young Marquesan and his wife and three children. He gave us an excellent midday meal of goat's meat and chicken, cooked in coconut milk, with taro and rice for vegetables. (Taro is a plant looking rather like a huge leek with broad leaves. It grows in swampy places, and only the bulbous root is eaten. When boiled this resembles a large mauve potato, and has a rich, creamy flavour.)

In the afternoon we were delighted when the native offered to take us back to Atuona in his *pirogue*; but putting to sea through the surf seemed to us a very hazardous proceeding. With all three of us aboard, the tiny craft's gunwales were only about three inches above the surface of the water. We skirted the cliffs so close that the spray fell all around us; the *pirogue* rode awkwardly in the confused backwash from the shore, and several times the crest of a wave flipped aboard, so that Carmichael and I had to bail for dear life, while the native paddled unconcernedly on.

It was an exciting trip; at any moment we expected the slapping top of one of the rollers to catch the boat unfairly and fill her to the gunwales; and, from our experience of the fatalism of Polynesians and other tropical races, we knew our native friend would have made no allowance for such an eventuality before it actually occurred.

After about half an hour's paddling we weathered the outermost point of the bay and turned westward. Once clear of the backwash the seas ran truer down the coast; the sails were set, and the little boat flew away before the trade-wind. During the next two hours we lay at our ease watching the headlands swing by and bay after bay open before us. The little boat, under a press of white canvas, flitted like a butterfly over the sea. We noted with interest the jungle-covered ridges and valleys across which we had struggled with so much heart-breaking effort the day before. Just before sunset the land-breeze crept out to us, and we drifted peacefully homeward through the heavy scented atmosphere of a tropical evening.

After being in Atuona for a week we began to long once more for the fresh, cool winds of the open sea. Jane suffered particularly from the hot weather, though Jessica seemed perfectly contented, having never been accustomed to anything else. There also appeared to be some malignant infection either in the atmosphere or in the sea of the Marquesas Islands; for all the bites which we had received in Nukuhiva began to turn into horrible festering sores. Every day more people were confined to the ship, and it soon became apparent that we were all in need of a change of climate.

Tempers, too, were beginning to grow uncertain, and *le cafard* assailed us all. The Marquesas Islands were all and more than we had expected them to be; the scenery was extravagantly beautiful, the atmosphere of mystery and thinly veiled barbarity which surrounded the native life was fascinating, but the whole tone of tropical life had begun to cloy; we became hopelessly lethargic, introspective, and lacking in energy to make the most of our opportunities. Doctor Stenhouse was becoming particularly depressed, and his depression began to influence all the others who lived aft. Before long several of us were hardly on speaking terms. George and I had a violent quarrel over such a trivial matter as a few pounds of taro; Carmichael became sad and listless; Lars grew morose and unapproachable, working from daylight till dark at the ship's rigging. Only Newell was still his cheerful, easy-going self, and we each of us began to rely more and more upon his friendship.

Jane very rarely went ashore now on account of the

heat; but occasionally I wandered off by myself. Once I walked up the valley in search of the ancient amphitheatre where the natives had been accustomed to hold the cannibalistic orgies of a hundred years ago.

Willie Marsh, who had been there, told us that the huge boulders of which it was made were still standing, apparently untouched by the years. In the centre was a rock upon which the chief of the tribe had sat, and round this were smaller boulders for his courtiers. Before the chief's throne was a deep pit into which the tortured bodies of the captives had been thrown—there to lie for several days until considered fit for human consumption. Beyond this pit again, a great semicircle of roughly fashioned stone seats rose tier upon tier against the hillside—enough to accommodate the whole tribe; while a hundred yards away was a low mound upon which the bones of the victims were said to have been piled. When some of the stones had been turned over and a few inches of soil had been scratched away, Willie and Sanson actually found ancient bones, which Sanson was able to identify as being human remains.

The present-day Marquesans look upon the neighbourhood of these *Maraes* with superstitious fear, and nothing will persuade a native to approach them at night. During my search for this particular one I came upon three deserted houses in the heart of the jungle. The doors and windows of all of them were open, and no sign of life was visible in their vicinity. There was a deathly hush upon the forest, so that I paused to listen, almost expecting to hear the dead warriors whispering to each other in the *Marae*, which I knew must be near by.

I was just about to walk on when a low, gurgling cough tore the stillness and held me rooted to the ground, hardly daring to breathe. It had come from one of the deserted houses, and, when I had recovered from the first shock, I crept forward to investigate.

As I drew nearer I heard a confused scuffling sound, accompanied by occasional thumps, coming from within the middle house, as though some heavy animal were dragging itself across the floor. I stopped and stood watching, and presently there appeared in the doorway a horrible apparition, with shaggy hair and slavering mouth.

Upon his hands and one knee, he dragged himself and the other useless leg out on to the verandah, then down the steps and across the few yards of grass which separated the house from the river. I felt sick with pity and disgust: this rotting remnant of a man looked as though he must be riddled with every filthy disease in hell. I dared not go near him, and I kept as still as I could for fear he should hear me. With loathsome contortions he dragged himself to the stream and drank like an animal, with his face in the water; then with a struggle he drew himself back.

As he turned he suddenly caught sight of me. He paused and lifted his head. For a full half-minute we stared at each other. From his glaring black eyes shone all the hate and misery of years of suffering. Never in all my life have I seen such a look of evil and despair. I stood horror-struck, unable to move. Then from his throat there swelled a low unearthly gurgle, rising to a howl, that was like devil's laughter. I sprang round and ran out of the jungle.

When I spoke to a friend at Atuona about the dying man in the forest he shrugged his shoulders.

"We have done all we can for him," he said. "There is no cure for his illness; he will die before the year is out."

"There are many others like him," he went on. "What would you? It is the legacy of the white man to these people."

CHAPTER XXVII
TROPICAL FOOTBALL

JANE, JESSICA AND I sailed with the others in the lifeboat to the island of Tahuata. On the north coast of the island we found the small bay of Hana Hevane; across it the coral had grown, leaving a gap a few feet wide, through which we pulled into the peaceful lagoon within.

We spent two glorious days living in a hut in the palm-groves that grew down to the beach.

On the first night we caught an eel, which Jane stewed over an open coconut-husk fire for supper. After supper we sat round the embers till nearly midnight. When we got up to go into the hut there was a terrific scurrying and scuffling in all directions; we sat down again, and in a minute or two we saw that we were surrounded by a ring of little green eyes watching us from the jungle. The place was apparently infested with rats; when we suddenly jumped up they all scuttled off as fast as they could. We started to walk away again, but soon found that the rats were not the only beasts abroad that night. The ground was pitted with land-crab holes, and, in the darkness, these loathsome monsters had crawled out in search of any offal or refuse fit for them to eat. They were all over the place—huge, bloated and disgusting, looking like a lot of crawling skulls, with beady black eyes, and one immense claw, about the size of a lobster's, held ready to defend themselves.

The possibility of being nipped by one of these brutes would have been enough to daunt the stoutest heart; but the fear of treading on one and feeling his offal-bloated carcase crunching beneath our bare feet, made us shiver; so as soon as we had shone the torch about us, to make sure of a clear path, we fled like frightened schoolgirls for the verandah of the hut.

Next morning I woke at dawn to hear a wild cock crowing lustily from a clump of bushes within a hundred yards of the hut. This was too good a chance to be missed, so, taking with me a point-22 rifle, I stalked, with exaggerated caution, in the direction of the bushes.

The cock crowed again, and next moment I saw a nice fat chicken sitting placidly upon a branch. I felt that the chance of a meal of fresh chicken justified my taking advantage of so unsporting a target, and anyway it was still quite dark; so, taking careful aim, I fired.

When I dashed into the bushes to retrieve the bird, I was almost knocked down by a cackling flurry of hens who flapped down about my head, and then trotted off towards the cooking shelter, where they strolled contentedly about picking up the scraps left from last night's meal. I had shot a farmyard fowl in its sleep!

At Hiva-Oa we played the only football match of the voyage. I must admit that we looked forward to the day of the match with some misgivings. Most of our opponents would be the grandsons of cannibals, so it seemed reasonable to suppose that the instincts of their ancestors still stirred in the hearts of some of them.

On the afternoon of the great day Scanty came aboard wearing a woeful expression.

"I 'ope you chaps is feelin' strong," he said, doubtfully. "The fellows ashore's just been showin' me what they used to do to 'em in the *good* old days."

"Still, it'll be all right," he added, cheering up a little, "so long as you win."

When we reached the football ground we were rather surprised to find our opponents dressed in smart green-and-white jerseys and wearing football boots. We saw that we were up against a keen and well-trained team; some of them were huge gorilla-like beings, with bulging muscles, and all of them were obviously eager to get at us. On the touch-line the whole of the rest of the tribe set up a roar, which sounded extraordinarily like a war-chant.

From the kick-off we played all out; but each time that one of us fell over there were shouts of laughter from the crowd, and as the game went on we felt more and more certain that their hereditary instincts might get the better of the Marquesans should we fail to win. George, who was refereeing, did his best for us; but we were hopelessly outclassed. He took care to be by that touch-line which was nearest to our boats when the game ended with the score at 7—0 against us.

At the sound of the whistle the crowd immediately rose, and some of them drew copra knives, but next moment the natives were busily chopping open water-melons, and hacking the tops off coconuts. Then we all sat down together to a mighty banquet of fruit and coco-nut milk.

While we were at Atuona we met the Bishop of the Marquesas, who has spent his life among the islands, and has written two books on Polynesian mythology; but our best friend was the storekeeper, Bob McKet-terick, an old Liverpool shellback. We used to go up to the store in the evenings to talk about ports and sailing ships and the joys of Blackpool on a Bank Holiday.

Bob had been sent ashore sick from a sailing ship, in Tahiti, twenty-five years before; and he had been in the islands ever since, either trading in cutters and schooners, or storekeeping for one of the big companies.

I asked him once whether he ever intended to go home.

"It's too late for that now, lad," he answered. "If Ah went 'ome now, Ah'd most likely be dead inside a six-month. Besides, Ah'm all right where Ah am, aren't

Ah? Plenty to eat, a little to drink, and t'natives lookin' at me as if Ah was t'local Lord Nuffield. What do *Ah* want to go 'ome for?"

Bob's greatest friend was Newell. "Thaat Newell!" he used to roar, slapping his sides. "'E is terrible. 'E was up 'ere last night tellin' me stories till four o'clock in t'morning. I never laughed so much before in all my born days."

For some time Bob had been building himself a yacht. "A yacht at anchor'll make t'bay look quite 'omely, won't it?" he said. "Besides t'Bishop give me a box of cigars for Christmas, so Ah moust 'ave a yacht, eh? Wouldn't be right not to."

On Tuesday, the 7th of December, the trading schooner *Moana* arrived from Tahiti. She brought for us ten hundredweight of potatoes, more than half of which were already rotten, while the rest became inedible within less than ten days. Doctor Stenhouse booked a passage aboard the *Moana*, and left in her next morning, bound for Tahiti. We were all extremely sorry to lose the "Doc"; he had been a very good friend to us from the first. But, apart from this, the loss of Doctor Stenhouse added considerably to our anxieties. We had many thousands of miles still to sail before reaching civilisation, and we did not enjoy the idea of having Jane and her three months' old baby on board without a doctor upon whom we could rely for advice. However, Dr. Stenhouse felt that he must go, so there was nothing to be done about it.

We had decided to call at one more South Sea island before continuing the voyage eastwards. Since we had already visited a semi-atoll and a purely volcanic group, several of the crew wanted next to see, if possible, one of the true atolls of the Tuamotu Islands. We sought the advice of the captain of the *Moana*.

"All the passes into the atolls are very narrow," he

said, "and the current sometimes races out of them at nine or ten knots."

"Of course," he went on, "you wouldn't really be in any danger even if there were a heavy race. You'd just pop out of the pass again, like a cork out of a bottle. I should try Hao if I were you; there ought not to be more than four or five knots of current in the pass there at this time of year."

So we settled on Hao; and at 4 A.M. on the 12th of December we hove-up our anchor and drifted gently out of Taa Hu Ku Bay.

When we left Hiva-Oa all of us aft were still in a very troubled state of mind; but no sooner had the islands faded upon the northern skyline than our worries seemed suddenly to fall from us, and we settled down thankfully once more to the daily rhythm of sea life. The trade-wind blew steadily, the sea glittered, and the sky was blue; within less than forty-eight hours it already seemed as though we had been at sea all our lives, and that our five weeks in the Marquesas Islands had been part of a fantastic and somewhat melancholy dream.

When we looked back upon our recent quarrels it seemed as though we had been lying under some malignant spell. Perhaps the curse of the Marquesas had been upon us. We shuddered as we thought of those deep forests and magnificent mountain gorges which lay brooding and deserted. Now that we had left them behind we suddenly saw them in a different light, not beautiful, nor magnificent, but inexpressibly sad. . . .

The voyage to Hao occupied five uneventful days.

CHAPTER XXVIII
THE TUAMOTUS

AT SUNSET on the 16th of December the palm-tops of Amanu shivered upon the southern horizon, and by midnight we were running down the western shore of that atoll. The moon was nearly full; the beaches shone dead white; the palms stood like lances against a brilliant sky.

The trade-wind, blowing warm and full, brought to us the wavering thunder of the surf and the hot dry odour of sun-baked coral. Under the lee of the island there was no swell; the *Cap Pilar* ran with square yards, like an enchanted castle, floating into fairyland.

Before dawn we picked up the north coast of Hao, and when the sun was high enough to show up the coral heads, we stood in towards the pass.

Hao is a true atoll, with a reef about 200 yards wide, and only six feet high, describing an irregular oval nearly sixty miles in circumference. There is only one pass into the lagoon, and it is rather difficult to recognise at a distance, owing to the ever-changing appearance of the palm-clumps which are the only landmarks.

We were not left long in doubt. As we approached the likeliest looking gap we could see an ominous white streak extending nearly half a mile out to sea. This, we knew, was one of the tide races, about which the captain of the *Moana* had warned us. Once again our chart was sadly out of date. Upon it was a picture of H.M.S. *Blossom*, no doubt a smart modern vessel in those days, sailing out of the lagoon under topsails and reefed foresail. However,

HAO ISLAND
(TUAMOTU ARCHIPELAGO)
The BOW ISLAND of CAP'COOK

Morai or East Pt {18°3'38"S.} By the French
{140°59'17"W.}

- - → - - CAP PILAR'S TRACK coming in
- - → - -   "   "   "   going out

Nautical Miles

LAGOON

Contains a multitude of coral knolls
which can easily be avoided by a
lookout from a loft

All this
part studded
with coral
knolls

Purdea
Bank

To Jima →
5000 ENTRANCE

from Hira Ua 500

Polynesian Village
Wells of fresh water
Suwahai's boring in 1840

ENTRANCE TO
HAO LAGOON

100 FATHOMS

MAGNETIC
Var.⁹
II.° E

MORAI

H.M.S. BLOSSOM COMING OUT.

S.P.1939

Drawn by Cyril Money

with this fine example and the happy simile of the cork popping out of the bottle to encourage us, we stood on under all plain sail.

When we reached the race we ran parallel with it, gradually edging over until we were fairly in the current. At first it seemed as though the *Cap Pilar* were held motionless in the grip of the tide, but after a little we saw that we were just able to stem it, and gradually we drew in towards the reef. As we approached the channel, which is less than fifty yards wide, the current grew stronger, and all round the ship the water boiled and seethed. On either side of us now the reef closed in like iron jaws upon the ship. Provided we could keep her stem on to the current there was very little danger, since we could see the coral only crawling beneath us; but the overfalls kicked up a huge sea, and the din was terrific.

It was this noise which nearly cost us the ship a few moments later. I had been directing the helmsman from a point of vantage in the fore rigging, but owing to the roaring of the waves he mistook one of my orders. I ought to have been directing him by signals instead of by shouts; but at the time this did not occur to me, so I was appalled by the sight of the *Cap Pilar's* head paying off rapidly to starboard!—towards the shore!—with the wheel, as I thought, hard a-port! Without a moment's hesitation the port anchor was let go, and there we stuck, with all our sails still set, but for the time being safe.

Our first idea was to clew up everything, and let the ship be carried out to sea (like a champagne cork, I hoped). But, when it was discovered that the sudden alteration of course had not been due to an eddy current, as I had at first supposed, there seemed to be no reason why we should not still be able to proceed; so we set every sail in the ship, and after getting our anchor, we crept into the lagoon without further incident.

It took us the rest of the day to beat across the lagoon to the native village, which lay about six miles dead to windward from the pass. The sailing conditions were ideal; just enough wind to keep the *Cap Pilar* sliding along at about four knots, yet not a hint of any swell. The lagoon was studded with coral heads which were nearly awash, but it was easy to avoid these with a look-out on the fore't'gallant yard.

About sunset we began to close in with the eastern shore of the lagoon, and a little later we came abreast of a small trading schooner, which was loading copra with her boats. Beside her we anchored, and by the time our sails were furled there were already several native outriggers alongside, and the usual exchange of fruit and friendly gestures began.

The islanders also brought sad news. " Did you see the *Mouette* ? " they asked.

" Yes, we saw her in the Gambier Islands, two months ago."

" Well, if you'd passed Amanu atoll before dark yesterday you might have seen her again."

Apparently she had tried to enter that lagoon only a few hours before we ourselves had sailed by. Her engineer had misunderstood one of the captain's signals on the engine-room bell, just as the helmsman of the *Cap Pilar* had misunderstood an order in the pass of Hao; but whereas we had been lucky enough to escape the consequences, the *Mouette* had struck first one side of the pass and then the other, after which she sank in fifteen fathoms of water.

After supper we settled ourselves in deck-chairs upon the poop. Near by sat four natives, two of them with guitars, and for hours they sang to us in the moonlight. Sometimes their song was gay, with an intricate pattern of words; next it was a lilting melody; then some ancient rune or saga. To all of them the singers improvised their own harmonies, and accompanied themselves on their guitars.

The moon blew over the horizon like a huge red balloon. As we gazed across the wrinkled grey face of the water to the reef, with its mane of glittering palms, we thought that here at last we had found our "Dream Island of the South Seas". We felt strangely unwilling to leave the ship. Out on the lagoon there was a great peace, and the warm sweet scent of the islands floated across to us like the breath of true romance. It seemed foolish to go ashore, there possibly to be disillusioned.

None the less we all did go ashore next day, and were met on the beach by the girls of the island.

Hao is less frequently visited by schooners than any of the other islands we came to, but the girls all wore print dresses rather than *pareus*. This, however, was their only concession to European civilisation—in every other way they followed the instincts and traditions of their ancestors.

Like most of the other Polynesian girls we met they were not very beautiful, and their figures were somewhat ungainly, but they had a great freedom of movement, and an unaffected shyness, which more than made up for their crude features and dark skins. They linked arms with us, and escorted us down the village street, where the whole population came out to nod and smile, and also to invite us into their houses; but the girls who had first taken possession of us only held on to our arms all the tighter, and bore us off to their own homes, where we were placed in chairs upon the verandahs and offered inelegant little home-made cakes, with cool sweet coconut-milk to drink. Then the guitars were brought out, and we sat for a long time upon the shady verandahs, while the girls squatted at our feet and played and sang to us, at the same time watching us gravely or smiling, ready to leap up to satisfy our slightest whim.

This was our introduction to the true South Sea Island life of which we had read so much. At first it seemed as though the natives must have read about it, too.

One of the first people we made friends with was the chief of Hao; he was over seventy years of age, and the only man on the island who spoke French at all fluently. I believe he owed his position entirely to this ability. He was quite embarrassing in his friendliness, which he usually expressed by a very maudlin fatherly attitude to us all.

To our astonishment we also found a solitary missionary living on the island. His real home, rather appropriately, was in the city of Inspiration, Arizona. He was a smart, typically American-looking young man of twenty, always dressed in neat white clothes, with a monogrammed pin in his tie. He was a very genuine and straight-forward Mormon, and we all had the greatest respect for him, while the natives obviously adored him.

If Jessica had been a little older she would have enjoyed those few days more than any of us, because from the moment we arrived she was the idol of the island. The Tuamotans are a declining race, like the Marquesans, and consequently they worship children with an almost religious fanaticism. Never once did we see a Tuamotan child beaten or even corrected, yet they all seemed to grow up into the most charming and unspoilt mortals.

The people of Hao were passionately fond of their own children, but they seemed to adore our little white baby even more; from morning until night there were always two or three of the islanders, both men and women, squatting about Jessica's cradle under the poop awning. While she was awake they sang her songs and played to her on the guitar; and when she slept they sat quietly watching over her. On account of this, Jane and I were able to spend much more time away from the ship in Hao. We knew that we could leave Jessica in perfect safety for an hour or two with the islanders; and whenever we took her ashore the girls of the village would cover her pram with garlands of sweet-scented flowers and vie with each other for the honour of pushing her up and down in the shade of the palm-trees.

CHAPTER XXIX
CHRISTMAS ON A CORAL ATOLL

THE EIGHT DAYS we spent at Hao passed like a fleeting dream. We swam or lay floating for long happy hours in the lagoon, poking about among the purple and yellow coral, and watching the brilliant little fishes darting from nook to nook of their limitless submarine flower gardens. Some of these fish were bright blue, other deep violet, and others orange or red or yellow with black patches—a whole aquarium in its natural setting. Whenever we went ashore, the natives made us welcome in their homes, and followed us about, ready to anticipate our smallest wish; each day was more enchanting than the last.

On this narrow circle of palm-clad reef there was nothing to see, nor any exhausting expeditions that you felt it your duty to undertake. You rowed in from the ship, picking your way carefully through the long line of fringing coral, and beached the dory on the clean white sand. Behind you the lagoon lay placid and lifeless in the glaring sunlight, then two minutes' stroll through the palms and you were watching the Pacific Ocean thundering all along the outer shore. The everlasting trade-wind blew cool and fresh against you, the sun shone brightly; there was nothing else to see in all Hao, and this fact in itself was enough to make the island a paradise for us.

One evening Newell and I went ashore together. When we reached the chief's house we heard that he was to conduct a service in one of the churches, of which there were three on the island, each of a different denomination, and each capable of seating the entire population of 134 people. The chief asked us to go with him, and we did not hesitate, although Newell became a little alarmed as we passed through the church doors. "D'you know the drill?" he whispered.

With charming tact, in case we might have come ashore without money, the old chief offered us each a 20-franc note to put in the offertory. As it happened, I had in my pocket a roll of notes amounting to about 120 francs; but, in view of the chief's thoughtfulness, I decided that it would have been ungracious not to accept his.

The service was simple and very earnestly supported by the congregation; afterwards we gathered in the chief's hut to drink coffee.

"*Mon dieu!*" exclaimed the old man suddenly. "I've lost the collection money!"

For some time we helped him search the path back to the church, until at last he gave it up with the pious observation "The Lord will provide." When we got back to the hut I suddenly noticed a roll of notes beneath the chair upon which I had been sitting. In triumph I handed them to the chief. His eyes glowed with religious fervour. "Praise the Lord!" he cried. "Did I not tell you He would take care of His own?"

Ten minutes later the chief put his hand in his own pocket and produced a second roll of notes!

"A miracle!" he cried. "The Lord has caused the collection to be doubled!"

I realised what had happened, and tried as tactfully as I could to recover a proportion of my money, of which we were very much in need for fresh provisions. But the chief appeared not to understand the significance of what I was trying to say, and in the end we left him still clutching the two wads of bank notes, and murmuring over and over again: "Truly the good God takes care of His own."

All the crew were enchanted with Hao, especially Willie Marsh. The girls were adorable, more than eager to make friends, and apparently prepared to be respectful, gay or

fascinating, entirely according to the tastes of their con-
sort of the moment. Willie Marsh always referred to them
as "young ladies", and treated them with the utmost
courtesy. Scanty, being a Sydney boy, called them
"donas", "lubras" or "tarts", depending upon his
mood, while other people spoke of them as "sweet little
girls", "native women", "wahinis", or just plain
"skirt".

They were none of these, and yet all of them; their only
desire was to entertain, serve and make happy the guests
whom "God had sent them"; but it was remarkable how
our tendency always was to give English or at least
worldly names to everything in the little paradise in which
we found ourselves. For instance, the natives used
secretly to brew a very horrible alcoholic drink from
bananas or from the hearts of palm-fronds; and this we
always referred to as banana beer, though in fact it was
hardly drinkable. Anyway, Newell apparently derived
great moral comfort from being able to talk about "going
ashore to have a mug of beer with the chief".

Throughout the cruise Newell had never been a ladies'
man. Whenever he happened to be at a loose end he
seemed to prefer the more jovial atmosphere of the tap-
room of an inn to the mere "walking out" which some of
the others favoured. "Beer is best," he always said. At
Hao he still made the same uncompromising pronounce-
ment, though it must be admitted that the tone in which
he now said it was somewhat lacking in conviction.

Newell and the chief were great pals. I think that it was
that suggestion of the patriarchal and the traditional about
the old man which attracted our second mate, who had
always been a faithful mourner of "the good old days".
But Newell himself gave a different explanation: the chief
had in his hut a remarkable old mahogany chest of
drawers; how it had even reached the island no one could
guess, but it had obviously been left there for the reason

that none of the drawers would open without the use of considerable violence, and no matter where you moved it about the floor it always remained rocking precariously upon one or other of its axes. Each time the chief tried to open a drawer in this " piece ", it *so very nearly* fell over, that Newell assured us he used to become rooted to that room for hour after hour in the vain hope that the old boy would one day pull it over on top of himself.

On Christmas Eve we forced ourselves to eat a huge meal of roast corned beef, roast potatoes and a Christmas pudding, the latter made by George and Jane from a recipe out of an American magazine. The pudding was good, but the rum butter which went with it was a riot. It must have been the most powerful rum butter ever produced —so strong that one of the teetotal members of the crew refused to touch it, while the other, who gallantly overcame his scruples, had to be assisted to bed. We had originally intended, that night, to build a huge fire upon the reef, and roast before it a whole pig—amid scenes of revelry befitting the surroundings and the occasion. But the islanders sent word that they wished to hold a great Christmas Day feast in our honour, and informed us that we had bought the only full-grown pig on the island, and would we please let them have it back for the banquet !

At noon on Christmas Day everyone went ashore in the two dories, while Jane, Jessica and I followed in the dinghy. We were met on the end of a small stone jetty by the chief and all the people of Hao. A group of young girls, all dressed in white, took charge of Jessica's pram, which they dressed with garlands of acanthus blossom; then we were all escorted in triumphal procession up to the village, preceded by a band composed of eight guitars. Jessica, in her pram, rolled along in solitary splendour at the head of the parade; it was evident that the whole show had been organised in her honour. Unfortunately, being only a little over five months old, she merely lay on her back and scowled.

The banquet took place in the village meeting-hall, which was festooned with flowers for the occasion; it puzzled us to know where so many flowers could have been found upon this apparently desert ring of dead coral. As soon as we were seated we were each crowned with an elaborate crown of flowers. Those of us who were lucky enough to get a wreath which fitted looked and felt like heroes. Throughout the feast the band kept up a stupendous volume of sound.

Jessica meanwhile was attended by half a dozen voluntary nursemaids in the cool interior of a near-by hut. When the meal was over she was wheeled once more on to the raised platform at the back of the hall. Then the old chief rose to his feet and made a long speech in a very tense voice; at the end of it there fell an expectant hush upon the company. The chief made a sign to two of the girls, who immediately lifted Jessica from her pram and held her up for all to see.

"We name this baby Queen of the Lagoon and the Islands," shouted the old man. He was answered by cheering and a gale of applause.

"We name her Atanua—Cloud within the Rainbow. May she live to remember her people."

She was crowned with a wreath of white flowers, while the natives gathered 'round in loving reverence. It was a magic moment in the life of our little girl, even though she was too young at the time to sense that magic; but one day, when she is much older, we shall tell Jessica Jane of her little island kingdom in the Pacific. Perhaps some time she will go back to them.

The day ended with a great dance. Wishing to return in some measure the islanders' kindness we got George to mix a few bottles of very weak brandy and lemon punch, which were to be our contribution to the evening's hilarity. We felt a little uneasy about this, but the quantity was not great, so I did not think that very much harm could result. However, to be on the safe side, we asked the chief to try some first.

"*Ah! c'est trop fort,*" pronounced the old man, who was deeply religious.

Whether this was idiomatic French or a plain statement of fact we did not know; but feeling rather ashamed of ourselves, we hastily gathered in what bottles we could still find, to keep them out of harm's way. But the chief apparently considered himself a superman, and that the drink which was too strong for his people was not necessarily too strong for him. So when a large number of bottles were safely collected in his hut, he filled a massive pewter pot (just presented to him by the ship) with the offending liquor, and, still muttering "*Trop fort—c'est trop fort*", he emptied half the contents down his throat at one draught.

We proceeded to pass the mug round as a kind of loving-cup. Beside the chief sat a fine buxom native woman called Fokahotu and never once did the mug pass these two without having to be replenished. Eventually Sanson, the only true Scotsman among us, was persuaded to sit to windward of the chief, in an attempt to reduce the old man's dose as much as possible; but the wily ruler then insisted on having the mug refilled *before* he drank, which made matters worse than ever.

The effect of the drink soon became evident and it was not long before the old chief's head fell forward and he was sound asleep. Thereupon the doughty Madame Fokahotu sprang up and strode boldly into the night, which immediately became loud with the noise of battle. We heard afterwards that she had thrown a ten-pound rock at her husband, who, according to her, had had "the effrontery to approach her in an inebriated condition".

Fokahotu was a fine specimen of female brawn, so we accepted this explanation without comment.

Meanwhile the revels were approaching a climax outside. In spite of the chief's self-sacrifice in keeping most of our *punch* from his people, the latter had not benefited very much by it, since they were well supplied with quantities of their own banana- and palm-frond beer. When we reached the assembly hut the more dignified European dances had long since given place to wild and unrestrained native "hulas", which the crew applauded frantically. At midnight some of us were anxious to get aboard, so we wound up the proceedings by joining hands with the islanders in the traditional way for the singing of "Auld Lang Syne". The natives all applauded us gravely, and there is very little doubt that most of them thought that this song must be an ancient British battle-cry or the National Anthem.

After this the girls all linked arms with us and the whole community walked us in procession down to the beach, singing all the way. We still remember some of the songs of Hao—lilting plaintive melodies, full of the sad fatalism of a dying race. Their eyes smiled upon us as they sang; we were their friends, and it made them unhappy to see us go.

When we reached the shore the men of the island ran our dories into the water, while the girls came one by one to kiss us all good-night and good-bye. As we pulled away across the lagoon we looked back at the cluster of white figures, painted with moonlight. They swayed in unison like a bank of lilies, and the lovely Hawaiian song of farewell floated out to us over the water, and followed us all the way to the ship.

But we did not all go aboard in the dory. The night was warm and still and odorous, and on the next day we were to sail away from the islands for ever. Small wonder then, that the sun was already beating fiercely upon the

reef next morning before the last of the Cap Pilarians returned to the ship; and most of them went about their
work that forenoon with the far-away look in their eyes of
those who have touched the heights and have not yet
altogether descended.

CHAPTER XXX
GOOD-BYE TO THE ISLANDS

ON BOXING DAY of 1937 we left Hao. Just before we weighed anchor the missionary and the old chief came out in an outrigger to say good-bye. The old man was still very much under the weather from the previous night's orgy but managed somehow to clamber unsteadily aboard, where he embraced us all loosely but affectionately. Unfortunately the windlass was already manned, and while he was still busy kissing the second mate our anchor left the bottom, and the *Cap Pilar* began to cast to port; so we were compelled to cut short the chief's farewells, rather unceremoniously, and bundle him over the side. Just then several other canoes filled with natives reached the ship; they were loaded down to their gunwales with green coconuts, and seeing that we were already under way, the islanders started to hurl the nuts on to our deck from both sides of the ship at once.

The crew, who were scuttling about from halliards to sheets and braces, had to run the gauntlet of a hail of parting gifts, and one or two of them were knocked off their feet by this very formidable confetti, each piece of which weighed between five and seven pounds. Soon, however, the square sails were set, and the *Cap Pilar*, gathering way before the trade-wind, quickly left the native boats astern.

Most of us had kept our wreaths of flowers, and now we threw them into the water and watched them float away out of sight. It was an act full of meaning and of sadness; we were saying good-bye to the South Seas. We were also saying good-bye to the island where our dreams of the South Seas had been transformed into reality. The climax of the cruise had been reached, but it was a worthy one, and, whatever might be the future of the voyage, it had now definitely achieved its objectives. It was with heavy hearts, but also with a feeling of triumph and fulfilment, that we sailed out across the calm lagoon.

With the current strongly astern of us we were through the pass in a flash and out into the open sea. We bore away from the reef, and then made down west of the island. Soon Hao was no more than an unevenly broken line upon the horizon; then it disappeared altogether, and we knew that our next sight of land would be the mountains of Peru, some 5,000 miles to the eastward.

The next six weeks were monotonous and uneventful, except for an epidemic of mild dysentery, which ran through the ship for about six days. The original sufferers had undoubtedly contracted the disease from drinking the banana beer of Hao, which was not brewed under the most hygienic conditions. Everyone in the ship was attacked at some time or other during the earlier part of that passage, and Jane and I were very alarmed in case Jessica should also get ill. We had heard of the dire effects of "summer sickness" on small babies, so we were meticulously careful to keep her away from the smallest chance of infection. One day, however, I found Jane rolling in agony in her bunk; she seemed to be suffering far greater pain than anyone else, but luckily she was better next day, and within a few days more the dysentery had left the ship; so we thought no more about this particular worry until we were very forcibly reminded of it two months later.

We experienced a good deal of light weather during this passage, and also ten days' steady northerly wind, which blew us across 1,600 miles of ocean without a single wavering in force or direction. But, at this stage, it seemed to us all that the fairest flowers had already been plucked, and the realisation that many thousands of miles must still be sailed before we eventually reached home, brought a vague sense of anti-climax to this period of our wanderings. In the forecastle particularly, one or two of the more temperamental spirits began to get on each other's nerves; and the mutual determination to avoid all quarrelling, which had characterised the earlier stages of the cruise, was temporarily allowed to lapse.

No serious disturbances resulted, but one afternoon the acting-cook and galley-boy started arguing about whether one of them had the right to tell the other to stir the pea-soup; it ended in their rushing out on to the main deck together, and going for each other hammer and tongs. The watch on duty, who were working aloft, applauded from the rigging, violently and derisively according to their sympathies; but the rolling of the ship caused many of the blows to miss their mark, and after each combatant had dived once or twice into the scuppers, under the impetus of his own misdirected efforts, they both became so exhausted that the issue had to be abandoned undecided.

As the days slid slowly by the arranging of each week's menu became a problem of a very acute nature. Although we had more than enough of essentials such as meat and flour, the four months which had already elapsed since leaving Auckland had taken a heavy toll of semi-luxuries such as jam, butter, tinned fish, tinned sausages, etc. The greatest hardship was our lack of potatoes and onions, which we had been quite unable to obtain for this part of the voyage, and George was faced with the task of concocting three meals a day out of corned beef, flour, rice, split peas and Lima beans. Of these we had plenty, but practically nothing else.

A typical day's menu was therefore as follows:

Breakfast. Curried beef and rice.
Lunch. Corned beef and fried rice; tapioca pudding.

Supper.   Minced corned beef and Lima beans; suet
pudding and treacle.

This sounds uninteresting, though adequate, for one
day, but when you are presented with varieties on the
same theme for seven consecutive days, and when you
know that it will be the same next week and also the week
after, even the most easy-going of mortals begins to look
about for somebody with whom to start an argument about
it. In the *Cap Pilar* the unfortunate scapegoat was George,
who was also the most suitable butt for everybody's " sug-
gestions ", because he treated them all with an unquench-
able good humour, leavened with just the right admixture
of contempt, to leave their authors something to grumble
about.

After about a month without any fresh meat or
vegetables our bottles of fortified lime juice were in heavy
demand; we longed for just one little grilled chop or a
spoonful of cauliflower; our blood grew meagre, and if
any of us had any sores they healed slowly. The only one
of us not affected by this state of affairs was Jessica.
Luckily Jane had taken a supply of tinned tomato juice
from Auckland to replace the oranges she had had in the
Islands; but apart from that Jessica demanded no special
attention.

Fresh water, of course, had to be strictly rationed, both
for drinking and washing. But we constructed a little
system of dams at the break of the poop; by means of
these, we caught enough rain-water to enable everyone to
have two good washes a week, and rinse out a few clothes
on Sundays as well.

Thirty-five days—thirty-six—thirty-seven. Slowly but
surely the line of dots which marked our daily positions
stretched out across the East Pacific chart, until at last, on
6th February, 1938, forty-four days out from Hao, we
caught sight of the foothills of the Andes, rising above a

bank of white cloud upon the eastern horizon. All that afternoon we stood northward along the Peruvian coast, fascinated by the sight of those historic hills, thinking, some of us, about Pizarro and the Incas, about Dons and pirates and desperate adventures, of stately galleons and gold.

The night fell damp and almost cold, due to the influence of the Humboldt current which sweeps up this coast. We felt a little uncertain of our position, because for many weeks now our wireless set had been out of order, so that we had had no opportunity of checking our chronometer by means of the time signals. But for many hours we continued upon our course, hoping to pick up the loom of the Palaminos light, situated upon an island on the southern side of Callao Bay. As we sailed on the land loomed nearer and nearer, and soon we could see clusters of little twinkling points that marked the villages; but still no friendly flashing gleam to reassure us. At last we dared go no farther, so we hove-to to wait for daylight.

When dawn came we found ourselves within a few miles of Callao. We also discovered that during the night one of the thick low-lying fogs, for which this coast is notorious, had obscured the light itself, while the villages lying more than 100 feet above sea level had been clearly visible at a distance of ten miles!

Our first contact with South America was made through a fisherman. None of us knew Spanish, but we had a pocket Portuguese dictionary, and by means of this we tried to converse with him. We tried to tell him that we had no chart of the Peruvian coast, and to enquire whether Callao harbour was quite open. As we developed our theme with encouraging smiles and gestures, we began to grow more confident, and went on to ask him to send us off a pilot. The fisherman's only answer was a wide gesture that looked suspiciously like one of relief; then he dived into the bottom of the boat, and reappeared holding two fine tunny. We realised that we could expect no other answer to our enquiries, so we cheered him heartily and caught the fish as he flung them aboard.

We spent that afternoon in constructing a rough plan of Callao Bay from the few facts and descriptions contained in the Admiralty *Sailing Directions*. With the aid of this plan and constant soundings we beat into the anchorage without any trouble, except for the half-hour we wasted in carefully avoiding two buoys, which we suspected of marking a wreck; in reality they indicated the deepest part of the main channel itself. No pilot came off to us, so, when it suddenly grew dark, we anchored at once, about half a mile north of the entrance to the inner harbour.

As darkness fell the waterfront of Callao lit up, while in the middle distance the city of Lima blazed into being at the feet of the mighty Andes. Here was civilisation again after five months of escape from it. Some of us were glad, and some were sorry. In any case our return was not too sudden; this, after all, was South American civilisation and Peruvian at that; it was not as though we had been looking at the lights of Hampstead or Muswell Hill.

CHAPTER XXXI
SNOW ON THE ANDES

NEXT MORNING the bay was shrouded in a damp and forbidding mist. Except for the fact that our anchor cable grew stolidly out before us into the slow, brown water we might as easily have been a thousand miles away in the middle of the ocean as at the very portals of a great and gaudy city.

Eventually there appeared a motor-launch bearing a portly individual in glittering uniform and a tall cadaverous man in plain clothes, wearing a broad-rimmed black hat, who turned out to be the medical officer of the port. The doctor refused at first to come aboard, and insisted that everyone should be lined up along the rail for his inspection. When we were all gathered he addressed us, for nearly a minute, in Spanish. No one understood a word of what he said, but his tone plainly suggested that something was amiss. In the end the officer in uniform shouted out in fluent English (or rather American):

"He says: 'You got any stamps—furrin stamps?'"

Instantly everyone dispersed to fish out odd letters and tear off the stamps they did not want. The doctor, thus appeased, came on board and signed all necessary documents without another word. After this I myself signed a declaration that the pilot had conducted our vessel, to our complete satisfaction, into the harbour; and the formalities ended with the usual expressions of goodwill and drinks all round.

We made a more varied collection of friends in Lima than in any other port upon our travels, and we found them without exception the most charming and generous folk. The Pacific Steam Navigation Company, for instance, offered out of the goodness of their hearts to act as our agents in all matters to do with the ship and the formalities of the port. We would have been lost without their unstinted assistance and the influence which they commanded.

Shortly after we arrived three destroyers of the Royal Canadian Navy also called at Callao, and we were caught in the whirl of gaiety which attended their visit. There were receptions and dances, which followed each other in quick succession. At these functions we met so many interesting and important personages that we quite naturally got their various names and occupations hopelessly mixed; many times, during our first week in Peru, we skated perilously upon the very brink of social disaster.

The squalid docklands of Callao, and the mean streets of the water-front, are not a very good preface to a visit to Peru; but as you pick your way through them you smile good-humouredly at the beggars and small boys, confident that Lima—"City of the Kings", built by Pizarro to be the capital of his Peruvian Empire—Lima will be different.

Seated, or more probably standing, in a very modern tramcar, you hurtle over the seven miles of parched earth that separates Lima from its port, at a speed which sometimes reaches over sixty miles per hour. The tramcar sways and lurches against the rails, outstrips all the motor traffic, and goes screaming round the bends. You hold your breath, and marvel at the emotionless expressions on the faces of the peasants who travel beside you. In less than twenty minutes you are passing the rows of dirty, windowless and often roofless red mud-houses that stand like hungry aliens on the outskirts of the city. Only a few moments later you are sailing down a fine broad street and into the Plaza San Martin, a square so spacious and magnificent that it might well be the envy of the proudest city of the world.

There are, if you care to look for them, some fine old houses of the Spanish colonial period, but Lima is mainly a city of very modern buildings. The most famous edifice is the great cathedral; but I must frankly confess that I was disappointed by it. I carried away with me an impression of painted pillars and elaborately fretted woodwork, contained within a hall of immense size, but of no particular shape. Ever since we had first thought of visiting Lima we had been looking forward to seeing in this cathedral the life-size statue of Santa Rosa, fashioned out of solid gold; when we beheld it, however, we were pardonably disappointed to find that it was *painted all over*. There were chapels all down one side of the cathedral, containing other figures in silver and gold, but each of them was completely hidden by paint.

The only figure which was not so decorated lay in a small glass-fronted case near the main entrance; it was the very decayed skeleton of a man. He appeared to have been about 4ft. 6in. in height; his frail and flimsy bones were varnished, which gave them a pathetically tawdry appearance; his head was precariously wired to his body, and now he lay upon his back under the inquiring gaze of any curious sightseer who might enter. Yet these were the remains of the terrible, the invincible Pizarro himself. Outside in the square stood his statue, showing a great bull of a man upon a fiery charger, a convincing memorial to one of the world's mightiest conquerors, Terror of the Incas, and Scourge of the Pacific coast; within the cathedral lay his actual body, an untidy bundle of bones, pointed out to a handful of common tourists by a guide, without even the dignity of a grave to hide his melancholy estate.

Those parts of Lima which have been planned on a grand scale, are grand indeed. There are the great squares with their fountains and statuary, triumphal arches, parks and palaces, and all the pomp befitting a mighty capital; from the city broad avenues, down the centres of which run beds of gaudy flowers, take you out to the residential districts of San Isidro and Miraflores. Here the houses are widely spaced among glorious gardens and age-old groves of olives, some of whose trees are said to be as old as the city itself. In Lima it never rains; or, at least, a short shower of rain in Lima is as rare as a week's continuous sunshine in Manchester; consequently all the public and private gardens are watered by a very elaborate system of irrigation, and they have to be completely submerged from time to time.

In spite of its lordly appearance Lima is a city of engaging contrasts. For instance, the grass in all the parks and gardens is well populated with fleas: everybody who is anybody in Lima (and even those who are not) harbours a flea or two from time to time. The drains and irrigation channels of the city are the undisputed province of a race of enormous rats, some of them as large as well-fed rabbits. But the most hideous, and also the commonest, fauna of Lima are the vultures, which can be seen perched in gruesome clusters in every part of the city; they are in fact, protected by law, because they are extremely efficient scavengers. All the same we could not help feeling that their presence, in large numbers, on a tree in the courtyard of one of the hospitals was in rather doubtful taste.

The most exciting incident of our sojourn in Peru was our journey over the Andes by train. We left the ship at dawn, and reached the station just in time to catch the train at seven o'clock. Of course Jessica had to come with us, so we strapped her cot to a flap-table between two seats.

For the first hour of the journey we trundled through

the dry cotton-fields of the Rimac valley; then the gradient gradually steepened, and soon the train began to wind its way between the reddish-brown foothills, liberally sprinkled with an ugly rash of cactus.

It was a memorable journey; one which took us back through centuries of history in a few hours. Modern buildings of stone and concrete soon disappeared in favour of a compromise between baked mud and corrugated iron, which gave place in its turn to the true *adobe* dwellings of the country Indians. Occasionally, in the less accessible valleys which we passed, whole villages and ruins stood deserted but almost intact, looking very much as thcy must have looked in the days when the Incas ruled. Soon the foothills became mountains, and the climb began in earnest. Immense cliffs hung above us, as we went crawling across the almost perpendicular sides of the valleys. It seemed to us as though even the train was making its first attempt to pick a way amongst those terrible crags: every few minutes it would come to a grinding halt, as though to scratch its head; then suddenly it would go into reverse, rattle over some points, and continue to push its way backwards up the next leg of its zig-zag track. Sometimes it would dive along the side of a gorge, clatter over a bridge at the head of it, and then rattle back along the opposite rock face, arriving after twenty minutes or so at a point little more than a quarter of a mile from where it had started. Occasionally it would fling itself from the canyon side and go swaying across some horrifying abyss upon a slender steel bridge. Thousands of feet below, a ragged ribbon of white marked the course of a torrent, while above us the fierce red cliffs hung, threatening. Once or twice when it seemed as though at any minute we might go toppling into eternity, our faithful little engine plunged (in the nick of time) into the friendly shelter of a tunnel.

About midday the beds of the gorges began to climb up once more to meet us, and it was evident that we were nearing the roof of the world. When we stopped at a station some 13,000 feet above sea-level, a light powdery snow was falling, and the wind was bitterly cold. Even the strongest of us found the rarefied atmosphere too much for him; but there was at least one compensation for enforced inactivity—it was apparently quite impossible, at this altitude, to get drunk. Some of the party made prodigious efforts to achieve this end, but without any apparent success.

From this point onwards the world of everyday receded very rapidly. We saw little knots of picturesque *adobe* hovels perched high up in the remoter gulleys like colonies of limpets. Sometimes the mountainsides near these hamlets were too steep for cultivation, so, perhaps a thousand feet below, would be a cluster of tiny plots, separated and surrounded by loose stone walls, two or three feet thick, which must have taken years to build. Each plot was of a different colour, and they lay here and there against the mountains, like occasional carpets to decorate the wilderness. The hillsides were pitted with little caverns, which marked the entrances to ancient gold and silver mines, probably first worked by the Spanish prospectors of many centuries before. Now and then a few Indians appeared, clad in felt hats and gaily coloured blankets. They were a fierce looking brood: the men lounged about unhampered by any burdens, while the women carried huge bundles, and usually a baby as well, slung in shawls upon their backs. Occasionally also we saw small herds of llamas, trotting by in their disdainful fashion. All this, as far as we were concerned, was life !

The train carried a doctor, who was provided with a bag of oxygen against the dreaded mountain sickness of high altitudes; but only a few of the Cappilarians suffered any inconvenience, while Jessica (as we had been promised) slept fairly peacefully throughout the journey. Early in the afternoon we reached the last of the tunnels, and from it the train ran out upon a desolate plateau covered with watery snow, and hemmed in on all sides by an unbroken rampart of jagged peaks. The next station was Ticlio, where a notice-board announced the highest point on the railway at 15,600 feet.

From here the rivers ran eastward into the Amazon, and we felt that we were already deep in the interior of South America. We soon found that we were also far beyond the influence of " the jolly ole' British Raj, what! " as Scanty, the cabin-boy, was so fond of calling it; for when we reached Huancayo about tea-time, we were surrounded on the platform by a howling mob of Indians, who tried literally to tear our luggage from our hands. We hung grimly on to our possessions, including Jessica and her pram. Just as the situation was beginning to get out of hand, a very ordinary red lorry burst through the ranks of our persecutors, and from it jumped two reassuringly hefty young men. They were Henry and Bill, come to fetch us from the American Magnetic Observatory. With a few deft oaths they extricated us from the rabble, and dumped us, together with our belongings, into various parts of the lorry.

There followed a nightmare drive. It had been raining for several days, and our hosts showed no surprise when they found the first suspension bridge we reached sagging pathetically, from only two of its hawsers, into the river. Out of the water below protruded the roof of a light lorry, while upon the nearer bank stood a little girl, with a jug of beer in her hands, crying bitterly.

Away we drove again, and soon we were hiccoughing across a desert, over which the road was no more than an ill-defined track. Several times we lost our way; soon it grew dark and bitterly cold; Jessica began to cry; we huddled together in the open back of the lorry, trying vainly to brace ourselves against the crashing bumps. For hours we struggled on through the pitch darkness, scrambling down the sides of ravines and battering our way across the moors. Now and again a native village closed round us without warning; there were no people in the streets, no lights, no windows in the houses, no sign of life anywhere, save an occasional skulking figure, or the distant howl of a dog. It was like driving through a city of sepulchres. About 10 o'clock we had to stop for Jane to feed Jessica, who then fortunately went to sleep. And on we went again. Suddenly Willie Marsh yelled: "Where's my parcel with all my things in it—anyone seen it?" No one had. "Strike me, it ain't a bleedin' joke." No one thought it was. Once more silence fell upon us, and we huddled more closely together.

The only high-light of those arduous hours was the indomitable good humour of friend Henry, without whose sunny presence we would have survived with difficulty. At last we found a bridge, and at about 11 P.M. we reached our destination, and went straight to bed.

Next day we did very little because, again on account of the altitude, a three-mile walk was as much as most of us could manage; but within that three miles radius we found a fairyland whose existence no one could have suspected. We found a canyon down whose bed flowed a mighty mountain torrent. We looked from the walls of this canyon upon a little lost world; there were villages and farms which had not changed in appearance for many generations. In a small field a man drove a yoke of oxen harnessed to a plough, formed of nothing but a pointed wooden stake. A little farther along another native squatted by a stream, apparently washing for gold. Along a track stalked a procession of llamas. We could see no way out of the canyon; perhaps the inhabitants had never bothered to look for one.

Of the journey back to Huancayo from the Observatory I need only say that by then the second bridge had followed the first into the river; and that we spent seven hours in search of yet a third bridge, which was happily still intact. Most of those seven hours were occupied in manhandling the lorry through an endless sequence of morasses. Jessica Jane encouraged us from a packing-case, carried from point to point along the roadside by her mother; the natives rode by on donkeys in a marked manner.

From Huancayo the journey down was an exact replica of the journey up, except that it was down.

After our jaunt over the Andes, we spent another week in Peru. We grew very fond of the country and its gay capital, where, although a few concessions were good-naturedly made to European customs, the most satisfactory answer to each of life's problems was still *mañana*. We loved the exhilarating dashes to and from the city in the high-speed tramcar, where the familiar notice: SMOKING IS FORBIDDEN read SMOKING IS FOR . . . , the remainder being covered by an advertisement for a popular brand of cigarettes. We liked to watch the gloating eye-balls of all the males within sight, steadfastly following the progress of each and every female who passed down the street. We began to understand the South American outlook on life, and to enjoy it.

In order to ensure a few months' respite from spending, we decided definitely to make the Galapagos Islands our next objective, and on Saturday the 26th of February, we were ready to sail.

It was precisely four hours before sailing-time when Jane was suddenly taken ill !

For an hour she lay on her bed, suffering agony, and as soon as she felt a little better we took her ashore to the American hospital. The diagnosis was acute appendicitis, necessitating an immediate operation.

It was a great shock, but there was no doubt that, in

spite of Jane's suffering, our guardian angel had once more averted a tragedy: had the attack been delayed by only a few hours we should already have been at sea. With the prevailing wind and the Humboldt current both carrying us irresistibly northwards, it would undoubtedly have taken us many days, perhaps weeks, to reach a port sufficiently civilised to maintain a good hospital. We also learned that Jane's attack of "dysentery" shortly after leaving Hao, had almost certainly been a first bout of appendicitis, and that even on that occasion her life may have hung by a thread.

But we could not possibly afford to let the ship and all her crew remain in Callao until Jane recovered, so there was nothing for it but to leave George to look after her and the baby, while the rest of us continued upon our way.

The operation took place next day, and was entirely successful. On Monday Jane was still grey and hollow-eyed, but definitely feeling better. She was asleep almost all day. About 2.30 in the afternoon I slipped out of the ward and made my way as quickly as possible down to Callao.

In the tram I met Henry from Huancayo Observatory; his cheerful banter was so comforting that I persuaded him to come aboard to see the ship get under way.

CHAPTER XXXII

A GALLEON SAILS FROM CALLAO

OUR CHEERY FAT FRIEND, the pilot, came aboard at 4 P.M. At 4.30 the launch *Casana* plucked us out from among the shipping and left us, with a gentle southerly wind, in the middle of Callao Bay.

At 4 o'clock next morning the light on the Huaura Islands showed up through the haze abeam; at dawn we could see Pelado Island about ten miles away to the eastward. At noon we were seventy-three miles north-west of Callao, and the voyage to the Never-Never Islands had begun.

Tuesday, 1st of March.

Ship painting continues; it looks as though the *Cap Pilar* will have the appearance of a millionaire's yacht by the time we reach the Galapagos.

In the afternoon there was a shoal of bonitos round the ship; Lars caught three, weighing about 20 lb. each.

An hour before sunset dark rain-clouds gathered in the east. Two miles away a huge sword-fish leaped, flashing bright against the cloud bank—Neptune spinning a silver coin.

Wednesday, 2nd of March.

We are running up the coast about twenty miles outside the steamer route. At dawn Mount Mongan was plainly visible abeam and remained in sight most of the day. At noon our day's run was ninety miles. The bonitos and the sword-fish are still with us.

In the evening a steamer came up on our port quarter,

about three miles off. As she passed a dark bank of clouds on the horizon we could see the white spouts from a school of whales bursting all round her. It looked as though she were being shelled.

This evening we got the wireless working, and for the first time for a year and a half, we heard the precise unimpassioned tones of the announcer giving the Empire news from Daventry.

Thursday, 3rd of March.

A giant ray was playing near the ship; leaping and falling back with explosions like gunfire. The sea is alive with fish of every kind. Towards evening a school of four sharks appeared astern—one a monster. We hooked the big one, but had to use our sea-boat lifting gear to get the brute aboard. Nine young sharks, ready to swim, were found inside her.

To-day the wind died away; but we were set nearly forty miles north-west by the Humboldt current, and our day's run was once more ninety miles.

Wireless out of order.

Friday, 4th of March.

The fish still keep company with us, but they are not nearly so numerous. There is hardly any wind to speak of; what there is comes from north of east. Our day's run dropped back to seventy miles, and it looks as though to-morrow's run will be a great deal less.

The wireless was working again to-night; once more we listened to the news from England. There is a depressing sameness about all the news these days.

Saturday, 5th of March.

Another day of light airs. This afternoon Scanty ran the clippers over my head. Close-cropped hair is one of the luxuries of seafaring which I have not been allowed to enjoy during the last eighteen months. Fishing continues.

Sunday, 6th of March.

Sixty miles in the right direction by noon to-day; but very little wind. During the forenoon one of the crew came to see me; he was in a terrible state of nerves. Maggs, who is acting ship's dispenser, decided that he ought to be put in the hospital for a few days. I am a little doubtful as to whether this will do any good, but it is worth trying.

In the evening it fell calm, and we put the dory over the side for Sanson to collect small beasts from the surface of the surrounding ocean.

All through the night we were dead becalmed. We began to wonder whether we should be forced, through shortage of stores, to give up the idea of reaching Panama, and go home round the Horn via Tahiti.

Monday, 7th of March.

Another quiet day. Both Lars and I got a touch of sunstroke. We forgot we had just had our hair cropped. We shall have to wear hats for a bit.

The run to-day was thirty-seven miles; once more the wind died towards sunset, and came off the land at night.

In the evening we went fishing again in the dory. We came across three sword-fish, lying with their curved scimitar-like fins and tails breaking the surface. We tried to stalk them, but they dived.

At dusk we pulled away half a mile ahead of the ship. Here we lay upon our oars.

Our little kingdom drifted slowly down upon us. Slatting of canvas, the rattle of chain sheets and the low murmur of casual conversation floated to us across the darkening waters. We lay in the boat smoking till the *Cap Pilar* came abreast of us.

Tuesday, 8th of March.

Still very little wind, mostly easterly. In the evening I sat on the poop, and talked about law with Donnelly. Now, for a few days I shall want to be a lawyer.

Wednesday, 9th of March.

The wind has definitely gone nor'-easterly now. If we have this weather after leaving the Galapagos, our chances of getting to Panama are very poor.

To-day *The Caterpillar*, " the organ of the forecastle ", was issued. Sanson and Donnelly are the editors; almost every member of the crew has contributed an article, a poem, or a drawing.

Thursday, 10th of March.

During the day the wind worked round to north; in the afternoon we put the ship on the port tack. At 9.30 P.M., after two hours' calm, the breeze came in from south-east once again, and we squared away.

It is several days after the change of the month; already the growing moon fills the night with a silvery breath. We are 300 miles from the coast of South America, but when the breeze goes to east, just before midnight, there is a soft fragrant hint of the land upon it. Last night again I talked for a long time with Donnelly.

Friday, 11th of March.

The current has turned contrary; at noon we had only made fourteen miles since the day before. We got more sights in the evening; we found the set to be still against us.

This evening we got the wireless to work after several

days of silence. Germany has attacked Austria. Perhaps it means nothing, or perhaps it means the end of civilisation; in any case it can't affect us at present, because there is no wind.

Saturday, 12th of March.

To-day the current set us twenty miles due east. If only we were on our way to Panama now, these variable winds and two days of east-going current would just make the difference between an easy passage, and, possibly, months of frustration.

We waited with great excitement for the wireless news to-night; but when it came it brought no declaration of war. Afterwards we all gathered on the poop to talk in the moonlight. Potter was at the wheel; his unemotional presence was very reassuring.

Sunday, 13th of March.

Steadily, at the rate of about forty miles a day, we progress. There were fish round us again: huge bonitos, which the boys hauled over the bowsprit rigging faster than they could be carried in to the deck. During the afternoon the wind freshened.

Monday, 14th of March.

To-day it blew light to moderate from due north. This was the best breeze we have had for over a fortnight. The Galapagos are now about 190 miles away. By midnight it was once more calm.

Tuesday, 15th of March.

Calm again, and only twenty-one miles from noon to noon.

We get London very clearly on the wireless. The Germans have marched into Austria. People are already being hunted all over the country. Hitler in Linz—police precautions—ultimatums. Next Czechoslovakia will be crushed between the two jaws of Greater Germany.

In the evening the wind came in again; this time from the south-east. The sails filled and went to sleep. The ship crept ahead—sweetly, softly, murmuring drowsily. A white moon, nearly full, walked up the sky—setting the sea a-glitter.

Wednesday, 16th of March.

Eleven miles to-day; the current turning westerly. All morning a school of bottle-nosed whales plunged and snorted round about. In the evening a mighty regiment of dolphins came charging down upon us from over the horizon. We could hear the tumult of their approach when they were still three miles away.

Stocks are falling on Wall Street. Franco is advancing. Hitler rages terribly. Mussolini doesn't care. The Japanese are in China, and now there is an "incident" between Poland and Lithuania. But there is still no wind.

Calm—dead calm. Not a breath to ruffle the water, or to smooth the creases from despondent-looking canvas, hanging—just hanging in bags and bundles from the yards. Picture-ship—picture-ocean, and a brilliant, boulderous burning sunset, signifying nothing.

Thursday, 17th of March.

Lars says Finland will never fight on the same side as Russia. Newell and I are definitely going to take up coasting when we get home. Over the wireless, to-night, we heard a debate on "The Road to Peace"; the word "war" occurred 257 times.

And the news? Japan regrets; America is concerned; the situation between Poland and Lithuania has assumed a more serious tone.

Southerly winds to-day, and a laughing sea. By noon

we had covered sixty-seven miles; only seventy-five miles left to go !

In the evening we went out in the dory to catch the little brown crabs which were scuttling about the surface of the sea, at great speed, in all directions.

We took photographs of the ship, and paddled slowly round her. Suddenly Newell said:

" This is what the chaps in the offices think we do all the time; and for once, by God, we're doing it ! "

At 5 o'clock it was quite cool, after a blazing day. Once more the western horizon went up in flames.

Half an hour before sunset there was the cry of " Land-ho ! " which rang out cheerily over the sea. We pulled back to the ship. From her decks the hills of Chatham Island were plainly visible in the nor'-west. We are seventeen days out from Callao to-day. Jane expected a telegram within ten days ! Oh, dear !

Friday, 18th of March.

Chatham Island sits upon the sea, spread out from its central heights like a heap of grey ashes, poured by a careless housemaid in heaven, upon God's immaculate front lawn.

No wind all day ! Only occasional " catspaws " to which we feverishly trimmed our sails. We strained and panted beneath a blazing sun, that, for the tenth time this voyage, passed immediately over our heads at noon. But before we could cast the ship or fill the sails, the flaw had passed by, and left us swinging ponderously round the compass, like a very old man attempting to waltz.

And all day Chatham Island lay squat and barren beside us. We began to loathe the sight of that island.

Saturday, 19th of March.

Dead calm all day; drifting steadily westward. We

may be swept past Wreck Point before the wind finds us again. If so, it might take us weeks to struggle back.

About 5 P.M. Chatham Island was blotted out by a squall of rain, whose greedy grey fingers of cloud reached out towards us, and brought a steady northerly breeze for an hour or so. Later calm again, and in the morning we had gained nothing.

Sunday, 20th of March.

At 6 P.M. we hove-to a few miles off the land. Lars took the lifeboat away with a crew of four men. They had provisions for several days. They were to buoy the channel into Wreck Bay, and stand by until we came.

The wind was moderate northerly. All day the *Cap Pilar* beat up the coast. Lars and his crew accomplished a very difficult and intricate task without a hitch, and at 4 P.M. we stood in towards where they lay. But the wind fell light, and the ebb-tide caught us and carried us down towards Schiavoni reef. For three agonising minutes the *Cap Pilar* hung in stays; then, as always, she paid off on the right tack and we stood out again.

By now the evening squall was black to windward; two more tacks laid us fair into the channel; after that we had little difficulty in " crabbing " down to the anchorage.

CHAPTER XXXIII

PROGRESSO AND WRECK BAY

AT 8 O'CLOCK NEXT MORNING the port officials came aboard, full of shouts and saluting. There were two of them, both exceedingly small, and dressed in dirty but fairly elaborate white uniforms.

They shook hands gravely, then fell to holding their temples and rolling their black eyes as though in pain.

"Very sick, me and Doctor," said one of them. "Last night very plenty whisky."

After routing out some aspirin tablets we proceeded to business. This consisted, on their part, of trying to extract from me £20, which I did not possess, for harbour dues. On my part, it consisted chiefly of trying not to laugh at their agonised expressions. In the end I signed a declaration to the effect that I had not known, before leaving Callao, that the dues in this little harbourless ocean desert would be four times as high as those in the largest port in the world.

The business concluded, we all went ashore. Our departure from the ship was attended by great ceremony, during which the Port doctor turned his head from time to time, and vomited quietly into the sea.

On reaching the shore we set off up the road to Progresso, the "capital" of these parts. The road was a broad, well graded highway, but, like those in the Andes, it was so deep in mud that walking upon it was a prodigious trial of strength.

Progresso itself is somewhat pathetically named. The first building of any size is the wreckage of a factory of some sort—huge boilers, rusted and desolate, sticking out of a tangle of vegetation; the bare iron framework of the structure; a few sheets of corrugated iron, some still attached to the girders, some on the cement beneath, and some lying where they had been blown amongst the scrub. Nothing more remains of some unfortunate pioneer's attempt at progress. There is a church, with only the skeleton of a tower, like the churches in Flanders during the Great War; also one large store, looking like a Swiss mountain post-office on the outside and a cow-shed on the inside.

This latter building appears to be the only weather-proof house of any size in the whole place, and, as in every other community, the store at Progresso is the meeting-place or club of the village. All day there are a dozen or more natives standing about, the women carrying their babies upon their backs, all staring fixedly at nothing. The floor of the place is covered with mud, and everywhere are animals or the signs of animals. Cows, pigs, goats, and even horses are brought inside by their owners, while the whole building is littered with cats and dogs who apparently live, love and fulfil every function of their existence amongst the bags of dry goods piled up at the back of the store.

Presiding over this Palace of Entertainment, we found the manager, in a white suit and white sun-helmet, with black leather boots and leggings. He was a very quiet, apologetic man, who gave one the impression that he was ashamed of not being able to speak English. This was very courteous of him in the circumstances, but also very confusing; because, instead of speaking in Spanish, a few words of which we might have been able to distinguish, he merely whispered more and more softly in some entirely unintelligible jargon of his own invention, at the same time making elaborate gestures, most of which were deprecatory.

However there was a clerk who spoke a little English, and we soon found that both of them had the dollar

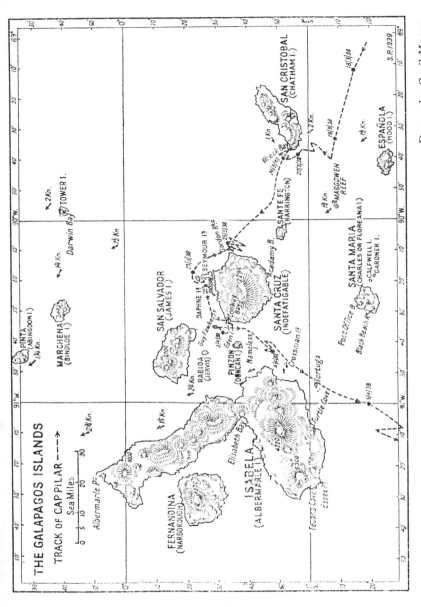

THE GALAPAGOS ISLANDS

TRACK OF CAPPILAR - - - ->

Drawn by Cyril Money

complex. Everything from matches to motor-cars cost a dollar, which would have been all right in its way had there been any motor-cars for sale; but since the most valuable article displayed was a Japanese pocket-knife, bearing the inscription "made in Europe", we had to protest that we were not wealthy Americans, but impecunious Englishmen nearing the end of a long cruise.

This candid statement of facts so overloaded the apologetic manager with a sense of unworthiness that his whispering trailed off into silence as he dumbly begged us to help ourselves, and in the end we were supplied with what we required at less than a quarter of the original price asked.

We had all imagined, before reaching the Galapagos, that they would be dry, parched, and barren. This was true of the coastal districts, but on the higher ground there was a healthy rain squall every evening at this time of year, and the whole countryside looked wonderfully green and fertile. On the way up to Progresso the track was lined with orange-trees, upon which there must have hung as much fruit as leaves. When we enquired the price of oranges we were laughingly told to bring sacks from the ship and gather as much fruit as we could carry away. Apart from the oranges, fresh meat was the least expensive item on our store-list. It cost us three farthings a pound! All the Galapagos cattle were wild, like the Marquesan herds, and had to be stalked and shot. The meat was subsequently cut up and hung in a shed, which was black with flies and stank horribly. This unhygienic treatment of the meat was, however, of no importance, since there is no disease, not even malaria, in these islands.

Most of the dwellings in the village are Indian hovels —very primitive, but apparently in good repair. They consist of open-work walls of sticks and posts, surmounted by thatched roofs. On account of their simple design they require little or no upkeep. The village street is, during the rainy months, a sea of mud; this mud seems to flow through the sides and in at the doors of the huts, where it is trodden into a soft smooth floor by the inhabitants. Garbage is strewn about near the dwellings, but all the Indians and their children appear to be remarkably healthy.

Beyond the village, surrounded by citrus-trees and plantains, we could see the corrugated-iron roofs of one or two European homes. Poor things—they looked hopelessly dilapidated. They were far too large for their owners to keep in repair, and their soft pine planking cried out for paint and oil. They seemed out of place in the jungle—pretentious and in ruins.

At Progresso—surely the last place on earth—we met a very fine gentleman and his charming wife. They were Monsieur and Madame Kobos. Monsieur was an Equadorian, brought up in the Galapagos and educated in Paris; his father had at one time been governor of the island, but subsequently lost his life during a revolt among the convicts. Madame was none other than the beautiful Norwegian girl spoken of by Robinson in *Deep Water and Shoal*. Karin is still very beautiful, although she is now the mother of four fine children, and looks after the house and family unaided.

Karin, her parents, and two or three others are the only survivors of a party of 300 Norwegians who tried to found a colony in Galapagos in 1926. The rest, we were told, returned to Scandinavia as soon as they discovered that life in the tropics demanded more hard work and less lotus-eating than they had imagined.

After ordering 20 lb. of beef for the ship Lars and I bought biscuits and chocolate for our lunch, and also, to our surprise, a bottle of tolerable beer. We decided that we were tired of walking, so, after once more firmly suppressing the dollar instincts of the manager, we arranged for two horses to be ready for us in half an hour. Our ride down to the beach was uneventful but very exhilarating. As soon as we reached the level ground at the bottom of the hill we found our horses eager to break into a canter; we arrived upon the beach in a cloud of sand and loose stones, like a couple of six-inch shells.

Apart from the inhabitants of Progresso there are quite a number of convicts on the Galapagos Islands; we were surprised by the lenient way in which they were treated. While Lars and I were waiting for a boat we sat and watched a group of prisoners being exercised on the beach. One youngster chose to be refractory, so his unfortunate gaoler was obliged to push him all the way round the track, thereby doing a double dose of punishment drill himself.

We spent three days in Wreck Bay. On our last evening there, M. Kobos took me up to Progresso to buy some pigs, which we intended to take away alive. It was pitch-dark by the time we reached the settlement. We picked our way carefully, I on horseback and Kobos on foot. When we arrived outside a native dwelling, Kobos spoke quietly into the darkness. He was answered by the dull querulous voice of a woman. Suddenly a light appeared: it was a girl with an oil-lamp. She crawled under the house and succeeded in driving out a few pigs and some chickens. I chose three of the pigs and twelve chickens; then without any further bargaining, we rode away.

Next day at six, through the breathless morning air, came the squealing of the three pigs, which had been brought down to the beach near the ship. We took the lifeboat inshore to collect the unhappy trussed-up animals, whose screams of rage echoed all round the settlement.

After breakfast I went to fetch the ship's papers, and to say good-bye to the Governor. By 10 o'clock there was a steady sea-breeze blowing up the coast, so we got under way and sailed out clear of the reef.

Navigating among the Galapagos Islands in a sailing ship is an exciting game. During the whole ten days we spent there the wind was light and fitful, except right inshore; and the current swirled westward through the group at between one and three knots—far too strongly for the boats to be of any use in pulling the *Cap Pilar* to safety when she got becalmed in a dangerous position. In many channels between the islands the tide eddies were so violent that, even with a moderate breeze, it was impossible to keep the ship under command. To add to our difficulties, there were a great many inaccuracies in our charts; several islands were marked a mile or more out of position.

We tried to work down the east coast of Santa Cruz Island to Academy Bay, but a nerve-racking twenty four hours, during part of which we were being swept up and down a reef-girt lee shore, in the darkness, by successive tides, persuaded us to give up the attempt. Instead, we visited the Seymour Islands, on the north side of Santa Cruz, where we had to make use of a "hearsay" anchorage, since there was none shown on our chart. Our only guide was a long sandy beach which we had heard casually described by an old beachcomber, when deeply under the influence of whisky.

We managed, however, to sound our way into a comfortable berth in nine fathoms, about half a mile off-shore.

CHAPTER XXXIV
THE NEVER-NEVER ISLANDS

IMMEDIATELY AFTER TEA we launched the dories and made for the beach. When still a hundred yards off we were greeted by a terrific uproar from a large colony of seals, who seemed to resent our arrival without being very much alarmed by it. Several males of various sizes swam out to meet the boat. They burst from the water all round us, poking up their fierce whiskery little heads and blowing prodigiously like indignant Clubmen.

On the beach the old cows rolled upon the sand with their babies; when we got ashore they did no more than bellow at us, without even bothering to waddle into the water until we walked right up to them. The irrepressible Peter Roach found an old cow-seal asleep on the sand, so he carefully lay down beside her and got Willie Marsh to take their photograph. He said that he would be ashamed to call himself a sailor without proof that he had a wife in every port.

When we had tired of watching the seals we turned inland. The sun was about to set; already there was a feeling of dusk in the air. As we set off across the wilderness of twisted volcanic rock a strange excitement possessed us. We might have been the first explorers to set foot upon a forgotten world. The island was covered with huge boulders of lava and fields of red pumice-stone, amongst which a little scrub grew sparsely. Here and there, above the rocks, a few gaunt, misshapen cacti raised their bloated heads. Occasionally a bird would flutter twittering before us, to disappear in the fading light. Our talk shattered the silence, like the voices of children singing in the dark.

Suddenly there was a ferocious guttural hiss from the rocks ahead; we stopped as if turned to stone. Sitting upon a boulder a few yards away, was a dragon!

He was the first dragon we had ever seen; but in every respect, except in size, he came well up to fairy-tale standards, and we now knew that we were indeed in another world. The monster which confronted us was about four feet long, with an ugly head, dangerous-looking mouth filled with sharp teeth, and a row of spikes running down his backbone. In colour he was yellow, orange, green and black, in patches all over his tough scaly hide. He hissed and spat at us furiously; one could almost imagine the smoke pouring out of his nostrils.

Although the Equator passes through the Galapagos group, we did not find them too hot, nor too damp, nor in any way oppressive. There is very little fresh water on the islands, and the vegetation is mostly scrub, but for us this disadvantage was more than balanced by their remoteness from civilisation.

And the fish! The ocean in these parts was teeming with fish of every fantastic shape and shade. White fish, blue fish, yellow ones, scarlet ones; fish of every imaginable colour or combination of colours. Round ones, flat ones, long ones, spiky ones, fish with teeth and fish with suckers; fish without tails, fish in tail-coats, fish in frills and fish in flowing gowns; fish like flowers, and fish like nightmares. And, all in their hundreds and thousands together, they flapped, fluttered and drilled among the coral, like clouds of confetti or autumn leaves.

After a while most of us were content to take the shore for granted and to devote ourselves entirely to the fishing. All our boats were in constant use—lifeboat, gig, two dories, dinghy, and an outrigger canoe (acquired by Roach in Hao, in exchange for an old gramophone). We took with us a flour-tin, into the bottom of which Potter had fitted a glass panel; when this was pushed into the water, you could see through it every detail of the sea floor in a depth of six or seven fathoms; we could actually *watch* the fish taking our bait. At noon each day, when the boats returned, they contained several hundred pounds of fish, which we then set about gutting and salting against the long windless voyage to Panama.

One morning Roach and Power took the outrigger over the reefs; but had to come back within two hours, because the weight of fish in the boat threatened to sink it, and there were several large sharks nosing round them.

In the lifeboat we went crunching our ponderous way between the islands. We sailed into coves and through the channels which, we thought, might never have been visited before. We were filled with a childish excitement at the rounding of each little headland, and every time we ran the boat in upon the sandy beaches between.

One day, when we were out pulling, we came across a shoal of large mullet, feeding on the surface. Immediately Newell, who is still a great stickler for naval procedure, decided that the lifeboat was now an armed transport, and set about engaging the enemy with his forward turret—Willie Marsh with a point-22 rifle. For the next half-hour we fought a thrilling action. We had two rook rifles, one forward and one aft, with which we blazed away about fifty rounds of ammunition, while the rowers pulled or backed furiously, trying to keep near the elusive shoal of fish. As each fish never showed more than an oval patch, about three inches long, above the surface, they were a very sporting target from a poppling lifeboat.

These days amongst the islands were quite unspoiled by any anxieties; there is really nothing a man could worry about in the Galapagos Islands. Most of the crew discarded all clothes, which seemed out of place among such wild surroundings. We spent three days on the

SUBAQUEOUS FANTASY
OR MARINE BIOLOGIST'S NIGHTMARE

Drawn by John Donnelly, *Boatswain*

Seymours, and another three in Conway Bay, on the western side of Santa Cruz.

At dawn on Sunday, 3rd of April we weighed and stood out to sea. At first we made up quite well along the western shore of Santa Cruz; but in the middle of the forenoon the tide turned, and we began to drift back again at over a knot. At 3 P.M. came a fresh land breeze with rain, and once more we went scurrying away down the coast. We made good headway until 6 P.M.; if only the wind had held for half an hour longer we should have been through the narrow channel between Nameless Island and the shore. But, just as darkness came, the wind died right away and we were left at the mercy of the current. Suddenly a powerful cross eddy caught us, and we began to drive straight towards the vertical-sided pinnacle of Nameless.

In the darkness it was impossible to see how close we actually passed; but, every minute, the roar of the surf upon the cliffs grew louder, and soon we could hear the barking of seals. It seemed as though we had ten minutes' grace at most before being dashed helpless against the cliffs.

At the last moment, however, the current appeared suddenly to split, and to pass round on each side of the island. Slowly the bearing of the cliff edge began to alter, until finally we were swept right round the rock into the open sea and safety on the other side.

For the next three days we struggled with fickle winds to claw off the land; but the current, which set strongly to the south-west down the coast of Isabela Island, was more than a match for us; we kept our anchors clear for instant use, and hoped for the best. We drifted down less than a mile off the Crossman Islands and half a mile from Tortuga.

We were bound for the island of Santa Maria, southernmost of the group, where the mysterious Baroness ——

was reputed to have lived with her five husbands. It was said that this Amazon ruled her " harem " with whip, gun, and a powerful forearm, and that they all existed in a state of complete barbarity. There had recently been rumours that one of the husbands had succeeded in escaping from his mistress, and that she had been murdered by two of the others; but no news from the island had reached Progresso for some months, so we were looking forward with considerable interest to finding out the true state of affairs.

At 9 A.M. on 5th of April the wind came in light but steady from E.S.E., and at last we stood away clear of the land. Santa Maria was visible about forty miles away to windward; it stood out bold and inviting upon the horizon. But during the afternoon the current dragged us away to the southward, and we never saw Santa Maria again, nor do we know to this day the fate of the hard-boiled Baroness ——.

CHAPTER XXXV
DRIFTING ON

April 6th.

We are now in such a good position from which to lay up to Panama that we have abandoned all idea of visiting Santa Maria, and decided to take full advantage of this lucky swirl of the current.

April 7th.

Dead calm again to-day, but a strong southerly current. For the last thirty-six hours we have noticed a remarkable phenomenon in the behaviour of the ship—she has been edging very gently astern. We are quite unable to account for this, as she does not cast in either direction.

Suddenly, about six bells in the afternoon, a huge fin broke surface close aboard on the port quarter. All hands, and Claude Maggs with his cameras, crowded to the ship's side; in a moment or two the dim outlines of a fantastic monster could be seen approaching the ship at a depth of about six feet. His movements were so slow as to be almost imperceptible, and he was of such a vast bulk and loathsome appearance that for fully a minute we all stood breathless with superstitious horror while he drifted upon us like an impending doom.

He turned out to be a whale shark, thirty-five feet long (one-third the length of the ship) and probably weighing about fifteen tons. He was obviously quite blind and harmless, but I am sure that none of us will ever see a more terrifying sight. His sinister sluggish movements and fantastic size were enough to make one's hair bristle; his body was covered with a rash of white spots. His mouth was fringed with loose and bestial-looking lips; in and out of it there swam and slithered obscenely white sucker-fish, like snakes on the Gorgon's head. He was the incarnation of blind brutality; the spirit of all earthly frightfulness.

For an hour or more we tried to catch the brute, and after repeated attempts we succeeded in manœuvring a noose of 2½-inch hemp so that he swam right into it. Immediately there was wild excitement; three men started hauling for all they were worth; the rest of us screamed like school children. But the moment he felt the weight of the rope upon his back the shark gathered way, so that the noose only closed on the extreme tip of his tail. For a few seconds the rope went humming taut, then it slipped clear, and the shark disappeared.

Almost immediately a light breeze came in to us from the north-east, and all that night we made good progress towards the South America coast.

April 8th.

The wind still blows steadily from the north-east; during the forenoon it has freshened into a merry breeze. By noon we had made seventy-seven miles, S. 31° E., since yesterday.

April 9th.

To-day we made sixty-four miles S. 39° E. The current is still with us, but the wind has fallen away.

At midday the sky clouded over; it rained all the evening. At sunset the wind hauled to E.S.E. so we went about, and were soon doing four knots N.E. on the other tack.

At tea-time to-day Scanty informed us that we had eaten our jam rations. We are not entitled to any more for three weeks.

If all goes well we should reach Panama about the middle of May.

Sunday, April 10*th.*

After a night of calms, rain squalls, and very variable easterly winds, we found at noon to-day that we had made sixteen miles due east.

The electric generator has failed for the first time for nearly two years. We shall have to depend on paraffin lamps and candles for a day or two.

This week McDonald is in his galley; "all's right with the world." I had a bet with Newell that we shall arrive in Balboa on 12th of May at 4 P.M.

April 11*th.*

The wind is still light and variable; but we've made another twenty-six miles N. 60° E. This week's best photograph: Don Alexander painting ship in nothing but a pair of shoes and tweed cap.

April 12*th.*

Trade wind at last! Forty-eight hours of this and we shall be across the Humboldt current.

For the past two days Lars has been in one of his morose moods, which usually mean that he has an incipient boil.

To-day they cleaned out the after-peak and sprayed it with creosote. The creosote hurts your lungs and eyes, so that you have to come up for air every few minutes. We shall put the sails in the after-peak.

April 13*th.*

The wind holds. By noon we had made seventy miles E.N. against nineteen miles of sou'-westerly current.

Lars has recovered his good humour, and has set the crew to touching up paintwork.

Willie Marsh brought me two badly mutilated ship's chisels; there was a gathering of the clan about them. I hope it will be all right; but the trouble has always been that the good men never do any wrong, while the scaly ones are apt to be incorrigible.

April 14th.

During the night the wind turned ahead; in the early morning we were obliged to go about and lay S.S.E., but not before we had made sixty good miles on the other tack.

The wind turned fair before midday, but it continues very unsteady with frequent squalls of heavy rain.

April 15th.

Good Friday, and so a holiday. The water this morning was very green, and much colder than usual, which shows that we are now in the Humboldt current. Sure enough at noon we had been set thirty-five miles N.W.

In bed to-night I started reading *Pepys's Diary*, whose cheerful complacence I find very restful.

April 16th.

The water temperature has dropped from 78° to 72°, and the air is quite fresh, so we put on our jackets after tea; during the night several of the boys wore overcoats at the wheel. We are seventy miles south of the Equator!

This afternoon our first pig was shot and butchered by Power and Roach.

Easter Sunday.

To-day we made eighty-five miles N. 50° E.; this evening our star sights showed that the current is trending a little east of north. We had roast pork, tinned spinach, tinned tomatoes, and red wine for supper. Afterwards Lars and I strolled up and down the poop talking of Finland and the Baltic.

The wireless has conked-out again; I don't suppose we shall get any more news this trip.

April 18th.

To-day we cross the Equator in 84° 20′ W. Lars's chief job at the moment is cleaning out the ship below decks. In the last few days tons of junk and rubbish have gone over the side. At 10 P.M. the wind went to south and freshened a little, increasing our speed from four to five knots.

April 19th.

Owing to the fact that the Sons of Neptune now out-number the uninitiated by 2 to 1, there was a proper Crossing the Line ceremony to-day.

With one of our foresails we rigged a large bath on the main deck; across this was laid the main boom.

Newell was King Neptune, and Jack Power was dressed as his queen; although the latter wore an inch or two of beard, his appearance was almost alluring.

Sanson was very realistically got up as a broken-down, drink-sodden quack, Willie Marsh was the barber, McDonald in charge of the whitewash spray, Roach and Jim Grant painters. Lethbridge did some very telling work with a bag of mouldy flour and a bucket of molasses.

The procedure was to bring each victim before King Neptune, who immediately ordered him to be washed. Thereupon he was ducked, painted, plastered with flour and treacle, sprayed with whitewash, lathered, shaved and finally ducked again. After this he was either made to sing, fight, or feed another victim with treacle, blindfold; this last punishment gave the best sport of all, but it only occurred once; on that occasion Blue tipped the entire bucket of treacle over Nobby Clayton's head.

The ceremony ended with a free fight.

April 20th.

At 6.40 A.M. the cat fell overboard. The ship was thrown into the wind, a dory cleared away, and by 6.55

the ship, complete with cat and dory, was once more upon her course.

The current is now easterly. At last we are safely out of the influence of the Humboldt. We have had wonderful luck; if things had gone differently we might easily have been swept away into the Doldrums, to lie there rotting for months.

April 21st.

To-day we logged sixty-two miles. In the evening we sighted the masthead lights of a steamer over the south-eastern horizon.

April 22nd.

The ship is now clear and clean below decks. In the afternoon we sighted a steamer on our port quarter. We stood over towards her and managed to attract her attention. She was the American S.S. *Lebore*. She agreed to send my radio telegram to Jane. We signalled that we expected to reach Balboa (at the southern end of the canal) on the 1st of May.

Before we had completed the message the wind hauled to N.W. and died away.

April 23rd.

Only twenty-five miles to-day. This afternoon our second pig, looking even sleeker and fatter than the first, was killed by Roach and Power.

Sunday, April 24th.

Thirty-seven miles to-day—no current. Pork, tinned carrots, and tomatoes for all meals.

April 25th.

Almost dead calm all day. In the evening the dory was

put over the side. Our star sights showed ten miles of
favourable current since noon.

April 26th.

Still no wind. Soon after lunch we sighted a steamer
bound south. We tried for half an hour to attract her
attention, but she did not stop. In the evening we raised
Cape Corrientes, thirty-five miles away to the nor'-east-
ward!

A hawk, which had been roosting on the t'gallant
yard, flew away as soon as we sighted land.

April 27th.

At dawn we were well in upon the coast of Colombia.
At about 6 A.M. it fell calm. At 9 o'clock Sanson noticed
some water snakes in a patch of debris which floated
past. We launched one of the dories. It soon returned
with a snake, which looked quite harmless. Sanson told
us that *all* sea snakes are venomous.

During the forenoon a large flying-boat passed us,
about five miles away to port. It was bound down to
Guayaquil in Ecuador. In the evening it passed us again
on its way back to Panama. Our position had not altered.

April 28th.

To-day, at noon, we were off the precipitous black
coast of the state of Panama, abreast of Ardita Bay. We
had made another sixty miles towards our journey's end.

April 29th.

In the evening we entered the eastern channel into
Panama Bay, with Cape Escarpado close aboard to starboard. Until 10 P.M. it was flat calm; we watched our
landmarks anxiously; but later the wind came sweetly
off the shore, and we stood away as we liked to the nor'-
rard.

April 30th.

At dawn we were well up the channel in amongst the islands of Las Perlas. It was a wonderful morning: hard slate-blue mountains and little tufts of cloud, like white handkerchiefs in the breast pockets of the hills.

In the afternoon we came in with a fleet of coasting schooners; for the first time in the whole voyage we had to remember the sailing ship rule of the road. At times we found these rules rather difficult to interpret; the wind was from the south, but every now and then a fresh squall would come sweeping down off the mountains, accompanied by heavy rain. On one occasion, when we had to brace up on the starboard tack for one of these squalls, we noticed, just before the rain blotted her out, that a schooner ahead, coming directly towards us, was also on the starboard tack.

May 1st.

All day we drifted down the northern shores of the bay, with the islands of the Perlas Archipelago clustered between us and the ocean. Pizarro had also sailed these waters in a ship about the size of the *Cap Pilar*. For seventy days he had beat doggedly against the trade winds and the current, before being compelled to give up the attempt. Then he marched his army through the jungles and over the mountains to the conquest of Peru. They must have been wearing steel armour on that march; how did they survive in such a jungle, over such mountains, and, above all, in such a climate?

By the middle of the afternoon we were nearing the fortress which guards the southern end of the Panama canal. As we looked out towards the islands and beyond them to the horizon we wondered how many of us, clerks, carpenters, builders, schoolmasters and the rest, would ever see the Pacific again.

Then another squall crept out to us, and filled our lazy

canvas. The little *Cap Pilar* heeled to the wind and drove ahead. Five minutes later we reached the anchorage. With the black fingers of the squall-cloud already curling above us to gather us in, our cable went clattering through the hawse-pipe.

At the very instant that the anchor touched bottom, a terrific explosion shattered the evening silence, and a vivid dagger of lightning streaked down our foremast. Potter, who was standing with one foot on the bight of the anchor cable, was thrown violently to the deck, but luckily no one was hurt. It was as though the heavens had fired a cannon to mark the end of our eight months' trek across the Pacific.

PART V

PANAMA AND THE SPANISH MAIN

CHAPTER XXXVI

THE RED EYE OF CAYMAN

THE CANAL MUST BE the hardest beset garrison of civilisation in the whole world. From Balboa, in the south, it marches boldly, flanked by its bodyguard of watch-towers and impressive concrete battlements, against the hosts of the jungle; only to disappear, before it has gone fifteen miles, among the waters of Gatun Lake. Twenty-five miles farther on it suddenly emerges at the head of a mighty stairway of locks, down which it steps in triumph, though a little self-consciously, like an only-just-victorious warrior, into the Atlantic.

The towns of Cristobal and Balboa, at the two ends of the Canal, a narrow strip of territory on either side of it and also a railway, are the property of the U.S.A. Panama City and Colon, which adjoin Balboa, and Cristobal respectively, belong to the Republic of Panama. The jungle is in undisputed possession of everything else.

We spent a week in Balboa, during which we beached the *Cap Pilar* on a mudbank to clean her, and once again we made a great many friends. If the reader is beginning to grow tired of hearing about the numbers of kind people we met wherever we went I can only assure him that we never wearied of meeting them. The officials of the Canal Zone (which meant everyone) were so tirelessly helpful and considerate that we felt a secret shame. We realised that we had allowed ourselves, on the slenderest evidence, to imagine that all Americans must be loud-mouthed, swaggering fellows, while actually all those we met were particularly quiet and courteous. We tried to give the Canal authorities as little trouble as possible, but they none the less insisted on working out elaborate schemes for reducing our charges to a minimum; it seemed that nothing which might help us in the smallest way was too much trouble for them. We hoped that in return we were able to convince some of our American friends that Englishmen do not habitually drink afternoon tea dressed in dinner jackets, nor refuse to call a spade a spade until they have been introduced to it.

In Panama the people live on ice. I do not mean that their diet consists exclusively of frozen water, but that every morsel of food they eat is brought in refrigerated ships, direct from the United States. Potatoes, greens, eggs, milk, butter, meat, fish, fruit—all come from the U.S.A. in cold storage, everything else is brought in tins.

By the time we reached Panama our supply of stores had run very low, so we laid in a complete fresh stock of provisions—enough to last us for the rest of the voyage. We found these provisions to be the best we had ever obtained, nor were they by any means the most expensive. Food for twenty-five people for three months cost us £120, exactly 8s. per head, per week.

On Saturday morning, 7th of May, we were taken in tow by two small launches, and escorted into the first of the great locks at Miraflores. The gates closed; the water swirled round us; in complete silence the *Cap Pilar* was lifted bodily out of the Pacific Ocean into the continent of America. Hardly a word was spoken between ship and shore during the whole of that remarkable journey. Powerful electric " mules " sent their wires aboard; they dragged us quickly through the Miraflores and Pedro Miguel locks, while ahead and astern of us and beside us steamers of all sorts, from tramps to 20,000-ton liners, followed exactly the same procedure.

About tea-time we anchored for the week-end in a

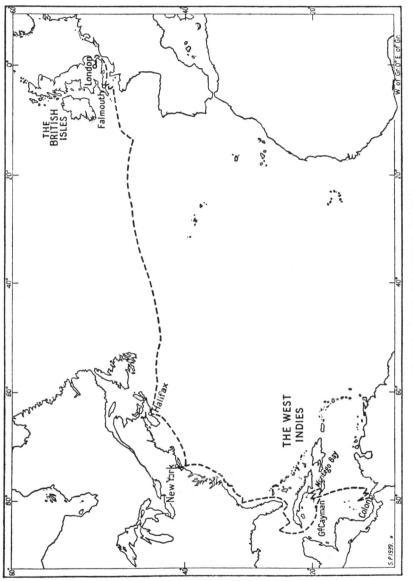

PANAMA AND SPANISH MAIN

shallow bight near the railway station of Gamboa; even before the launches had departed we already had visitors from the shore.

Extract from *The Caterpillar:*

OUR IMPOSSIBLE VISITORS

" Which way does the ship go ? "

" Do you do much night sailing ? "

" Are you really one big happy family ? "

" Did you go by train from Sydney to New Zealand ? "

" You come from South Africa ? But you're not black, are you ? "

" Do you ever have to go up on the cross-bars ? "

Among our visitors were three merry, freckled-faced American schoolboys, who might have jumped straight out of a story by Mark Twain; they wanted to take us alligator hunting. We arranged to have our gig and life-boat in the water ready to start at nightfall.

At 7 P.M. Jake, the eldest schoolboy, and his pals were once more aboard, this time armed with electric torches and two wire nooses attached to the ends of sticks. We asked them whether we ought to take guns, but they were almost offended by the suggestion: "We always catch 'gators alive with these nooses," they said; "there ain't no sense in killing 'em."

It was a night of bright moonlight—really too bright for hunting alligators. Jake thought it was unlikely that we should actually catch any; but he promised us that we would see one.

There was not a breath of wind as we shipped our oars and pulled towards the jungle. The water " guggled " quietly against the boat; the steady " chunk " of the oars beat out over the surface of the lake, upon which lay a silvery haze shot with moonlight. When we had gone a few hundred yards from the ship Jake stood up in the bows to guide us in and out through a forest of tree-stumps, sticking weirdly out of the flat black water. In another ten minutes we reached the edge of the forest. We lay upon our oars, and drifted silently in beneath the trees.

For several minutes nobody spoke. The dank smell of rotting wood poured out of the jungle. We sat peering into the night. Suddenly the beam of Jake's electric torch shot out ahead of us. It wavered along the bank into the black shadows beneath the trees, swung out over the lake, then back again under the trees, backwards and forwards. All at once it hesitated, then remained fixed on a point about fifty yards away. " 'Gator ! " came a harsh whisper; we shuddered with excitement. We followed the direction of the beam; there, at the end of it we saw, glowing fiercely like a warning in the darkness, the twin red eyes of Cayman.

Under the hoarsely whispered commands of our young leader the boat crept silently forward; but at the first dip of the oars the eyes vanished, as though instantaneously switched off.

We relaxed and paddled on. Soon we saw another pair of eyes, and then another; but we were never able to get nearer than a boat's length from them before they dropped, without a ripple, below the surface. About half a mile farther on we came to an opening in the trees which marked the mouth of a backwater. We turned inland, and the jungle closed over us and around us. For a while we pushed cautiously through the gloom, until at last the trees parted overhead and the waterway broadened. The backwater led us farther and farther from the Canal; the boats went swishing through fields of water lilies; we passed the derelict hull of a ship, whose uneven timbers stuck gruesomely out of the mud, like the ribs of some huge prehistoric animal.

A little way on, the channel narrowed once again;

soon we could make no more progress. For a few minutes we sat smoking and listening to the voices of the jungle which began to wake in the trees around us. The forest seemed to be full of birds; harsh grating cries, weird rattles, and an oft-repeated single note, like the striking of a deep ship's bell, rang out and were answered.

Suddenly Jake held up his hand: "There's an ocelot out hunting to-night," he said dramatically. We listened in silence; none of us knew what to expect—the roar of a ravenous tiger or the yowling of a love-sick tom-cat.

A piteous cry like the wail of a tiny baby broke the stillness: "There he goes," whispered Jake, "he sounds hungry." I felt the hair creeping on my scalp; so frail, so eerie a plaint in the darkness, seemed to double its menace.

The moon was now well up, and our boats glistened white against the forest. Jake thought it unlikely that we should see any more alligators that night, so we drove the boats in through the lilies towards the bank. No sooner had we laid aside our oars than there came a hoarse cry of: "Light! Light! Give me the light!" We held our breath. There was dead silence, as Jake leaned gingerly forward over the bows. Suddenly: "Got 'im," yelled Jake. With visions of a threshing, snarling monster and the water lashed to bloodstained foam for twenty yards around we crowded forward to his assistance. But he needed no help. Aloft, in one hand, he bore triumphantly his wriggling capture; it was a baby alligator, perfect in every detail, but exactly seven inches long. In spite of everything our alligator hunt had been a success.

On Monday morning the launches once more took us in tow, and for an hour or two we plodded over the desolate expanses of Gatun Lake. On either hand the jungle stretched away unbroken to the distant hilltops.

Most of the lake had once been forest too; wide expanses of it, which were filled with tree-stumps, like fields of anti-tank defences, testified to the only mistake made by the men who had cut the Panama Canal. Apparently it had been considered unnecessary to clear the jungle before flooding the area which is now Gatun Lake; it was assumed that the water itself would soon rot away the trees. In actual fact they had become petrified instead of decaying, with the result that no boat can now stray far from the limits of the dredged channel, without the risk of being impaled on these stone-hard spikes.

We reached the farther shore of the lake and dropped quickly and silently through the locks into the sea. Beside us a cruising liner popped as unconcernedly up into the lake. Half an hour later we anchored off the wharves of Colon.

We spent only five days in Colon; it is doubtful whether we could have stood even one more. I do not remember that the sun shone for more than half an hour a day during the whole of that week, yet the steamy, sweltering heat was overpowering. From early morning until night our clothes clung to our bodies. Colon was the only port we visited in which we definitely suffered from the tropical climate; in fact it will interest most people to know that during our whole two years of voyaging, including a year in the tropics, the thermometer in the *Cap Pilar's* chart-house never once registered more than 91° F.

The day after the *Cap Pilar* reached Colon the Italian liner *Orazio* brought Jane, George, and Jessica Jane from Peru. Newell and I travelled back by rail to Balboa to meet them.

It had been two and a half months since I had seen Jessica; she had grown almost beyond recognition. When I burst into their cabin she gave me one sour look, then howled with indignation at the sight of me. She was over nine months old, and could very nearly walk.

They had all travelled third class on the steamer, and Jessica had been a great favourite with the crew. One evening Jane had returned from dinner to find Jessica's bunk empty. After searching anxiously through the third class accommodation, she eventually found her baby in the firemen's forecastle. Jessica was being dandled upon the knee of a grimy stoker, while his messmates did their best to amuse her with comical faces and animal noises.

On 14th of May we hove up, and beat laboriously out between the breakwaters into the Caribbean; our next port was to be Kingston, Jamaica. There was a fresh trade wind coming in from the north-east, kicking up an awkward cross sea, which set the *Cap Pilar* jumping like an ill-tempered bronco. This was the first sea we had met for over half a year, so it was not long before many of the ship's company began to feel once more the first stirrings of a malaise which they had hoped never to know again.

For five weary days the *Cap Pilar* thrashed doggedly into the teeth of a relentless weather. We found that the whole nature of the voyage had once more changed: not only had we passed from the Pacific into what seemed almost like home waters; but the long peaceful caravanings across thousands of miles of ocean had given place to a state of affairs in which a new country lay before us at every tack. In the evening we turned from the mountains of Panama, and next day at noon Costa Rica was under our lee: Colombia, Nicaragua and Honduras; we approached each in turn within a period of a few days. We were sailing, like the pirates of old, upon the Spanish Main; romantic-sounding names such as the Gulf of Darien, Baranquilla and Pearl Cay Lagoon

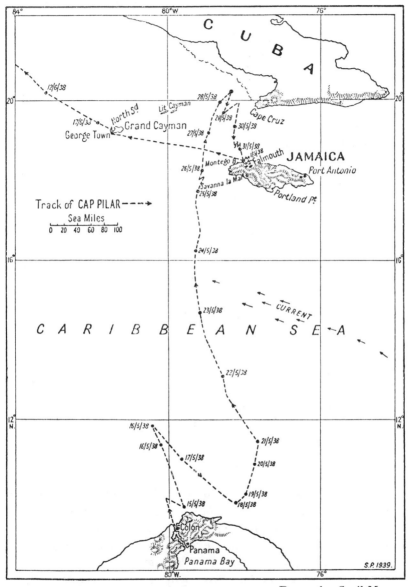

Drawn by Cyril Money

PANAMA TO JAMAICA

appeared upon our charts; we liked to keep a look-out for patrolling frigates, and to train imaginary cannon upon the merchant ships who passed us.

On the fifth day out we were a hundred miles west of Cartagena; here at last the wind fell light and uncertain. We had hoped to make good easting under the influence of a counter-current, running along the southern shores of the Caribbean, and then to dive northwards across the powerful main west-going stream, in the hopes of just fetching Kingston if we were lucky. But unfortunately we found no counter-current; so, when the wind fell light, we decided to strike out at once upon the starboard tack, and, in the event of being swept past Jamaica, to try our luck again in the currents on the south coast of Cuba.

We had our hearts in our mouths as we headed away into the open Caribbean. From hour to hour during the days which followed we watched every degree of leeway the *Cap Pilar* made; we trimmed and re-trimmed our sails to gain all possible advantage over the wind and current. A whole week dragged out, and still we were holding our own; at one time it looked as though we might just manage to struggle into slack water under the lee of Jamaica; but next day we felt, for the first time, the full strength of the west-going current, and all our hopes of ever reaching Kingston vanished in a few hours.

Now, once again, there were signs of restlessness throughout the ship. The best part of the voyage was behind us; there were some on board who wanted to abandon the attempt on Jamaica and to call instead at Havana on the way to New York. Others were still very eager to see Jamaica at all costs; we found it very difficult to discover the true will of the majority. In view of the conflicting opinions it seemed safer to stick obstinately to our original intentions, so we held on across the wind, and eventually came in with the coast of Cuba, just fourteen days out from the Panama.

We had no luck with the currents here either, though the set was never actually against us; but, by carefully watching every smallest shift of the wind, we managed at long last to make the few all-important miles of easting; then we once more stood away south, determined to catch a turn round the last rock in Jamaica or die in the attempt.

In the afternoon of the seventeenth day we saw mountains ahead of us, and in the evening we carried the sea breeze right in upon the coast. We could see the houses of Montego Bay lining the shore only three miles to windward; we stood on until the very moment that the breeze died at sunset. For three hours after that we backed and filled in the dead air and a lumbering swell, losing ground visibly; then the first stray puffs of land breeze brought peace to the labouring ship, and all through the night she held position against the stream. Next day at noon we anchored abreast of a steamer who was loading bananas for Liverpool, and what had seemed like the longest passage of the cruise was over at last.

CHAPTER XXXVII
JAMAICA IS SO BRACING

WHEN WE ARRIVED IN Jamaica we heard that serious rioting had broken out all over the country. But as yet there was no sign of any disturbance in Montego Bay, and nothing could possibly have looked more peaceful than the sleepy white town, stretching haphazard along a mile of water-front. Jane and I lived ashore for a week in a very beautiful hotel, where we could dive directly into the sea off the verandah, and the bright lazy fish made an ever-changing flower-garden beneath our bedroom window.

Later it became necessary for me to spend a day or two in Kingston on ship's business. In order that Jane should be able to come with me we got a very capable trained nurse to look after Jessica while we were away. We also hired a sturdy American car, and on the first Sunday after our arrival we drove away, with George in the back, looking, with his bushy black beard, like a Sikh bodyguard. We had been advised that we ought to go armed, so upon the back seat of the car beside him, George laid a massive point-four-five Webley revolver, which caused him so much embarrassment that he insisted on wrapping it up in brown paper before we started.

Throughout Sunday we drove across the island; Monday we spent in Kingston; on Tuesday we drove back again by another route. In all that time we saw no sign of any disturbance, except on one occasion, when a little boy cried out at sight of George's beard, and threw an orange at us from the top of a steep bank. George

320

drew himself up sternly, whereupon the little boy threw another orange. We drove hastily away.

When we returned to Montego Bay we heard that there had been riots in the town itself, and that many of the crew had been enrolled as special constables. I found them in the courtyard of the police station wearing brand new white sun helmets, and carrying either rifles or shot-guns.

The special constables consisted of the white men who could be spared from their work, as well as a surprising number of coloured men, who no doubt felt that order must at all costs be maintained in the island. Most of the specials were naturally young men, and some of these boys seemed to treat the whole affair as though it were a thrilling holiday, like a week-end's grouse-shooting.

I am not competent to give an opinion upon the relative merits of the two sides in the Jamaican dispute; but it is safe to say that most of the strikers' demands for higher wages and better living conditions were manifestly just; in fact almost all the planters to whom I spoke expressed themselves eager to satisfy these demands as soon as legislation in England should secure a sufficiently high price for sugar to make such concessions possible.

"We do not want to exploit labour," they said, "it is you in England who exploit it by paying us a ridiculously low price for our sugar and by buying surplus Cuban sugar at cut prices. The average English family spends at most 7½d. a week on sugar; if they only increased this sum to 9d. a week our difficulties here would be solved."

In Kingston I spoke to a shifty-eyed, brutal-looking street-corner lounger. He was apparently out of work, so I asked him what his trade might be.

"I's a public speakah, boss," he told me. "I don't have no trade."

I asked him where he spoke.

"Oh, all over the country," he answered, with pride, "Savann-la-Mar, Black River, Lucea, Falmouth. I been in all those places last week."

"They had riots in those towns last week. Were you there during the riots?"

"No, sah. I left before the riots. I's a public speakah," he added indignantly, "not a rioter."

Unfortunately these "orators" were hardly ever to be found at the actual scene of a riot. They spent their time touring the countryside (at whose expense nobody knew), stirring up the ignorant and normally easy-going negroes to acts of violence, which did nothing to further their cause, and often resulted in one or two of them being shot. One of the most frequent forms of sabotage was the burning of cane-fields, which was equally disastrous for the owners and their labourers, and was probably done by these same "orators" as a means of deliberately aggravating the unemployment problem.

But it was very difficult to find anything helpful in some of the points of view expressed by white people in Jamaica. A friend of ours, for instance, said one day: "There'll be more trouble here next Monday. The strikers are going to hold a meeting at A——."

"Perhaps there won't be any trouble if the Specials don't go up there," I suggested.

"Oh, but we want them to make trouble," was the calm reply, "so that we can teach them a lesson."

Another man we met summed up a long discourse on the rights and wrongs of the situation with the astounding declaration that "What the niggers seem to forget is that they came (*sic*) to this country as *slaves*. Now they want to own the place." I am ashamed to say that we shirked the responsibility of making any answer.

There was a fine swaggering "Hell's Angels", "Ralph the Rover" and "Kiss me, Hardy, ere I die" atmosphere about a few of the youngest Specials. One patrol even called themselves the "Suicide Squad", though it is unlikely that they were ever exposed to any abnormal danger, unless it was from the inexpert use of their own firearms. The other side, according to reports from the secret police, had only one rifle and one revolver between them.

Most of the strikers' escapades were pathetically ineffectual, and there was very little *organised* resistance to the police; but occasionally the roads were half-heartedly barricaded, and the flying squads ambushed and stoned. None of the Cappilarians were ever injured, though one night the patrol to which Carmichael was attached was held up and came under revolver fire, while he himself was bowled over by a piece of rock.

Another patrol was also stopped by a barricade. When they got out of their car to clear the road they saw a white-shirted figure running across a neighbouring field. The patrol leader immediately gave his men the order to fire, and a fusilade of bullets went ripping after the unfortunate fugitive, who may only have been an inquisitive passer-by, frightened by the arrival of the police. The "target" was first sighted at about 200 yards, and was very difficult to distinguish in the darkness; but the Specials continued to fire until the man suddenly appeared to fall, after which they drove away without even bothering to investigate.

Labour demonstrations usually took the form of hunger marches. Upon one placard, typical of those generally carried, stood the roughly scrawled words: "THIS IS A HUNGRY MARCH. THE UNDERSIGN APPEAL TO GOVERNMENT FOR WORK." In point of fact it looked as though such placards were regarded, by those who followed them, more as free passes for a day's holiday and a communal outing than as a genuine appeal for work. You could often see the demonstrators laughing and singing as they went. We even heard of a house-boy who asked one morning to have his breakfast half an hour early to enable him to join a " hunger march " in a town some distance away. It must, however, be admitted that a great many of these marchers always brought their machetes with them; but, although these long-bladed axes would undoubtedly have been the most effective and barbarous weapons imaginable, we never heard of their being used as such.

There is no doubt that rioting did occur while we were in Jamaica, and that, if it had been allowed to get beyond control, there would eventually have been an appalling loss of life on both sides. Even so, the shooting of demonstrators by hastily armed bands of civilians, who had had no previous training in the administration of authority, was, to say the least, regrettable. The working people very naturally objected to being potted at by gangs or daring young sportsmen, and there were several occasions when the arrival of a car-load of Specials immediately transformed a meeting into a riot. On the other hand, we had nothing but admiration for the regular police and the military; they were always firm, but exceedingly patient. We felt that if Specials had not been allowed to operate, except under the command of the Regulars, there would have been very few incidents to which exception could have been taken. The working people seemed to have an instinctive respect for men in uniform, and a very understandable hate for the irregulars, whom they suspected (sometimes with good reason) of bearing them an entirely personal malice.

We had been looking forward for some months to getting a fresh coat of green paint on the *Cap Pilar's* top sides, ready for her visit to New York. But in Montego Bay there were unfortunately so few people left aboard the ship that I was tempted to accept help from the shore to make certain of having the job finished before it was time to leave. In a weak moment I gave in to the repeated solicitations of a merry rogue, with a perpetual grin, called Jackson, who waylaid me about half a dozen times a day wherever I went in the town.

"You give me the job of painting ship, boss," he begged, "and I get the first coat on in one day; I have three friends to help me."

"Have you ever done any painting before?" I asked.

He seemed hurt by my question. "Don't ask me that, boss, I'm Jackson of Montego Bay. I paint anything." So next morning at seven o'clock Jackson and his three friends started work.

Lars greeted their arrival with a look of profoundest mistrust, and refused to accept Jackson's flattering description of his own abilities. But, sure enough, by the evening the *Cap Pilar* wore a glistening fresh coat of paint; as I pulled out to her, I was looking forward to at least a grudging admission from Lars that my idea had been a good one.

He met me at the gangway. "Did you say Jackson could paint anything?" he asked, gloomily.

"That's what *he* said."

"Well he's painted everything," Lars said shortly.

Jackson had certainly been as good as his word. The deck, the varnished poop rail, the rigging and even the white paintwork of the deckhouses were daubed and spotted with green; in the middle of the main deck stood the maestro himself, covered from head to foot in paint till he looked like the devil in a Christmas pantomime. He was engaged in a violent argument with his "friends" over the matter of payment; unfortunately he still held a pot in one hand and a brush in the other, so his wild gesticulations sent a shower of paint in all directions. It eventually took Lars longer to clean up the mess than it would have taken to paint the ship.

On the 11th of June we sailed away to the westward, leaving Montego Bay basking in the hot sunshine as peacefully as on the day we had arrived.

CHAPTER XXXVIII

FOLLOWING THE GULF STREAM

AUGUST AND SEPTEMBER are the two months during which West Indian hurricanes most frequently occur, although a few have been recorded as early as June and as late as November. We were therefore anxious to be well on the way to New York by the beginning of July. But the Cayman Islands lay directly in our path, so we felt justified in spending a day or two there before leaving the tropics for good.

On 13th of June we sighted the low sandy coasts of Grand Cayman, the largest of these islands. By the evening we were anchored off George Town, the capital of the group.

The Caymans were discovered by Columbus in 1503. In those days they were alive with turtles and alligators, from the latter of which they received their name. Later they became an important re-victualling station both for ships of war and for pirates. The buccaneers of those days (some, but not all, of whom were pirates) also derived their name indirectly from the alligators and the turtles, whose flesh they used to smoke over a sort of grill called a "buccan". The islands are quite flat and lie only a few feet above sea-level on a foundation of coral, like the atolls of the Pacific; consequently they are extremely vulnerable to hurricanes, and as recently as November, 1932, the settlement on one of them was completely destroyed, with a loss of over sixty lives.

We found the Caymans as interesting as any of the islands we had visited; we wished we could have stayed there longer. We made the acquaintance of the very magnificent and very gracious Commissioner of the

Island, the Dormant Commissioner Mr. Panton, and several other dignitaries of the community, who all did their best to make us welcome.

The population is partly white and partly coloured; many of the families are said to be descended from ship-wrecked sailors, and even from pirates. Certainly the atmosphere of the fierce old buccaneering days still colours the life of the islands: ancient cannon and cannon-balls are a common sight, and the very existence of the settlement depends upon a fleet of smart, exceptionally speedy schooners, which the islanders build themselves.

If they were not so remotely situated the Caymans would soon become famous for their schooners, which are the fastest in the Caribbean. They are constructed of hard wood brought from Central America; yachts for European and American owners have actually been built at George Town. There are three families of ship-builders, who hand down the secrets of their trade from father to son. Most of the schooners they build are of very shallow draught, so as to enable them to fish for turtles upon the banks, which lie scattered along the Nicaraguan coast.

During the hurricane season their topmasts are struck, and they are anchored in the lagoon. A bad hurricane will blow many of them into the mangroves, but they rarely suffer much damage. When the blow is over the islanders go and dig them out of the trees.

We found that a great many of the Caymaners had been to America; and that during the days of prohibition they had been extensively employed in rum-running. Incidentally we had filled up our own barrel in Jamaica, with rum at 12s. 6d. per gallon. George now decided to draw off a bottle, and was somewhat disappointed to see that it was a clear colourless liquid. Nothing daunted, he took a good pull. Next moment, with a yell of pain, he spat it out; but not in time to prevent the inside of his mouth from being sore for several days afterwards. The kindly saloon-keeper ashore diagnosed our "fire-water" as 180 per cent overproof; he very obligingly diluted it for us and added the necessary burnt sugar, which gives to rum its brown colour. Out of only half the contents of our barrel he made twenty-two bottles of rum, which were about 100 per cent overproof; then we filled the barrel again with water. The final product, which had cost us roughly 1s. a bottle, was much enjoyed for its great potency wherever we went. We never succeeded in finishing the barrel however; at the end of the voyage, in order to avoid the enormous duty upon it in London, it was emptied sadly and ingloriously into the dark waters of the East India Dock.

North of George Town, round a small headland, an immense sweep of sandy beach stretches clean and white for five unbroken miles. Every afternoon we used to sail across to this beach in one of our boats; not a house nor any sign of habitation was in sight, so we pulled off all our clothes, ran down the hot sand and dived straight into the sea. There we would lie for many hours, coming out now and then to dry in the blazing sun, until it was time to sail back again to the ship.

On the last night of our stay we went to a dinner-party, wearing boiled shirts, in the true "outpost of Empire" manner. After dinner we attended a ball, where our host made a very moving oration, in which, while the advantages of an education at Winchester and Oxford were clearly stated, it was pointed out that membership of the great British Empire to a large extent atoned for any lack of further social background. Then we all danced the "Big Apple".

Next morning at dawn we once more proceeded to sea. Two days later, just as it was getting dark, we sighted the lighthouse on the westernmost point of Cuba. A few hours afterwards we passed out of the Caribbean, and into the Gulf of Mexico.

For three days we remained almost stationary. We had tried to hug the Cuban coast too closely, and were deservedly punished for trying to cut off corners in a sailing ship. Half a knot of counter-current cancelled any advantage we managed to gain from the few vagrant puffs of wind which found us; while five miles farther out to sea a trim little Cayman schooner sailed daintily past and disappeared over the horizon.

At Panama we had achieved, for the first time, a really appetising variety of stores. The credit for this must go to Lethbridge, who had been in charge of the catering in George's absence.

When George returned from Peru he blandly announced that he had been studying Spanish methods of cooking. We awaited the results with interest, and also with considerable misgivings. This, we felt, was a "fast one", calculated to curtail our rights of free criticism and self-determination. But the first dish he provided was a huge success; it was a sort of super-charged macaroni cheese, containing various quantities of almost every known spice. It appeared on the menu once a week, and was always referred to as "George's mess". Unfortunately, before we reached New York, the weevils once more invested our macaroni; every stick housed about a dozen little black insects, who refused to come out, no matter how hard the cook blew. The remedy was to serve "George's mess" only in the evening, when the livestock passed unnoticed if boldly attacked in a poor light, and did not in any way detract from the flavour of the dish.

At last we drifted out into the wind again; but it came

in light and fluky, and our progress was painfully slow. The month of June was fast drawing to a close, but still we lay idling across the hot waters of the Gulf of Mexico. The hurricane season was at hand. Anxiety began to weigh heavily upon us. Would we never find the Gulf Stream to carry us, upon its broad reliable back, into the comparative safety of the Atlantic? Then, quite suddenly, two days later, we began to feel an easterly drag. Within twenty-four hours we were moving towards the southern end of Florida in the grip of a steady two-knot current.

We swept round into the straits between the mainland and the Bahama Islands, where the current quickly increased to three and then four knots. On the last day of June we could see the tops of the skyscrapers of Miami, sticking up above the western horizon, like a fabulous Arabian city in the desert. Although there was very little wind we swung on up the coast at six or seven knots, so for the moment we gave up worrying about calms and tropical cyclones. We made a trapeze and hung it from the fore-yard-arm; every afternoon we staged a swimming gala, complete with high diving and acrobatics. Even Jessica, who was eleven months old, took part in the festivities; in a canvas harness attached to one of the ship's lifebuoys, she floated gurgling amongst the rest of the swimmers.

We were now in one of the busiest shipping lanes in the world; day and night the steamers went thumping past us in an endless procession. We listened eagerly to the wireless news from Europe: for a time we seriously wished that we could have turned, and sailed back into the solitude of the wide Pacific. Civilisation was once more close at hand; we felt it reaching out for us. Only a few days longer could we lie unmolested upon the sea, while the steamers went hurrying by, hurrying northward, hurrying home to England.

VOYAGING DIGEST

—from *The Caterpillar*

All figures calculated from London until Noon on 6th of July, 1938.

Distance travelled	32,500 miles
Average speed at sea	4 knots
Average speed, including harbour time	2 knots
Average speed from Capetown to Sydney	6 knots
Time at sea	345 days
Time in port	309 days
Time altogether away from London	654 days
Time spent in the tropics	310 days
Best day's run	221 miles
Best week's run	1,246 miles
Best day's run under all plain sail	207 miles
Number of times we have anchored	38 times
Most times we have anchored in one port—Rio	7 times
Highest temperature experienced at sea	91° F.
Lowest temperature experienced at sea	43° F.

CHAPTER XXXIX

NEW YORK

WE WERE ABOUT thirty miles south of Sandy Hook when Howard Hughes took off upon his flight round the world. We had got a breeze at last, and, about tea-time that day, we hove-to within hailing distance of the pilot cutter.

The pilot was a very prince among jovial good fellows. He swung himself over our rail with his coat on his arm, his collar unbuttoned, and his tie loosened at the neck in the popular American manner.

"Well, I do declare," he boomed, "and which of you boys is the Captain here? Are you the Captain? Well, Well! Pleased to meet you, Captain. My name's Stenson." And he shook hands heartily, handed me an evening paper and looked round the ship, all in one movement. We almost wondered whether the pilots of New York were chosen on social as well as on seafaring merits; because the most genial host in the world could not have made us more whole-heartedly welcome to his house than did the first New Yorker we met to the United States of America.

In a few minutes we had the *Cap Pilar* upon her course, and heading for the entrance of the Swash channel.

"We're doing fine," cried the pilot, grinning, "We'll be up at quarantine by 6 o'clock. Say, I'm just going to take a good look at this dandy little ship of yours. I've never had a sailing ship before. It certainly is an experience for me." And he went forward.

With a strong flood-tide and a moderate breeze astern of her the *Cap Pilar* was making a good seven knots; in

333

a very short time we were well in amongst the buoys, which seemed to walk past us like telegraph-poles on the railway. Then suddenly the wind died, and a moment later came in again from south-west, so we were obliged to brace the yards sharp up on the port tack and steer as close to the wind as she would go. Even so she would barely lay her course; if we had not had the pilot aboard we would have made at least one tack to get round the first elbow in the channel.

But pilots, of course, are not dependent upon buoys and beacons.

" What's your draught, Cap? " asked this one.

" Eleven feet."

" Eleven feet, eh? Then there's plenty of water over that bank for us. We won't trouble to weather the buoy."

A little bit later: " I wonder what the depth *is* here? " remarked the pilot in a tone of mild interest. George, who had the lead line ready in his hand, immediately took a cast. " And a quarter—three! " he called.

" No foolin'! " cried the pilot. " Three and a quarter fathoms! I never would have thought there'd be an inch over thirteen feet on this very spot. This ole river's never the same two days running. You never can tell from one day to the next how the banks are going to shift! "

We grinned—a little weakly, I fear—at this revelation; but soon we also became infected with the pilot's philosophic attitude.

Six o'clock; once more the wind fell light, then died away altogether, leaving us drifting at about two knots into the main fairway.

Unfortunately we were rather near the western side of the channel when the wind failed, and soon it was obvious that the tide was not running true and that it would carry us straight down upon the very next buoy.

"Well, ain't that a pity?" said the pilot. "Just when we were doing so fine. You couldn't turn her around, could you?"

"We could with the anchor."

"Oh, you don't want to let go any anchors before you have to. Don't want to give you boys more work than we can help, do we?"

Whatever we were going to do there was not much time to lose. The buoy in question weighed many tons, and the ship was lying broadside across the tide, driving along at an alarming rate. Lars walked forward and stood by the starboard anchor with his maul ready to let go at a moment's notice.

Suddenly there came a little gust of wind from seaward. As fast as we could we ran down all the headsails, clewed up the square sails, and hauled the mainsail and spanker to windward. For seconds that seemed like days there was no result, then gradually she began to move astern and cast to starboard. The buoy was quite close now; for a moment it looked as though it would still just foul our jib-boom rigging; then we were past, and with clear water ahead of us once again.

"That was great!" grinned the imperturbable pilot, "I've often wondered how a sailing ship would get out of a jam like that." His cheerfulness did not diminish in the least when the wind almost immediately died away and left us drifting stern first up one of the busiest fairways in the world.

At 10 P.M. we anchored off the quarantine station; next morning early the various authorities boarded us and vied with each other to make our path easy. The pilot refused to leave us; he even insisted on taking me ashore to make arrangements for a berth. He and I took the ferry across to Manhattan and spent several hours in chasing about the city between the various offices, in which we were received with universal acclaim. Eventually we returned to the ship with the virtual freedom of the city bestowed upon us.

It was a glorious morning, with a steady south-westerly breeze whipping across the Hudson River.

"Boy! What a day for a sail," cried the irrepressible pilot. "We can sail her right up to the pier with a breeze like this."

After lunch we hurried aboard and lost no time in getting the anchor up. Then, under every sail we could set, and with the tide once more in our favour, we went booming up the crowded river towards the city. Soon we could make out the slender spires of the down-town skyscrapers, tapering splendidly above the haze; a little farther, and the whole incredible pile of Manhattan was plainly visible, like a fairy citadel—like a cluster of orchids—like anything you will, that is miraculous or magnificent or dramatic. We were in no mood for cynicism on that morning in July. The sun shone brilliantly, the wind sang, the white caps went skipping from shore to shore; the *Cap Pilar*, fresh painted from trucks to waterline, sailed superbly up the fairway, one of a proud procession of liners, tramps and pleasure steamers. Past the Statue of Liberty—past Ellis Island—past Brooklyn Bridge, upon which two of my great-uncles had once worked as painters. The wind dropped a bit, and it was just 6 o'clock when we reached the Battery. The river was thick with ferries, taking the business people home across the river. They jostled past us ahead and astern; they swept up close beside us. The people on them crowded to the rail to wave and shout their greetings, so that several of the boats took an alarming list under the uneven weight.

The pilot had taken off his shirt so as to feel more at home amongst us. He waved and called to the tug skippers and to his comrades upon other ships.

One of the tug masters came alongside to put a line aboard us, then sheered away again. " Pity not to let her sail right home," he shouted.

So the *Cap Pilar* sailed on up the line of wharves, past street after crowded Manhattan street. It was an exciting time, and New York, almost the last place we came to, was the first which immediately fulfilled our greatest expectations.

At last we began to furl our sails: directly we had done so the tug slipped us, with remarkable precision, into our berth at the end of 34th Street West—almost in the shadow of the Empire State Building.

Next morning Howard Hughes was back again from round the world, having covered fifteen thousand miles in the time it frequently took us to do fifty.

In New York we led a butterfly existence which has left no vivid impressions; but we enjoyed ourselves like slum children in a field of daffodils. For a brief two weeks we left the future to look after itself as we flitted inconsequently from one extravagant pleasure to the next. We were all of us country cousins with a vengeance; whenever we encountered one another, at the end of a day's energetic sight-seeing, we gabbled together excitedly about all the wonders we had seen. One evening we went to the largest cinema in the world, but were unable to get seats; so, determined only to deal in superlatives, we visited instead the highest building in the world and had supper in a restaurant on the 100th floor.

From 9 A.M. until 5 P.M. every day I was occupied

with the usual pilgrimage to the down-town quarter of the city. No matter how long the *Cap Pilar* remained in any port, it never seemed long enough for me to be able to make an end of all the business attendant upon her arrival and departure.

I had the greatest admiration for the American business men whom I met and for their methods. It seemed as though they realised what a hideous bore "business" could be, and they therefore tried to lighten the burden with every little kindly act they could think of. It may be unorthodox to mix business and pleasure; but, frankly, I found the working day in New York far easier to get through than in any other city, and I felt exceedingly grateful to the gentlemen who pressed me with invitations to "come along over to the club and meet the boys", who were anxious to "have us know their wives", and who always kept a bottle of whisky in the office safe and a good looking secretary ready "to fix you a highball" at a moment's notice.

"If we *have* to spend most of the day in checking each other's arithmetic," they seemed to imply, "then for the Lord's sake let's fit in a little hearty good fellowship to make up for it."

Two days after we arrived Jane's sister Mary "came to town" from her home in Canada; and we made this the excuse for an orgy of night life, which we soon found more exhausting than a long gale at sea. We spent the evening in one or two Harlem "hot spots", fascinated to ecstasy by the wild gay dancing of the coloured people. We went to a cabaret, and were successfully thrilled by the sight of bare-breasted dancing girls, dutifully pouting at the funny man's innuendos. We dined in "tuxedos" at a restaurant, famous for its association with Camel cigarettes. We even paid 15s. each to see a chorus of beautiful South Sea Island girls, performing their native songs and dances.

We watched Howard Hughes driving up Broadway in a snowstorm of " ticker tape " and waste paper. We did business on Wall Street, saw life in Greenwich Village, and drove at breathless speeds on the Express Highways. One day I made a pilgrimage to the house in which my grandfather and his brothers had lived nearly a hundred years ago; it was one of a row of semi-detached buildings in a street not far from the waterfront. The ground floor was a shop, outside which hung a placard marked " Soda "; there had probably never been any garden.

Some of the crew went to Coney Island; the sober Les Lethbridge and Colin Potter were reported to have been caught on three successive nights by a shower of rain, and forced to take refuge in the stalls of the French Follies. From after supper until midnight one evening we all went rowing on the lake in Central Park.

George probably enjoyed New York the most, and this was entirely due to his magnificent black beard. The first time he went ashore he was greeted by cries of: " Hi-ya, House of David! " from a score of passers-by, and waiters in restaurants would whisper in his ear: " Ball player—huh? " and become almost embarrassing in their attentiveness. He soon found out that there was a baseball team, who all wore beards as a publicity stunt. Thereafter, by meeting all enquiries about his athletic skill with silence and an amiable smile, the wily George managed to cash in on a good deal of very generous hero-worship.

After a week in New York Jane and Jessica travelled back to Canada with sister Mary, and a few days later we also were ready to leave.

We said good-bye with real regret to a city which had made us so heartily welcome: our berth had cost us nothing; the Dalziel Towing Company had done prodigious feats of towing for little more than the price of the coal consumed; and everybody else, who ought really to have fined us, stopped us, stung us, and nailed writs to our mast for the numberless misdemeanours which we were for ever committing, appointed themselves instead our tireless allies and guardians from the Awful Powers whom they represented.

CHAPTER XL

FOG ON THE BANKS

On 25TH OF JULY the *Cap Pilar* towed down the Hudson and out through the Narrows. At the very moment of departure we lost one of our company, Sydney Marshall the Australian, who had found himself a job aboard a racing yacht. We had been looking forward to celebrating his twenty-first birthday aboard the ship, but we were denied the pleasure, and except for a charming Christmas card which he sent us after our return to England we have heard nothing of him since the moment he skipped over the rail into the tug.

When we got outside the wind was contrary, so we spent the afternoon at anchor near the Scotland lightship. But about 9 P.M. a light breeze came in from the west, and soon we were under way again bound for Halifax.

The following morning we passed the Fire Island light-vessel, and altered course for the Nantucket. But we were destined never to see it, because, for the whole of the rest of the voyage to Halifax, with only two short intervals, we were groping about uneasily in a thick and clammy fog.

All next day the fog continued, and throughout the following night. We crept gingerly onwards, sounding all the time, and gazing perpetually into the dripping darkness. We could see no more than a ship's length ahead; from our navigation lights the yellow, green, and red beams struck out into the grey gloom like feelers.

Day and night, night and day, we kept the foghorn braying. It made a howling, shattering din, which went seeking ruthlessly into the uttermost corners of the ship, strangling conversation, tearing through our sleep; the crew relieved each other every hour at the hand-wheel, which worked the bellows. Regularly, once every minute, the three wild notes blared out; in the interval between the watch strained their ears for an answer, but no answer came. Occasionally we heard the distant growl of a steamer's siren, but never a sound from the gloom around us. Slowly, by means of the lead-line, we felt our way along the edges of the banks.

At dawn, after the first night of fog, a fishing boat suddenly loomed out of the darkness, almost under our jib-boom. All her crew must have been asleep, for they had made no attempt to answer our fog signals. We just managed to avoid running them down. Before we had recovered from the shock another ghostly vessel appeared close on our port bow. We were in the thick of a whole fleet of fishermen, none of whom were making any attempt to blow their foghorns.

On the third morning we estimated that the Nantucket light-vessel was less than ten miles away. We listened eagerly for her fog signal, but not a sound broke the stillness. Suddenly the faintest tremor of a noise caught our anxious ears; quickly it swelled into the steady chugging of a small diesel motor. Cyril Money, who was working our foghorn, put forth all his energy to produce the loudest possible sound. There was no answer; but almost immediately the dim shape of a trawler appeared out of the swirling whiteness. We hove-to and shouted to the trawler to do the same; then we launched a dory and pulled alongside him to ask whether he knew our position. The trawlermen were as uncertain as we were of the exact position; but they very nearly filled our boat with mullet and cod, for which they refused any sort of payment, so we readily forgave them their neglect of fog signals.

We sailed on. The fog grew thicker. We hove the lead

more often, and clung desperately to twenty fathoms round the Georges Bank.

In the afternoon of the fifth day out of New York there was a sudden clearing of the mist, through which we were able to snap a fairly good sight of the sun. This, coupled with a simultaneous sounding, gave us an idea of our position and allowed us to lay a more accurate course for the Halifax light-vessel. Soon afterwards the fog came down again as thick as ever; we continued, wailing dismally upon our way.

During the forenoon of the seventh day the visibility increased to about three miles; we expected to pick up the lightship in the early afternoon. Two o'clock came, and three o'clock, but still no sign of her; we began to wonder whether we had not after all sailed past her. We had just made up our minds to heave-to and wait when the red hull, with HALIFAX painted upon it in large white letters, appeared out of the mist less than a mile away on the starboard bow. We altered course towards the land; but hardly had we trimmed our sails when we were once more enveloped in a blanket of fog, this time thicker than ever before, so that we could see no more than a few yards on either side of the ship.

The entrance to Halifax Harbour is long and narrow; but the wind, though light, was still blowing fair; so we felt that we must at all costs take this opportunity of reaching port without delay. We knew that right ahead of us now was the tongue of a bank, lying in sufficient depth of water for the *Cap Pilar* to be able to sail straight across; so we decided that if we were able, by means of constant soundings, to recognise this shoal when we reached it, we would then steer directly into the harbour mouth; if we failed to find the shoal there would be no alternative but to stand away out to sea and wait for clear weather.

Everyone was gathered on the main deck, eagerly

listening, as the leadsman called each successive depth.

" Eighteen — seventeen — nineteen — eighteen "; then suddenly: " *Fifteen—twelve—seven* ", in three successive casts. According to our sailing directions there was no tide running, so we noted the time and continued sounding. " Seven—six—seven—six—five—five and a half—six." Anxiously we watched the clock; we must be almost at the edge of the bank again now. " Six— six—six—six—*seven—nine—twelve—fourteen*." Hastily we compared our calculated distance between reaching and leaving the shoal with the contours marked upon the chart. We were all right.

Once more we altered course and slid quietly onwards. We tried to get rough bearings of the fog signals from two lighthouses on shore. There was hardly a ripple on the sea beside us; we wondered whether there would be sufficient swell to make the bell-buoys toll. We heard the low note of a steamer's siren coming down upon our port side; she passed quite close, but we saw no sign of her—only the wash of her bow-wave slapping against us. We hoped we were heading directly for the outermost buoy; if we could only find this the rest would be easy.

We could hear the distant muttering of surf. We knew the land was close; but how far could you hear the surf on a day like this? It must be well past sunset now, the white fog turned to grey and seemed to pile upon us. In complete silence we crept along, while from the rigging aloft, on the forecastle head, and in every part of the ship, twenty-five pairs of ears were straining into the gloom for the first faint note of warning.

" What's that? " came a loud whisper from someone. " Yes—there it is again! "

Next minute we all heard the mysterious creaking boom of a whistle buoy. We laughed at each other with sudden relief; the sound seemed to come from a great distance. " There was no need to worry about finding that buoy," we said. "Why, you can hear the damned thing two miles away at least." But we were wrong; almost before we had finished speaking the huge steel structure of the buoy appeared beside us, and was soon swallowed again by the mist astern.

From now on there was no difficulty in picking our way from buoy to buoy until finally, at 8 o'clock, we suddenly burst through the fog, and the city of Halifax lay twinkling welcomely before us. Without more ado we clewed up all sail and anchored to wait for daylight.

Thoughts of home had now definitely begun to cast a shadow over all our plans and activities. In Halifax most people contented themselves with a few unambitious walks into the forest that stretches for miles on every hand. But one or two of the crew made a memorable expedition by Indian canoe, up the river and through a chain of beautiful lakes, into the depths of the wilderness. Three others preferred to hitch-hike their way down the coast, and eventually arrived at Lunenburg, a little old-world Nova Scotian port, where they found a big four-masted schooner engaged in a regular trade with the West Indies. They also saw the famous schooner *Blue Nose* fitting out there for the autumn racing.

My only expedition was nothing more ambitious than a twenty-four hour train journey across Canada to fetch Jane and Jessica; but I found this more interesting than I had expected, because in the train I met a burly fellow, only a few years older than myself, who told wonderful tales of the prohibition days on the U.S.A. coast. It appeared that this man had been a smuggler himself, and his tales suffered not at all on account of their improbability.

One of these stories concerned a gang of young English ex-naval officers who had been "in the game" in the early nineteen-twenties.

" I've worked for Italians and I've worked for Greeks, and you know where you are with those hombres," said my friend. " If they're going to take you for a ride they tell you so, and no foolin'. But these God-damned English yeggs—ugh!—it makes me shiver to think of those babies. One night they asked me to dinner aboard their ship. All glittering brass and white uniforms, and a quartermaster at the gangway, just like a man-o'-war, But when we sat down to dinner—ough!" He shuddered visibly this time. " I tell you, I'd sooner sit in with a bunch of coiled cobras than spend five minutes in the saloon of that ship again. It was: ' Pleased to meetcha, old boy,' and ' Hev another glass of port, wontcha, ole chap?' and all the time they were talking you thought you could feel the barrel of a point-forty-five sneaking in alongside your backbone—ugh! Those were the toughest boys I ever had to do with."

He mentioned their names. By an odd coincidence I had met one of them in the Austrian Tyrol, whither he had retired to live comfortably upon the proceeds of a year or two's rum-running. He had told me how their smuggling had consisted simply of steaming straight into New York Harbour and unloading cases of champagne into a fleet of waiting lorries. He was a particularly polite, kindly individual. Apparently his somewhat cold and formal manner had completely unnerved this rugged Canadian, who was convinced that the outward charm had been merely a mask to cover the most callous and sinister designs.

The members of the Royal Nova Scotian Yacht Squadron took us firmly to their ample collective bosom, made us all honorary members, and smote boldly the rock of Canadian prohibition so that it brought forth whisky.

But the most exciting event in Halifax was when Potter and McDonald, who had made friends with a man who owned a wireless telephone set, actually spoke for ten minutes each to somebody living at Croydon. Most of us only heard about it afterwards, but it had a strangely disquieting effect upon us all. The weather was cool, there was a fog in the air at nights, and England— there was England just across the way—within speaking distance.

We suddenly realised that this last little journey over the Atlantic—about 2,500 miles—was one of the shortest ocean passages we had ever made. It ought not to take us much more than a fortnight to reach Falmouth. And all at once we felt an overpowering longing to see those little green fields again.

CHAPTER XLI

HOME FROM HALIFAX

ON THE 14TH OF AUGUST we sailed away from Halifax with the magic words "Falmouth—for orders" upon our Customs' clearance. Our hopes of a smart passage across the Atlantic soon faded. Before light, variable winds we trickled gently eastward. One week—two weeks—three weeks; but never any wind to help us home.

Home! Homeward bound! No words had ever thrilled us half so much. The keenest adventurer among us had looked forward less eagerly to raising a South Sea island than he now longed for his first sight of England. As the passage dragged on we fell into a mood of contentment which no tricks of the weather were able to dispel. It no longer seemed to matter how lightly the wind blew so long as each day brought us a few miles nearer to Falmouth.

On 5th of September the wind went to north-east and blew freshly for a day and a half, sending us scurrying close-hauled into the Bay of Biscay. There, once more, we were becalmed in brilliant weather. It was as though the *Cap Pilar* were unwilling to leave the open ocean; as though she demanded one last moment of sun-bathed idleness before carrying us to the end of our journey.

At dawn on 6th of September the horizon was dotted with red and white sails; soon we were surrounded by the ships of the French tunny fleet, stout little sixty-foot cutters with a long rod stuck out on either side. In the afternoon we pulled over to the nearest tunnyman. Her crew welcomed us aboard, and begged us to choose the finest fish in their icebox as a present.

348

All through the afternoon the *Cap Pilar* and the tunny-fisher sailed in company while we sat in the latter's cabin, drinking the wine of Bordeaux and talking idly of ships and fishing, and cabbage-patches in the winter, just as though we had been gathered in some water-front tavern ashore. Then we took all except one of her crew aboard the *Cap Pilar* to taste Jamaica rum, admire the baby, and to share our morbid interest in the 6 o'clock news from Europe.

When we switched on the wireless we were greeted by a series of sharp crackles and a few pops, followed by a mulish silence, which no amount of twiddling and rattling could break.

"What about another glass of Bordeaux," suggested the captain of the tunnyman hopefully; "there'll be wind to-night, and we shall have to say good-bye."

Thankfully we abandoned our efforts and set ourselves instead to making the most of this happy deep-sea meeting.

Towards nightfall the wind freshened from the south-west. The tunnyman sailed up alongside us to re-embark her crew. With a final wave and a shouted farewell she hauled to the wind and stood south, while the *Cap Pilar* went bowling away to the north-eastward at a steady seven knots.

Almost every day now we met some steamer through whom we were able to send a wireless message home. On Wednesday, 7th of September, we were sixty miles from the Lizard; in the afternoon a friendly tramp circled twice round us while we sent a long message by international code, asking him to warn Lloyd's and all our relatives that we expected to reach Falmouth next day.

The following morning, however, found us close-hauled again to a fresh north-east wind which headed us off relentlessly towards the coast of France. For five days after that we tacked incessantly, fighting for every mile to windward—fighting to get home. The wind continued to freshen; by 9th of September it had become a moderate gale. The sky was cloudless but a dense haze lay upon the horizon, reducing the visibility to about three miles. Occasionally a steamer or two would jump into cumbrous existence out of the mist and go snorting past us. Eagerly we signalled for a weather report, but now they all appeared to be in too much of a hurry to pay us any attention.

"There must be a war on," said Willie. "The blighters is all too busy watchin' for submarines to take any notice of a sailing ship."

But we no longer suffered from the nightly gloom with which the wireless news had formerly loaded us. The crisis, if there still was a crisis, seemed remote and unimportant compared with the nearness of England. The wind was now set in the north-east. We kept the *Cap Pilar* pounding into it.

In the South Sea Islands Lars and the duty watch had set up new shrouds and backstays for the entire fore and main riggings. Throughout the voyage we had been sewing new sails. So we hung on to a cloud of canvas, and the *Cap Pilar* flogged her way backwards and forwards between France and England like a great white bird fluttering against the bars of her cage.

At 2 A.M. on 10th of September the masthead lights of a large warship appeared close upon our starboard quarter. There was a brilliant moon which must have made our sails shine out in the darkness. As she approached a light began to wink from her yard-arm. Now, at last, we would be able to get a reliable weather report.

"What ship?" she signalled.

We gave our name and port of origin. As soon as she

had received them we began to ask her for the latest weather forecast. But she must have imagined that we intended to ask her name because she acknowledged the first "What" of our message with a curt "No".

"Good sailing! Good night," she added politely, and before we were able to repeat our request, omitting the first offensive word, she had wallowed out of range, and we were left to tack patiently on.

During the night of 10th of September the wind began to take off slightly. At daybreak on 11th of September we saw the Lizard. By breakfast-time we were becalmed close under the cliffs of Cornwall.

As we gazed at the land we realised that this would be the last occasion upon which we would stand together to watch the coasts of a new country drifting out to meet us. Brazil, the Cape, Tasmania, Peru, and now England—how alike they all looked at this distance, how wild and how deserted!

About the middle of the forenoon the faintest ripple was seen approaching us from the nor'-west. Ten minutes later it reached us and brought with it the sweet clean smell of the English countryside. Soon the *Cap Pilar* was once more forging ahead. Then the mist vanished, and we could see the whole coast of Cornwall, from the Lizard to Dodman Point. The Colonials out of the watch below rushed on deck to catch their first glimpse of "home".

"Not a bad little place," said Scanty. "But what d'you call them funny little green patches?"

"Those are the green fields of England."

"Fields! D'yer mean paddocks?" exclaimed Scanty, in genuine astonishment. "Cor bli'! Why don't they put a roof over 'em?"

During the afternoon the wind drew back to north; all through the night we worked slowly up the coast.

Now we were suddenly in a desperate hurry and eager to try every laborious strategy to cheat or take advantage of the tides.

Early in the morning on 12th of September we laid into Falmouth Bay. With the flood-tide well under our bow it was clear that the last hour of the voyage was at hand.

"Ready about." "Lee-oh!" The *Cap Pilar* swung into the wind and fell off upon the other tack. The crew moved quickly and efficiently to their stations. The lee sheets came home, the braces were coiled down with a meticulous neatness. Every action had about it an air of finality. It was the last board.

Twenty minutes later we were at anchor, surrounded by a crowd of motor-boats and launches. Fathers, mothers, sisters, brothers waved to their bearded kinsmen in the *Cap Pilar* and clamoured to come aboard. Most of them had been waiting in Falmouth ever since we had signalled from sixty miles south-west of the Lizard, five days before. One family brought with them three crates of lettuces, another a haunch of beef. Then came a mother, as though to the relief of a beleaguered garrison, with sacks of cabbages, baskets of fruit, and loaves of fresh white bread. As soon as the greetings were over we asked for newspapers; but one glance at the banner headlines was enough for most of us. "Crisis! *Crisis*! CRISIS!" Just before we had left London in 1936 the German army had marched into the Rhineland. On the day of our return the fate of the whole world seemed to depend upon a speech, which was to be made that very night in Nürnberg. Hastily we turned to the sporting pages.

Later in the day the *Cap Pilar* towed into Falmouth Harbour. In the evening Scanty insisted upon bathing Jessica and putting her to bed so that Jane could have dinner ashore with the rest of us.

We stayed a week in Falmouth—a week filled with all the usual "ship's business", but this time against a background of ultimata, famous flights, and urgent Cabinet meetings.

In contrast to the momentous happenings of the day, our light-hearted adventure in the *Cap Pilar* seemed a disappointingly trivial affair. Two years ago we had looked upon our voyage as a gesture of defiance in a gloomy world. Now that gesture had assumed more the appearance of a facetious grimace.

We were home again from round the world, with twelve out of the original seventeen—twelve burly, broad-shouldered sailors, hardly recognisable as the same bunch of ordinary young men who had sailed with us from England. We also brought thirteen others, and a baby girl. A rugged fishing schooner had been transformed, by the efforts of Lars, into a staunch and beautiful little ship. But in September, 1938, these achievements seemed a feeble contribution to the world's peace of mind.

One evening Lars and I strolled into a water-front tavern. Against the bar stood two old fellows, talking earnestly.

"I went aboard 'er after she anchored," one of them was saying. "They're as queer a crowd as ever brought a ship into Falmouth. Not like they was in my time."

"Ar," said his companion, sympathetically.

"I was standin' 'avin' a yarn wiv one of 'em when up comes another lad, wantin' ter get by wiv a bucket of water. An' what d'yer think 'e said, eh?" The old boy paused to take a long, vehement swig at his glass. "'E said 'Excuse me, George'. That's what 'e said. After a two years' voyage—'Excuse me, George'. *Blimey!*"

"Good job 'Itler didn't 'ear 'im," he added, grimly.

By this time Lars was grinning broadly. " May be the voyage did some good after all," he muttered.

It was decided that the *Cap Pilar* should be laid up in London for the winter, so Jane and Jessica once more left us and drove home to Wimbledon by car. Roach signed off, and set out to walk to Nottingham, which he hoped to reach before the steeplechasing season opened. Carmichael went to stay with relatives in Scotland. The day after they left " Smithy ", of all people, turned up on board, eager to help us sail the ship round the coast.

On Monday, 19th of September, we picked up our anchor for the last time, and beat out of Falmouth Harbour with threats of war whistling about our ears.

After we had weathered Start Point a strong southerly wind with rain and poor visibility kept us pinned to the English coast. We threaded our way anxiously through several fleets of drifters and a long line of merchant shipping.

Our wireless set was once more working. During the run up-Channel the news grew steadily worse. We began to wonder whether we should get to Dover before the Straits were blocked by a field of mines.

At midday on the 20th of September we reached Portland Bill, cheered by the report that Mr. Attlee had demanded the recall of Parliament. We were interested to hear, as we passed St. Alban's Head, that his demand had been refused.

On 21st of September, off Brighton, we learned of Czechoslovakia's acceptance of the Anglo-French proposals. Then the wind began to fail. We struggled on to Beachy Head, where the wind died right away and left us in a drizzling rain upon a sea as grey and lifeless as a sodden dishcloth.

We listened eagerly for the news bulletins which were given every few hours. . . . London was digging trenches in all her parks—we were becalmed. . . . Men were being called up—we were becalmed. . . . Mr. Chamberlain was flying to Godesberg—we were becalmed.

Singly and in hurrying groups the steamers thundered past us. A powerful German liner swept by, ignoring our salute. From time to time we heard the drone of aeroplane engines above the clouds. Into the silence of a wind-forsaken ocean came the growing murmur of a world gathering itself for some great upheaval. But at sunset on 22nd of September we were still becalmed off Beachy Head.

That night the wind once more began to blow. At midnight we shipped the pilot at Dungeness. By breakfast on 23rd of September we had rounded the South Foreland and passed into the Downs. The wind backed from west to south-west. We carried the tide to the north-east Spit buoy, where we altered course into the London river.

The wind backed slowly towards south. Close-hauled upon the port tack the *Cap Pilar* was just able to lay fair up the channel. We joined the stream of shipping; but we were only doing six knots, so the steamers continued to pass us one by one.

Suddenly, however, we noticed a tiny coaster of the type usually drawn by John G. Walter in *Punch*. She was half a mile away on our starboard bow and we were gaining on her!

If we managed to pass her she would be the only steamer that the *Cap Pilar* had overtaken during the past two years. We trimmed our sails to the final inch. A fresh excitement ran through the ship as we gradually crept closer to the other vessel.

Soon we drew abreast of her, and all at once I was struck by something familiar in her appearance. Surely that deckhouse amidships was the galley in which I had passed one of the earliest six months of my seafaring

356 THE VOYAGE OF THE *CAP PILAR*

career when I had sailed as cook, bos'n, and entire ship's company of the motor-vessel *Woolbyrne*, under the orders of a nineteen-stone captain and three officers.

The name on her bows was not the same, but that might easily have been changed; so as we passed her I hailed:

"Is that the old *Woolbyrne*?"

"Yes. Who are you?"

"I'm the cook."

When Scanty, who was below, heard that we were passing the *Woolbyrne* he rushed on deck.

"Where's Skipper's old ship?" he shouted excitedly. Then his face fell. "Lumme, Skipper! Where's the rest of it?"

The wind died to nothing, and as night fell the grey mist rose from the river and seemed to gather us in. Upon the full flood-tide we glided slowly up Sea Reach, through the Lower Hope and into the Iron Bight. In the darkness we crept along unnoticed, except by the outward-bound steamers, who, seeing our green or red light, probably swore impatiently at "another blasted spreety blocking the fairway."

One of Watson's tugs found us off Shorn Mead and soon had his hawser aboard. Quickly we towed through the glare of Gravesend, past Greenhithe, past the training-ship *Worcester*, up Long Reach to Purfleet. For a few minutes the urgent tumult of Erith pulsated around us; then followed the quiet of the marshes beyond, with the piping of a flight of whimbrel flying south above us. Autumn was upon the land; the night air was damp and soft against our faces. We reached the East India Docks, from which we had set out exactly two years before waving like heroes to a large crowd. Now we came sneaking back to London in the dead of night with not a soul to welcome us.

By 3 A.M. on the 24th of September we were safely

berthed. We spent the remainder of that day in cutting down the sails and making all snug for the winter. In the evening we gathered at Stone's chop-house, Picca-dilly, for a farewell supper. The low oak-panelled room became thick with smoke and the smell of fried onions and beer. Everybody made speeches. We insisted that nothing could take from us the memories of all we had seen and done together. We made plans to meet again each year. Out in the street the newsboys were crying special editions of the evening papers.

Next day the whole world shouted "War and Disaster!" Hastily we wound up our affairs and went our ways.